Poetry 1900 to 1965

*An anthology
selected and edited by*

George MacBeth

Longman

with

Faber and Faber

LONGMAN GROUP LIMITED
London
Associated companies, branches and representatives
throughout the world

Introduction and notes
© Longman Group Ltd (formerly Longmans, Green & Co Ltd) 1967

First published 1967 in conjunction with Faber and Faber Ltd
Seventh impression 1974

ISBN 0 582 34150 7 (cased)
ISBN 0 582 34151 5 (paper)

NOTE ON THE EDITOR

George MacBeth was born in Shotts, Scotland, in 1932. He was educated
at King Edward VII School, Sheffield, and New College, Oxford, where
he read Greats. Since 1955 he has worked for the BBC Third Programme
as the Editor and Producer of a number of poetry programmes including
'The Poet's Voice', 'Poetry Now' and 'The Living Poet'. He is also a
frequent broadcaster and interviewer in poetry programmes.

He is the author of two books of his own poems. 'The Broken Places'
(Scorpion Press, 1963) and 'A Doomsday Book' (Scorpion Press, 1965).
He also has edited 'The Penguin Book of Sick Verse' (1963), 'The Penguin
Book of Animal Verse' (1965) and 'The Penguin Book of Victorian Verse'.

In addition to writing poetry and editing anthologies, he frequently
lectures about poetry and reads his own poems and in 1964 he wrote,
produced and appeared in a poetry cabaret show at The Establishment
Club.

Printed in Hong Kong by
Dai Nippon Printing Co. (H.K.) Ltd

Acknowledgements

We are grateful to the following for permission to reproduce copyright material:

Andre Deutsch Ltd for 'War Poet', 'The Image', 'Translation', 'Brahms Peruses the Score of *Siegfried*' and lines from 'Mythological Sonnets' and 'To X' by Roy Fuller, and for 'Not Waving But Drowning', 'Fafnir and the Knights', 'The Jungle Husband' and 'I Remember' by Stevie Smith from *Not Waving But Drowning*. The author and Chatto and Windus Ltd for 'The Ants', 'To an Old Lady', 'Letter II', 'This Last Pain', 'Note on Local Flora', 'Aubade', 'Missing Dates', 'Just a Smack at Auden', 'The Teasers' and 'Let It Go' from *Collected Poems* by Professor William Empson. Faber & Faber Ltd for 'Musée des Beaux Arts', 'Gare du Midi', 'Who's Who', 'Consider', 'The Novelist', 'Missing', 'Edward Lear', 'Epitaph on a Tyrant', 'Rimbaud', 'Dear Though the Night is Gone', 'Miss Gee', 'Oh What is that Sound', 'The Managers', 'Lakes', 'Vespers' and lines from 'The Witnesses' and 'The Orators' by W. H. Auden; 'The Love Song of J. Alfred Prufrock', 'Preludes', 'Rhapsody on a Windy Night', 'Gerontion', 'Burbank with a Baedeker; Bleistein with a Cigar', 'Whispers of Immortality', 'The Fire Sermon', 'The Hollow Men' and 'Little Gidding' by T. S. Eliot; 'Snow', 'Sunlight on the Garden', 'Bagpipe Music', 'Autobiography', 'Cradle Song for Eleanor', 'Prayer Before Birth', 'Brother Fire,' 'The Suicide' and lines from 'Autumn Journal' by Louis MacNeice; 'The Wound', 'Incident on a Journey', 'On the Move', 'Black Jackets', 'Considering the Snail' and 'My Sad Captains' by Thom Gunn; 'The Thought-Fox', 'Esther's Tomcat', 'Hawk Roosting', 'View of a Pig', 'Relic', 'An Otter', 'Pike', 'Snowdrop', 'Thistles' by Ted Hughes; 'Horses', 'The Combat', 'The Interrogation', 'The Good Town' and 'The Horses' by Edwin Muir; 'How to Kill', 'Landscape with Figures', 'Aristocrats' and 'Vergissmeinicht' by Keith Douglas; 'Broadcast', 'Faith Healing', 'Home', 'Toads Revisited', 'Water', 'The Whitsun Weddings', 'Days', 'A Study of Reading Habits', 'Ambulances' and 'An Arundel Tomb' by Philip Larkin; Rupert Hart-Davis Ltd for 'A Dead Mole', 'Cuckoos', 'The Fear', 'Passing the Graveyard' and lines from 'Into Hades' by Andrew Young, and 'Evans', 'Poetry for Supper', 'Iago Prytherch', 'Ninetieth Birthday', 'Those Others', 'To a Young Poet', 'Tramp' and 'On the Farm' by R. S. Thomas. Longmans, Green & Co. Ltd for 'Was he Married?' 'Poor Soul, Poor Girl!', 'Croft' and 'Après la Politique, la Haine des Bourbons' by Stevie Smith from *Selected Poems*. The author for 'Seven Hunters', 'At Porthcothan', and 'The Forenoon' (from a cycle of poems entitled 'Herman Moon's Hourbook') from *Torse 3*, and 'Navajo Children, Canyon de Chelly, Arizona' and 'Lenau's Dream' from *Nonsequences* by Christopher Middleton, both published by Longmans, Green & Co. Ltd. John Murray (Publishers) Ltd for 'Pot Pourri from a Surrey Garden', 'A Subaltern's Love Song', 'Indoor Games Near Newbury', 'Devonshire Street, W.1' and lines from 'Summoned by Bells' from *Collected Poems* by John Betjeman. Mr Harold Owen and Chatto and Windus for 'Exposure', 'Arms and the Boy', 'The Show', 'Insensibility', 'Dulce et Decorum Est', 'Futility', 'Anthem for Doomed

v

Contents

vii

xi

Details of the Record

This 12″ LP offers a representative sample of the poetry in the anthology.

The Readers: Hugh Dickson, Harvey Hall, Frances Horovitz, Ted Hughes, Basil Jones, George MacBeth, Patrick Magee and Stevie Smith.

Contents
Side One

Side Two

How to read a poem

Normally when someone reads a newspaper, or indeed any other piece of prose, he lets his eye run down the page and from side to side and takes in the sense of the words through his eyes. He doesn't pay any attention to the sound that they would make if he were reading them aloud, or the shape and arrangement of them on the page. The method he uses is called 'silent' reading. In classical times this process was unknown. When a Greek or Roman or even a medieval man wanted to read something, he spoke the words aloud to himself. The speed of silent reading has undoubtedly enabled us to take in large amounts of information much more quickly. Unfortunately, it has caused a complete neglect of words as things.

In reading a popular newspaper, or a Government document, this doesn't perhaps matter very much. Most prose nowadays is written to convey a group of ideas as clearly and quickly as possible without much concern for its structure and music. Poetry, on the other hand, is more solid and more resonant. No one can read a poem unless he realises that it is a physical object as well as an abstract vehicle for conveying ideas. A poem has a material existence like a piece of music or sculpture or a plate of meat. It can't be appreciated or understood unless it is read aloud to oneself, or at least mouthed to oneself to obtain the feel of the words. Listening to a poem read aloud by someone else (as one might listen to a friend or a relation reading a letter at the breakfast table) is not enough. A poem must be 'played' by the reader himself so that he creates his own sound through the feel of the words as he speaks them. He must exercise his own jaws and let his own saliva run so that he 'tastes' the poem in his mouth as he might taste a piece of food. Ideally, of course, this method of reading should be applied to any piece of writing which aspires to be a work of art, whether it be in prose or in verse.

Perhaps I can make the method of reading I have in mind clearer by comparing it with the way one speaks to someone who is deaf, exaggerating the movements of one's lips in the formation of the sounds. It is well worth trying to do this without making any sound at all and concentrate one's attention for a moment purely on this matter of 'feel'. Once a reader has grasped this vital difference between mouthing and silent reading, the difficulties of understanding poetry can be broken down into three groups. Some of the difficulties arise purely from the appearance of poems on a page. Normally prose is printed in such a way as to fill up the available space in as economic a way as possible. The words are arranged in arbitrary symmetrical lines across and down the page and the reader is not supposed to pay any attention to them as such, except perhaps as a specimen of good or bad typography. A poem, on the other hand, is always laid out on the page in a way which has some significance. The line endings are usually printed so as to mark some rhythmical point in the poem's development and the lines are often grouped into sections or stanzas of equal numbers in a way which helps the poet to make the structure of the poem clear.

This visual difference between poetry and prose has unfortunately created an impression that the sound of the poem is *logically* connected in some way with its shape on the page. This is not so. Some prose is laid out in a careful pattern, in the way that verse is, to give an extra grandeur or elegance to it. Inscriptions on tombstones are a good example. Although these are usually written in prose, they are laid out in a neat pattern of varying long and short lines to make an attractive architectural arrangement. The same is true of many of the words in advertisements. These are arranged to weave in and out of an arrangement of pictures. Nevertheless, in each case the words are not meant to be read as verse. The line endings are meant to appeal to the eye but not to affect the reader's phrasing or rhythm. On the other hand, words can sometimes be set out in a prose poem as in prose and yet be intended for reading aloud to oneself in the way other verse is. Critics sometimes seek to show that a piece of so-called verse is really prose, with no metre and rhythm of its own, by setting it out on the page without line breaks. This is a stupid device. For example the following lines by W. B. Yeats are still in a recognisable rhythm whether they are printed as verse or as prose:

'Never shall a young man, thrown into despair by those great honey-coloured ramparts at your ear, love you for yourself alone and not your yellow hair.'

Never shall a young man,
Thrown into despair
By those great honey-coloured
Ramparts at your ear,
Love you for yourself alone
And not your yellow hair.

Of course, the point about this example is that the rhythm is a fairly obvious one and can be easily picked up without the help of the line lay-out. Usually the point of the line lay-out is to act as a guide to the poem's metre and rhythm and in some cases without it we should find it very difficult to pick these up. One advantage of the slow, mouthing reading I am recommending is that it will help to concentrate attention on the shape of the poem and so enable the reader to use the guidance it offers about the poem's structure. For example, it will enable him to count numbers of lines as he goes and hence recognise, for example, a sonnet. If you know that a sonnet has fourteen lines, a slow reading of a poem which reveals that it has fourteen lines will enable you to classify it correctly and there will be a number of other features about it which are likely to become clear – its rhyme-scheme and stanza structure, for example.

Once the usefulness, and also the limitations, of the line lay-out and appearance of a poem are clear, there remain two sets of difficulties: those connected with sound, and those connected with sense. As a general rule, I think it is a good thing to read every new poem through at least twice before beginning to think about it. The first reading should be for the general meaning and the second reading for the general sound. Later readings will begin to connect the two. The first reading, for the general sense, should entirely concentrate on treating the poem as if it were a piece of prose and getting the phrasing and the emphases right. Someone once said that a paragraph of prose was like a flight of bombers, only some of which were carrying a lethal load. He meant that out of perhaps two hundred words only twenty-five per cent need to be heard to convey the main sense of a passage. The target will be hit if these words get through. For example, in my last sentence the four key words are 'target', 'hit', 'these' and 'through'. Target hit these through. This compressed telegraphic group of words conveys the crucial sense of the passage and these are the four words which must, therefore, take the emphasis when the sentence is read aloud.

In a radio news broadcast, the announcer will carefully stress the key words so as to make the meaning of his bulletin clear even if through lack of attention on the part of his listeners or interference from other sound sources some of the words go astray. If, however, the *key* words go astray the chances are that what he has to say will not be clear. It will also be unclear if he stresses the wrong words. The radio announcer's technique provides us with a model for our own mouthing of a poem at a first reading. It should aim to pick out and heavily stress the key words so that the basic meaning is built up in our minds. Once the main emphasis or sense has become clear the passage as a whole will be clear. There are, of course, a number of complications. The poem, if it is a rich and complicated one, may allow an alternative way of stressing a particular sentence. Nevertheless, if the reader's preliminary work is carefully done, it will reveal this possibility to him. The important thing to grasp is that some ways of stressing are emphatically ruled out by the poet. A bad actor in Shakespeare will sometimes emphasise a word which is appropriate to his own interpretation of the role he is playing but not allowed by Shakespeare's text. The reader of a poem should try to avoid being this kind of bad actor.

After the reader has got some idea of the general sense of the passage, he should read it again concentrating entirely on its sound. This second reading will produce a pattern of stresses in some cases quite different from the pattern produced by reading for sense. This is because the metre and rhythm of a poem create its own tune and a poet is quite often concerned to play off this tune against the natural tune of the sense. Later readings of the poem will, of course, reconcile these two. Let us compare, for example, two possible readings of the opening lines from Andrew Young's poem 'Passing the Graveyard' (p. 55):

I sée you did not trý to sáve

The boúquet of white flówers I gáve;

So fást they wíther on your gráve.

The accent lines here indicate where I think the stresses for sense might fall. On a second reading for sound, however, the accents would fall like this:

I sĕe | you dĭd | nŏt trý | tŏ sáve |
Thĕ bou | quĕt óf | whĭte flówers | Ĭ gáve; |
Sŏ fást | thĕy wí | thĕr ón | yŏur gráve.

This second reading has made it clear to the reader that the poem is written in eight-syllable iambic lines in which a metrically short syllable is succeeded in each line four times by a metrically long syllable. The bar lines and notation marks make clear how this works. Of course, in a final reading no one would stick strictly to the stressing of this second reading for sound. Its purpose is simply to reveal the structure of the poem to the reader. Eventually he will hit on an effective compromise between the first. reading and the second, as I said earlier. The point of the second reading is that it reveals, for example, the metrical significance of the word 'did' in the first line and 'on' in the third line. Although these are unimportant in reading for sense alone they must be borne in mind in a reading for sound because they have their part to play in the structure of the iambic line.

Most of the English poetry we are familiar with is written in this di-dum, di-dum sort of iambic metre and it is one of the easiest metres for us to recognise. Its opposite, a trochaic metre which goes dum-di, dum-di, dum-di, is also easy to recognise; so are dactylic metres which go dum-di-di, dum-di-di, or anapaestic ones which go di-di-dum, di-di-dum. Many twentieth-century poems, however, are written in looser metres which are more difficult to recognise. For example, many are written in a sort of stress accent metre which depends on the number of natural sense stresses in a line. Here is an example from R. S. Thomas's poem 'Poetry for Supper' (p. 225):

Lísten, nów, verse should be as nátural

As the small túber that feeds on múck

And gróws slówly from obtúse sóil

To the white flówer of immórtal beáuty.

The accent marks indicate how the stresses fall and counting them shows that there are always four to a line. The difference between this method of stress and the iambic one used by Andrew Young is that there is no distinction between the emphasis revealed by the first reading for sense and the second one for sound. The poet is aiming at greater naturalness by using the natural stresses of everyday speech and simply grouping them together in given numbers to a line. This method was first used extensively by the great Victorian poet Gerard Manley Hopkins, whose poems were first collected in book form in 1918, long after his death. Hopkins said that there could be as many as three unstressed syllables in a foot, together with one stressed one. Earlier writers had believed that there could only be two unstressed syllables in a foot to one stressed. They had also said that there must be at least one unstressed syllable in a foot. Hopkins said that a foot could consist simply of one stressed syllable.

Here is the passage from 'Poetry for Supper', again with the accent marks, the notation and the foot arrangement indicated:

Listen,| now,| verse should be as| natural|

As the small| tuber that| feeds| on muck|

And grows| slowly| from obtuse| soil

To the white| flower| of immortal| beauty.

In the first line the word 'now' is a single stress put on its own and the phrase 'verse should be as' is a foot with one stressed syllable (the word 'verse') and three unstressed ones (the words 'should be as').

This kind of thing is extremely common in twentieth-century poetry from Auden and MacNeice onwards. As I've indicated, it is an easy kind of poetry to read because the sense and the sound stresses coincide. What the reader must do if he is to understand the structure of the poem, however, is to *count* the number of stresses in each line. This will help him to stress a line correctly in case of doubt, and at the same time will increase his pleasure in the poem's form as a work of art. The word 'metre' simply means 'measure' and it is perhaps best defined in terms of the old-fashioned word 'numbers'. Poets sometimes used to speak of their verses as numbers, in the way singers nowadays might speak of their songs. The advantage of the word 'numbers' is that it does remind us of the basic definition of metre: *metre is mathematics*.

Once this definition is grasped the syllabic metres used by poets like Dylan Thomas and Thom Gunn become clearer. The point about a syllabic metre is that there are a fixed number of syllables in each line but no fixed number of stresses, as in R. S. Thomas's poem. This means that the first reading for sense will reveal the emphasis structure of the poem and the second reading for sound won't alter it. The second reading for sound will in fact really become a reading for counting. Here is an example of some lines in syllabics from Thom Gunn's poem 'Considering the Snail' (p. 303):

> The snail pushes through a green
> night, for the grass is heavy
> with water and meets over
> the bright path he makes, where rain
> has darkened the earth's dark. He
> moves in a wood of desire,

There are seven syllables in each line of this poem. The stresses and pauses should be exactly as if the passage were written in prose, possibly with a slight pause at the end of each line, although the practice of poets varies in this respect.

Apart from poems in stress accent forms, and in syllabics, as well as poems in traditional metres, this book contains a number of poems in free verse and one (W. H. Auden's 'Vespers' p. 181) in prose. Those in free verse are often aimed at depending on cadence or grouping of phrases in such a way that the reading depends on either a slowing down or a speeding up of the normal speed at which prose is read. Here is a passage from the beginning of D. H. Lawrence's poem 'Bat' (p. 38) which is written in free verse:

> At evening, sitting on this terrace,
> When the sun from the west, beyond Pisa, beyond the
>   mountains of Carrara
> Departs, and the world is taken by surprise . . .

There is no fixed number either of stresses or of syllables or of feet in these lines. Lawrence is giving form to his writing simply by the placing of commas and the arrangement of the words in lines. The commas, which are more frequent than usual in prose, compel the reader to move more slowly. This gives the poem a swooping, or undulating, effect. Lawrence himself once had this to say in a letter to Edward Marsh about the rhythm of his own poetry: 'I think I read my poetry more by length than by stress – as a matter of movements in space than footsteps hitting the earth. ... I think more of a bird with broad wings flying and lapsing through the air more than anything, when I think of metre ... it all depends on the pause, the natural pause, the natural lingering of the voice according to the feeling.' This is very useful to keep in mind in reading Lawrence's own free verse and the free verse of someone like Stevie Smith.

The free verse of T. S. Eliot, however, in a poem like 'The Waste Land', for example, is rather different. It sometimes depends on quick changes from stress accent writing to metrical jingles to very loose writing like Lawrence's own. The reader must always be on the alert for Eliot's changes of gear. Here is a passage from 'The Fire Sermon' (p. 87) which illustrates this point:

And along the Strand, up Queen Victoria Street.

O City city, I can sometimes hear

Beside a public bar in Lower Thames Street,

The pleasant whining of a mandoline

And a clatter and a chatter from within

Where fishmen lounge at noon: where the walls

Of Magnus Martyr hold

Inexplicable splendour of Ionian white and gold.

    The river sweats

    Oil and tar

    The barges drift

    With the turning tide

The first four lines here are fairly traditional iambic penta-
meters with ten syllables in the line arranged in the familiar
di-dum, di-dum pattern. There are one or two mild variants
from this but the basic pattern is clear and the notation marks
show how it works. From the fourth line onwards a stress
accent pattern takes over. The number of stresses to the line,
however, is irregular to begin with. The accents indicate that
there are three main stresses in line five, four main stresses in
line six, three in line seven and five in line eight. After this, in
lines nine, ten, eleven and twelve, there are two main stresses
in each line as the accents indicate.

W. H. Auden's poem, 'Vespers', as I have already indicated,
is really a kind of prose. Here is a passage from it:

'In my Eden a person who dislikes Bellini has the good manners
not to get born: In his New Jerusalem a person who dislikes
work will be very sorry he was born.'

The way to read this poem is to recognise that it tends to
break up into two halves in each section in the way that a
number of passages in the Bible do. This is because Hebrew
poetry depended on a kind of division of this sort which is
reproduced in the translations and I think that Auden in this
poem is imitating that effect.

Once a reader has grasped the way that the poem should be
formed in his mouth to bring out the main pattern of stresses
of sense and sound, there will still be a number of difficulties
which may confront him. These are likely to concern the
central plot of the poem, incidental references in it which are
unclear to him, and in some cases the imagery and syntax which
the poet is employing. At this point I hope that the notes in this
book may prove of considerable further help. As the reader
will see, each poet's work is preceded by a brief introduction
and succeeded by a group of notes. These notes are designed to
be read after the poems (and later together with them) as a
stimulus to thought about them and an aid to explanation of
their central difficulties. They present the editor's view of the
poem's central subject together with his analysis of their
metrical and rhythmical structure. On the whole they do not
provide elucidation of difficult references. The notes should be
treated rather as an extension of the introduction and read as a
straightforward narrative from beginning to end.

A last word of advice to give the reader before he goes on to the poems, concerns what one might call the 'language' of poetry. In theory, there is no distinction between the language of poetry and prose except in rhythm. We all know, however, that in practice poetry tends to be much more compressed, more rich and more allusive than prose. The poet usually aims to get his effects in less space than the prose writer and he is often dealing with very complicated states of mind. A man in love, or a man on the edge of a nervous breakdown, is less able to speak plainly and clearly than a man describing what he had for lunch or where he went on his holiday. He may use everyday experiences of this kind to convey his feelings and his attitudes but the chances are that they will be presented in a very eccentric and unprosaic way. Sometimes, like a telegram, a poem will omit a number of connectives, so that the reader has to fill in the full details of the message for himself. Sometimes the poem will use a metaphor which we may not understand or sometimes even recognise. Here, for example, is the beginning of Dylan Thomas's poem, 'The Force that through the green fuse drives the flower' (p. 236):

> The force that through the green fuse drives
>   the flower
> Drives my green age; that blasts the roots of trees
> Is my destroyer.
> And I am dumb to tell the crooked rose
> My youth is bent by the same wintry fever.

Despite the fact that the metre of this poem is the familiar di-dum, di-dum, di-dum of traditional iambic, the poem is not likely to strike most readers as an easy one. Once the overall sense has been grasped – that the poem is about the subjection of all life, animal and vegetable, to the same laws of nature – the details may still puzzle. After the word 'rose', for example, and before the word 'my' in the fourth and fifth lines, the word 'that' has been missed out. This is a simple case of a telegraphic device. It gives the poem extra concision. Such omissions are not always as easy as this to notice. The reader must always be on his toes.

Moreover, in the first line of the poem the word 'fuse' is a metaphor. Because of the alliteration of 'f' sounds in the line, however, the reader is less likely to have his attention drawn to it. Dylan Thomas has made it sound completely natural and unobtrusive. This is a great merit in his writing but at the same time one must be alert and not miss its enrichment of the poem's meaning. If we substituted the word 'stem' the sense would be similar but not the same. Thomas manages to give the forces of nature the energy of an electric charge by using the term 'fuse' and this affects our sense of nature's destructiveness as well as its power because we think of fuses in connection with lights which can give us a shock or perhaps even more so with bombs, which can kill. It should be stressed, however, that the appreciation of a poet's vocabulary of metaphor and diction will always come at a third or later reading of his poem. Appreciating poetry is not a matter of noticing incidental beauties, or picking out isolated good lines and phrases. The main thing is to get the central point about the poem and its overall rhythmical structure clear. Imagery and diction and their influence on a poem's impact should be assessed later.

The last thing to be said is this: poetry is for me the greatest of the arts. It is the one art in which English-speaking people have always excelled, and it is the one art which can be practised at any time and in any place by writer or reader. When a poem is known by heart it can stay in the mind for a lifetime and affect everything that happens to a man or woman for good or for ill. No painting or building or piece of music can at the same time remain so memorable and so meaningful. In the First World War when asked what he was fighting for, Wilfred Owen replied: 'The English language.' This book will not have failed if it makes readers see what Wilfred Owen meant.

George MacBeth

W. B. Yeats

William Butler Yeats was born at Sandymount in Ireland in 1865 and died in France in 1939. In the course of his long life he gained a reputation as director of the Abbey Theatre (the Irish National Theatre) and as an Irish senator as well as a poet. Although he never achieved the success in public life of his near contemporary, the Italian writer D'Annunzio, or the widespread public acclaim of his exact contemporary, the English writer Kipling, Yeats shared their fascination for poetry as a public art, almost a branch of rhetoric, and also their concern for the passion and the ceremony of an essentially right-wing attitude to life. The achievement and the limitation of Yeats lay in his attempt to make a reactionary philosophy seem sensible and honourable in the context of the twentieth century. Despite the predominantly liberal-socialist ethos of the postwar period, he has maintained and increased his reputation among poets and readers. He is now generally regarded as the greatest English poet of the century and has indeed been called (by Kenneth Allott) 'the greatest English poet since Wordsworth'.

Yeats is not, however, an English poet at all; he is an Irish poet. His work can be seen as falling into three periods: the early rather misty, mythological poems of the Celtic twilight period, the concrete particularising poems of his middle years and the more dandified, violent mythological poems which occupied him at the end of his life. His greatest successes seem to me to have been achieved in writing about his friends and the causes for which they spoke, fought and died. Irish history and Irish politics came alive to Yeats through the doings of people he knew and loved. His best work is a commentary on the history of a whole country at the establishment of its freedom, a period of agonising crisis seen through the eyes of a particularly sensitive and involved member of it. Ireland was still small enough in the early twentieth century for one man to feel its problems personally and mould great poetry out of them. No English poet has been able during the last fifty or sixty years to do this for more than one particular region. This more than anything else establishes Yeats's pre-eminence.

To a Wealthy Man who Promised a Second Subscription to the Dublin Municipal Gallery if it Were Proved the People Wanted Pictures

You gave, but will not give again
Until enough of Paudeen's pence
By Biddy's halfpennies have lain
To be 'some sort of evidence',
Before you'll put your guineas down,
That things it were a pride to give
Are what the blind and ignorant town
Imagines best to make it thrive.
What cared Duke Ercole, that bid
His mummers to the market-place,
What th' onion-sellers thought or did
So that his Plautus set the pace
For the Italian comedies?
And Guidobaldo, when he made
That grammar school of courtesies
Where wit and beauty learned their trade
Upon Urbino's windy hill,
Had sent no runners to and fro
That he might learn the shepherds' will.
And when they drove out Cosimo,
Indifferent how the rancour ran,
He gave the hours they had set free
To Michelozzo's latest plan
For the San Marco Library,
Whence turbulent Italy should draw
Delight in Art whose end is peace,
In logic and in natural law
By sucking at the dugs of Greece.

Your open hand but shows our loss,
For he knew better how to live.
Let Paudeens play at pitch and toss,

Look up in the sun's eye and give
What the exultant heart calls good
That some new day may breed the best
Because you gave, not what they would,
But the right twigs for an eagle's nest!
December 1912

A Coat

I made my song a coat
Covered with embroideries
Out of old mythologies
From heel to throat;
But the fools caught it,
Wore it in the world's eyes
As though they'd wrought it.
Song, let them take it,
For there's more enterprise
In walking naked.

In Memory of Major Robert Gregory

I

Now that we're almost settled in our house
I'll name the friends that cannot sup with us
Beside a fire of turf in th' ancient tower,
And having talked to some late hour
Climb up the narrow winding stair to bed:
Discoverers of forgotten truth
Or mere companions of my youth,
All, all are in my thoughts to-night being dead.

4

Always we'd have the new friend meet the old
And we are hurt if either friend seem cold,
And there is salt to lengthen out the smart
In the affections of our heart,
And quarrels are blown up upon that head;
But not a friend that I would bring
This night can set us quarrelling,
For all that come into my mind are dead.

III

Lionel Johnson comes the first to mind,
That loved his learning better than mankind,
Though courteous to the worst; much falling he
Brooded upon sanctity
Till all his Greek and Latin learning seemed
A long blast upon the horn that brought
A little nearer to his thought
A measureless consummation that he dreamed.

IV

And that enquiring man John Synge comes next,
That dying chose the living world for text
And never could have rested in the tomb
But that, long travelling, he had come
Towards nightfall upon certain set apart
In a most desolate stony place,
Towards nightfall upon a race
Passionate and simple like his heart.

V

And then I think of old George Pollexfen,
In muscular youth well known to Mayo men
For horsemanship at meets or at racecourses,
That could have shown how pure-bred horses

And solid men, for all their passion, live
But as the outrageous stars incline
By opposition, square and trine;
Having grown sluggish and contemplative.

VI

They were my close companions many a year,
A portion of my mind and life, as it were,
And now their breathless faces seem to look
Out of some old picture-book;
I am accustomed to their lack of breath,
But not that my dear friend's dear son,
Our Sidney and our perfect man,
Could share in that discourtesy of death.

VII

For all things the delighted eye now sees
Were loved by him: the old storm-broken trees
That cast their shadows upon road and bridge;
The tower set on the stream's edge;
The ford where drinking cattle make a stir
Nightly, and startled by that sound
The water-hen must change her ground;
He might have been your heartiest welcomer.

VIII

When with the Galway foxhounds he would ride
From Castle Taylor to the Roxborough side
Or Esserkelly plain, few kept his pace;
At Mooneen he had leaped a place
So perilous that half the astonished meet
Had shut their eyes; and where was it
He rode a race without a bit?
And yet his mind outran the horses' feet.

IX

We dreamed that a great painter had been born
To cold Clare rock and Galway rock and thorn,

To that stern colour and that delicate line
That are our secret discipline
Wherein the gazing heart doubles her might.
Soldier, scholar, horseman, he,
And yet he had the intensity
To have published all to be a world's delight.

X

What other could so well have counselled us
In all lovely intricacies of a house
As he that practised or that understood
All work in metal or in wood,
In moulded plaster or in carven stone?
Soldier, scholar, horseman, he,
And all he did done perfectly
As though he had but that one trade alone.

XI

Some burn damp faggots, others may consume
The entire combustible world in one small room
As though dried straw, and if we turn about
The bare chimney is gone black out
Because the work had finished in that flare.
Soldier, scholar, horseman, he,
As 'twere all life's epitome.
What made us dream that he could comb grey hair?

XII

I had thought, seeing how bitter is that wind
That shakes the shutter, to have brought to mind
All those that manhood tried, or childhood loved
Or boyish intellect approved,
With some appropriate commentary on each;
Until imagination brought
A fitter welcome; but a thought
Of that late death took all my heart for speech.

An Irish Airman Foresees his Death

I know that I shall meet my fate
Somewhere among the clouds above;
Those that I fight I do not hate,
Those that I guard I do not love;
My country is Kiltartan Cross,
My countrymen Kiltartan's poor,
No likely end could bring them loss
Or leave them happier than before.
Nor law, nor duty bade me fight,
Nor public men, nor cheering crowds,
A lonely impulse of delight
Drove to this tumult in the clouds;
I balanced all, brought all to mind,
The years to come seemed waste of breath,
A waste of breath the years behind
In balance with this life, this death.

A Song

I thought no more was needed
Youth to prolong
Than dumb-bell and foil
To keep the body young.
O who could have foretold
That the heart grows old?

Though I have many words,
What woman's satisfied,
I am no longer faint
Because at her side?
O who could have foretold
That the heart grows old?

I have no lost desire
But the heart that I had;
I thought 'twould burn my body
Laid on the death-bed,
For who could have foretold
That the heart grows old?

The Scholars

Bald heads forgetful of their sins,
Old, learned, respectable bald heads
Edit and annotate the lines
That young men, tossing on their beds,
Rhymed out in love's despair
To flatter beauty's ignorant ear.

All shuffle there; all cough in ink;
All wear the carpet with their shoes;
All think what other people think;
All know the man their neighbour knows.
Lord, what would they say
Did their Catullus walk that way?

Memory

One had a lovely face,
And two or three had charm,
But charm and face were in vain
Because the mountain grass
Cannot but keep the form
Where the mountain hare has lain.

Upon a Dying Lady

I

Her Courtesy

With the old kindness, the old distinguished grace,
She lies, her lovely piteous head amid dull red hair
Propped upon pillows, rouge on the pallor of her face.
She would not have us sad because she is lying there,
And when she meets our gaze her eyes are laughter-lit,
Her speech a wicked tale that we may vie with her,
Matching our broken-hearted wit against her wit,
Thinking of saints and of Petronius Arbiter.

II

Certain Artists bring her Dolls and Drawings

Bring where our Beauty lies
A new modelled doll, or drawing,
With a friend's or an enemy's
Features, or maybe showing
Her features when a tress
Of dull red hair was flowing
Over some silken dress
Cut in the Turkish fashion,
Or, it may be, like a boy's.
We have given the world our passion,
We have naught for death but toys.

III

She turns the Dolls' Faces to the Wall

Because to-day is some religious festival
They had a priest say Mass, and even the Japanese,
Heel up and weight on toe, must face the wall
– Pedant in passion, learned in old courtesies,
Vehement and witty she had seemed – ; the Venetian
lady

Who had seemed to glide to some intrigue in her red
    shoes,
Her domino, her panniered skirt copied from Longhi;
The meditative critic; all are on their toes,
Even our Beauty with her Turkish trousers on.
Because the priest must have like every dog his day
Or keep us all awake with baying at the moon,
We and our dolls being but the world were best away.

IV

The End of Day

She is playing like a child
And penance is the play,
Fantastical and wild
Because the end of day
Shows her that some one soon
Will come from the house, and say –
Though play is but half done –
'Come in and leave the play.'

V

Her Race

She has not grown uncivil
As narrow natures would
And called the pleasures evil
Happier days thought good;
She knows herself a woman,
No red and white of a face,
Or rank, raised from a common
Unreckonable race;
And how should her heart fail her
Or sickness break her will
With her dead brother's valour
For an example still?

Her Courage

When her soul flies to the predestined dancing-place
(I have no speech but symbol, the pagan speech I made
Amid the dreams of youth) let her come face to face,
Amid that first astonishment, with Grania's shade,
All but the terrors of the woodland flight forgot
That made her Diarmuid dear, and some old cardinal
Pacing with half-closed eyelids in a sunny spot
Who had murmured of Giorgione at his latest breath –
Aye, and Achilles, Timor, Babar, Barhaim, all
Who have lived in joy and laughed into the face of
    Death.

Her Friends bring her a Christmas Tree

Pardon, great enemy,
Without an angry thought
We've carried in our tree,
And here and there have bought
Till all the boughs are gay,
And she may look from the bed
On pretty things that may
Please a fantastic head.
Give her a little grace,
What if a laughing eye
Have looked into your face?
It is about to die.

Easter 1916

I have met them at close of day
Coming with vivid faces
From counter or desk among grey
Eighteenth-century houses.

I have passed with a nod of the head
Or polite meaningless words,
Or have lingered awhile and said
Polite meaningless words,
And thought before I had done
Of a mocking tale or a gibe
To please a companion
Around the fire at the club,
Being certain that they and I
But lived where motley is worn:
All changed, changed utterly:
A terrible beauty is born.

That woman's days were spent
In ignorant good-will,
Her nights in argument
Until her voice grew shrill.
What voice more sweet than hers
When, young and beautiful,
She rode to harriers?
This man had kept a school
And rode our wingèd horse;
This other his helper and friend
Was coming into his force;
He might have won fame in the end,
So sensitive his nature seemed,
So daring and sweet his thought.
This other man I had dreamed
A drunken, vainglorious lout.
He had done most bitter wrong
To some who are near my heart,
Yet I number him in the song;
He, too, has resigned his part
In the casual comedy;
He, too, has been changed in his turn,
Transformed utterly:
A terrible beauty is born.

Hearts with one purpose alone
Through summer and winter seem
Enchanted to a stone
To trouble the living stream.
The horse that comes from the road,
The rider, the birds that range
From cloud to tumbling cloud,
Minute by minute they change;
A shadow of cloud on the stream
Changes minute by minute;
A horse-hoof slides on the brim,
And a horse plashes within it;
The long-legged moor-hens dive,
And hens to moor-cocks call;
Minute by minute they live:
The stone's in the midst of all.

Too long a sacrifice
Can make a stone of the heart.
O when may it suffice?
That is Heaven's part, our part
To murmur name upon name,
As a mother names her child
When sleep at last has come
On limbs that had run wild.
What is it but nightfall?
No, no, not night but death;
Was it needless death after all?
For England may keep faith
For all that is done and said.
We know their dream; enough
To know they dreamed and are dead;
And what if excess of love
Bewildered them till they died?
I write it out in a verse –
MacDonagh and MacBride
And Connolly and Pearse
Now and in time to be,

14

Wherever green is worn,
Are changed, changed utterly:
A terrible beauty is born.
September 25, 1916

The Second Coming

Turning and turning in the widening gyre
The falcon cannot hear the falconer;
Things fall apart; the centre cannot hold;
Mere anarchy is loosed upon the world,
The blood-dimmed tide is loosed, and everywhere
The ceremony of innocence is drowned;
The best lack all conviction, while the worst
Are full of passionate intensity.

Surely some revelation is at hand;
Surely the Second Coming is at hand.
The Second Coming! Hardly are those words out
When a vast image out of *Spiritus Mundi*
Troubles my sight: somewhere in sands of the desert
A shape with lion body and the head of a man,
A gaze blank and pitiless as the sun,
Is moving its slow thighs, while all about it
Reel shadows of the indignant desert birds.
The darkness drops again; but now I know
That twenty centuries of stony sleep
Were vexed to nightmare by a rocking cradle,
And what rough beast, its hour come round at last,
Slouches towards Bethlehem to be born?

Sailing to Byzantium

I

That is no country for old men. The young
In one another's arms, birds in the trees
– Those dying generations – at their song,
The salmon-falls, the mackerel-crowded seas,
Fish, flesh, or fowl, commend all summer long
Whatever is begotten, born, and dies.
Caught in that sensual music all neglect
Monuments of unageing intellect.

II

An aged man is but a paltry thing,
A tattered coat upon a stick, unless
Soul clap its hands and sing, and louder sing
For every tatter in its mortal dress,
Nor is there singing school but studying
Monuments of its own magnificence;
And therefore I have sailed the seas and come
To the holy city of Byzantium.

III

O sages standing in God's holy fire
As in the gold mosaic of a wall,
Come from the holy fire, perne in a gyre,
And be the singing-masters of my soul.
Consume my heart away; sick with desire
And fastened to a dying animal
It knows not what it is; and gather me
Into the artifice of eternity.

IV

Once out of nature I shall never take
My bodily form from any natural thing,
But such a form as Grecian goldsmiths make
Of hammered gold and gold enamelling
To keep a drowsy Emperor awake;

Or set upon a golden bough to sing
To lords and ladies of Byzantium
Of what is past, or passing, or to come.
1927

The Road at My Door

An affable Irregular,
A heavily-built Falstaffian man,
Comes cracking jokes of civil war
As though to die by gunshot were
The finest play under the sun.

A brown Lieutenant and his men,
Half dressed in national uniform,
Stand at my door, and I complain
Of the foul weather, hail and rain,
A pear-tree broken by the storm.

I count those feathered balls of soot
The moor-hen guides upon the stream,
To silence the envy in my thought;
And turn towards my chamber, caught
In the cold snows of a dream.

Leda and the Swan

A sudden blow: the great wings beating still
Above the staggering girl, her thighs caressed
By the dark webs, her nape caught in his bill,
He holds her helpless breast upon his breast.

How can those terrified vague fingers push
The feathered glory from her loosening thighs?
And how can body, laid in that white rush,
But feel the strange heart beating where it lies?

A shudder in the loins engenders there
The broken wall, the burning roof and tower
And Agamemnon dead.
                                    Being so caught up,
So mastered by the brute blood of the air,
Did she put on his knowledge with his power
Before the indifferent beak could let her drop?
1923

Among School Children

I

I walk through the long schoolroom questioning;
A kind old nun in a white hood replies;
The children learn to cipher and to sing,
To study reading-books and histories,
To cut and sew, be neat in everything
In the best modern way – the children's eyes
In momentary wonder stare upon
A sixty-year-old smiling public man.

II

I dream of a Ledaean body, bent
Above a sinking fire, a tale that she
Told of a harsh reproof, or trivial event
That changed some childish day to tragedy –
Told, and it seemed that our two natures blent
Into a sphere from youthful sympathy,
Or else, to alter Plato's parable,
Into the yolk and white of the one shell.

III

And thinking of that fit of grief or rage
I look upon one child or t'other there
And wonder if she stood so at that age –
For even daughters of the swan can share
Something of every paddler's heritage –
And had that colour upon cheek or hair,
And thereupon my heart is driven wild:
She stands before me as a living child.

IV

Her present image floats into the mind –
Did Quattrocento finger fashion it
Hollow of cheek as though it drank the wind
And took a mess of shadows for its meat?
And I though never of Ledaean kind
Had pretty plumage once – enough of that,
Better to smile on all that smile, and show
There is a comfortable kind of old scarecrow.

V

What youthful mother, a shape upon her lap
Honey of generation had betrayed,
And that must sleep, shriek, struggle to escape
As recollection or the drug decide,
Would think her son, did she but see that shape
With sixty or more winters on its head,
A compensation for the pang of his birth,
Or the uncertainty of his setting forth?

VI

Plato thought nature but a spume that plays
Upon a ghostly paradigm of things;
Solider Aristotle played the taws
Upon the bottom of a king of kings;
World-famous golden-thighed Pythagoras
Fingered upon a fiddle-stick or strings
What a star sang and careless Muses heard:
Old clothes upon old sticks to scare a bird.

Both nuns and mothers worship images,
But those the candles light are not as those
That animate a mother's reveries,
But keep a marble or a bronze repose.
And yet they too break hearts – O Presences
That passion, piety or affection knows,
And that all heavenly glory symbolise –
O self-born mockers of man's enterprise;

VIII

Labour is blossoming or dancing where
The body is not bruised to pleasure soul,
Nor beauty born out of its own despair,
Nor blear-eyed wisdom out of midnight oil.
O chestnut-tree, great-rooted blossomer,
Are you the leaf, the blossom or the bole?
O body swayed to music, O brightening glance,
How can we know the dancer from the dance?

Death

Nor dread nor hope attend
A dying animal;
A man awaits his end
Dreading and hoping all;
Many times he died,
Many times rose again.
A great man in his pride
Confronting murderous men
Casts derision upon
Supersession of breath;
He knows death to the bone –
Man has created death.

For Anne Gregory

'Never shall a young man,
Thrown into despair
By those great honey-coloured
Ramparts at your ear,
Love you for yourself alone
And not your yellow hair.'

'But I can get a hair-dye
And set such colour there,
Brown, or black, or carrot,
That young men in despair
May love me for myself alone
And not my yellow hair.'

'I heard an old religious man
But yesternight declare
That he had found a text to prove
That only God, my dear,
Could love you for yourself alone
And not your yellow hair.'

Byzantium

The unpurged images of day recede;
The Emperor's drunken soldiery are abed;
Night resonance recedes, night-walkers' song
After great cathedral gong;
A starlit or a moonlit dome disdains
All that man is,
All mere complexities,
The fury and the mire of human veins.

Before me floats an image, man or shade,
Shade more than man, more image than a shade;

For Hades' bobbin bound in mummy-cloth
May unwind the winding path;
A mouth that has no moisture and no breath
Breathless mouths may summon;
I hail the superhuman;
I call it death-in-life and life-in-death.

Miracle, bird or golden handiwork,
More miracle than bird or handiwork,
Planted on the star-lit golden bough,
Can like the cocks of Hades crow,
Or, by the moon embittered, scorn aloud
In glory of changeless metal
Common bird or petal
And all complexities of mire or blood.

At midnight on the Emperor's pavement flit
Flames that no faggot feeds, nor steel has lit,
Nor storm disturbs, flames begotten of flame,
Where blood-begotten spirits come
And all complexities of fury leave,
Dying into a dance;
An agony of trance,
An agony of flame that cannot singe a sleeve.

Astraddle on the dolphin's mire and blood,
Spirit after spirit! The smithies break the flood,
The golden smithies of the Emperor!
Marbles of the dancing floor
Break bitter furies of complexity,
Those images that yet
Fresh images beget,
That dolphin-torn, that gong-tormented sea.
1930

Old Tom Again

Things out of perfection sail,
And all their swelling canvas wear,
Nor shall the self-begotten fail
Though fantastic men suppose
Building-yard and stormy shore,
Winding-sheet and swaddling-clothes.

Lapis Lazuli

(For Harry Clifton)

I have heard that hysterical women say
They are sick of the palette and fiddle-bow,
Of poets that are always gay,
For everybody knows or else should know
That if nothing drastic is done
Aeroplane and Zeppelin will come out,
Pitch like King Billy bomb-balls in
Until the town lie beaten flat.

All perform their tragic play,
There struts Hamlet, there is Lear,
That's Ophelia, that Cordelia:
Yet they, should the last scene be there,
The great stage curtain about to drop,
If worthy their prominent part in the play,
Do not break up their lines to weep.
They know that Hamlet and Lear are gay;
Gaiety transfiguring all that dread.
All men have aimed at, found and lost;
Black out; Heaven blazing into the head:
Tragedy wrought to its uttermost.
Though Hamlet rambles and Lear rages,
And all the drop-scenes drop at once
Upon a hundred thousand stages,
It cannot grow by an inch or an ounce.

On their own feet they came, or on shipboard,
Camel-back, horse-back, ass-back, mule-back,
Old civilisations put to the sword.
Then they and their wisdom went to rack:
No handiwork of Callimachus,
Who handled marble as if it were bronze,
Made draperies that seemed to rise
When sea-wind swept the corner, stands;
His long lamp-chimney shaped like the stem
Of a slender palm, stood but a day;
All things fall and are built again,
And those that build them again are gay.

Two Chinamen, behind them a third,
Are carved in lapis lazuli,
Over them flies a long-legged bird,
A symbol of longevity;
The third, doubtless a serving-man,
Carries a musical instrument.

Every discoloration of the stone,
Every accidental crack or dent,
Seems a water-course or an avalanche,
Or lofty slope where it still snows
Though doubtless plum or cherry-branch
Sweetens the little half-way house
Those Chinamen climb towards, and I
Delight to imagine them seated there;
There, on the mountain and the sky,
On all the tragic scene they stare.
One asks for mournful melodies;
Accomplished fingers begin to play.
Their eyes mid many wrinkles, their eyes,
Their ancient, glittering eyes, are gay.

What Then?

His chosen comrades thought at school
He must grow a famous man;
He thought the same and lived by rule,
All his twenties crammed with toil;
'What then?' sang Plato's ghost. 'What then?'

Everything he wrote was read,
After certain years he won
Sufficient money for his need,
Friends that have been friends indeed;
'What then?' sang Plato's ghost. 'What then?'

All his happier dreams came true –
A small old house, wife, daughter, son,
Grounds where plum and cabbage grew,
Poets and Wits about him drew;
'What then?' sang Plato's ghost. 'What then?'

'The work is done,' grown old he thought,
'According to my boyish plan;
Let the fools rage, I swerved in naught,
Something to perfection brought';
But louder sang that ghost, 'What then?'

Beautiful Lofty Things

Beautiful lofty things: O'Leary's noble head;
My father upon the Abbey stage, before him a raging
  crowd:
'This Land of Saints,' and then as the applause died
  out,
'Of Plaster Saints'; his beautiful mischievous head
  thrown back.

Standish O'Grady supporting himself between the
    tables
Speaking to a drunken audience high nonsensical
    words;
Augusta Gregory seated at her great ormolu table,
Her eightieth winter approaching: 'Yesterday he
    threatened my life.
I told him that nightly from six to seven I sat at this
    table,
The blinds drawn up'; Maud Gonne at Howth station
    waiting a train,
Pallas Athene in that straight back and arrogant head:
All the Olympians; a thing never known again.

Roger Casement

(After reading 'The Forged Casement Diaries' by Dr Maloney)

I say that Roger Casement
Did what he had to do.
He died upon the gallows,
But that is nothing new.

Afraid they might be beaten
Before the bench of Time,
They turned a trick by forgery
And blackened his good name.

A perjurer stood ready
To prove their forgery true;
They gave it out to all the world,
And that is something new;

For Spring Rice had to whisper it,
Being their Ambassador,
And then the speakers got it
And writers by the score.

Come Tom and Dick, come all the troop
That cried it far and wide,
Come from the forger and his desk,
Desert the perjurer's side;

Come speak your bit in public
That some amends be made
To this most gallant gentleman
That is in quicklime laid.

The Spur

You think it horrible that lust and rage
Should dance attention upon my old age;
They were not such a plague when I was young;
What else have I to spur me into song?

Long-legged Fly

That civilisation may not sink,
Its great battle lost,
Quiet the dog, tether the pony
To a distant post;
Our master Caesar is in the tent
Where the maps are spread,
His eyes fixed upon nothing,
A hand under his head.
Like a long-legged fly upon the stream
His mind moves upon silence.

That the topless towers be burnt
And men recall that face,
Move most gently if move you must
In this lonely place.

She thinks, part woman, three parts a child,
That nobody looks; her feet
Practise a tinker shuffle
Picked up on a street.
Like a long-legged fly upon the stream
Her mind moves upon silence.

That girls at puberty may find
The first Adam in their thought,
Shut the door of the Pope's chapel,
Keep those children out.
There on that scaffolding reclines
Michael Angelo.
With no more sound than the mice make
His hand moves to and fro.
Like a long-legged fly upon the stream
His mind moves upon silence.

John Kinsella's Lament for Mrs Mary Moore

A bloody and a sudden end,
    Gunshot or a noose,
For Death who takes what man would keep,
    Leaves what man would lose.
He might have had my sister,
    My cousins by the score,
But nothing satisfied the fool
    But my dear Mary Moore,
None other knows what pleasures man
    At table or in bed.
What shall I do for pretty girls
    Now my old bawd is dead?

Though stiff to strike a bargain,
    Like an old Jew man,
Her bargain struck we laughed and talked
    And emptied many a can;
And O! but she had stories,
    Though not for the priest's ear,
To keep the soul of man alive,
    Banish age and care,
And being old she put a skin
    On everything she said.
What shall I do for pretty girls
    Now my old bawd is dead?

The priests have got a book that says
    But for Adam's sin
Eden's Garden would be there
    And I there within.
No expectation fails there,
    No pleasing habit ends,
No man grows old, no girl grows cold,
    But friends walk by friends.
Who quarrels over halfpennies
    That plucks the trees for bread?
What shall I do for pretty girls
    Now my old bawd is dead?

Notes

TO A WEALTHY MAN WHO PROMISED A SECOND SUBSCRIPTION TO THE DUBLIN MUNICIPAL GALLERY IF IT WERE PROVED THE PEOPLE WANTED PICTURES. This scornful piece of rhetoric is a little unfair. After all the rich man, Lord Ardilaun, had already given one subscription. Wouldn't Yeats have been better occupied addressing his poem to the ordinary citizens ('Paudeen' and 'Biddy') who had not as yet given anything? The parade of examples of artists and patrons from the Italian Renaissance has the effect of elevating a rather violent and perhaps even snobbish outburst of indignation. As so often with Yeats, we are swept away by the Irish blarney without pausing to consider the implications of the words.

A COAT. This short poem, published in *Responsibilities* in 1914, is a direct comment on, and renouncement of, Yeats's poems of the 1890s. It is a plain statement of the kind approved by the last two of its own lines.

IN MEMORY OF MAJOR ROBERT GREGORY. One of Yeats's major poems in his plain, middle style. The new house referred to in the first line is the tower at Thoor Ballylee which Yeats was settling into in 1919 and 1920. This tower is really a square medieval castle beside a mill and a millstream and its situation and associations form the background for the poem. Yeats was always fond of calling his dead friends back to mind. Lionel Johnson was one of the finest minor poets of the 1890s. He committed suicide in 1903. John Synge is best known as the author of *The Playboy of the Western World*. He died in 1908. George Pollexfen was the poet's uncle. The reason why Yeats concentrates on Major Gregory in his poem is not only perhaps the one which he gives in the last line and a half. His real fascination with Major Gregory now that he is settling into his own castle is that this friend combined the virtues of the artist and the man of action. 'Perfection of the life or of the work', to quote Yeats's own words in another poem, seemed an unreal choice in the case of Major Gregory. The early death of this friend serves Yeats as an emotional trigger for the attitudes he wants to dwell on.

AN IRISH AIRMAN FORESEES HIS DEATH. The tone of this poem has struck some commentators as Fascist. Based again upon Gregory, it really expresses the romantic individualism of an intellectual flier like D'Annunzio, or, later, St Exupéry. The poem's philosophy might be summed up in the familiar early nineteenth-century lines: 'One crowded hour of glorious life/Is worth an age without a name.' Kiltartan Cross is quite near to Yeats's home at Thoor Ballylee.

A SONG. An early example of a favourite form of Yeats's – a song with a refrain. The point of the refrain, the heart growing old, is contradicted by many of Yeats's last poems which rail at the inadequacies of the body while the mind and the spirit is still unimpaired.

THE SCHOLARS. A light, scornful poem about the failure of academic critics to understand the text they are studying. The Roman poet Catullus lived in the first century B.C. and wrote almost entirely about his own love affairs.

MEMORY. This graceful lyric refers to Yeats's inability to be won by other women while he still remembered Maud Gonne, the Irish agitator and beauty with whom he was fascinated over many years.

UPON A DYING LADY. This great early poem, about Mabel Beardsley, foreshadows the attitudes which Yeats finally summed up years later in 'Lapis Lazuli'. The poem exemplifies and praises the quality of 'gaiety transfiguring all that dread'. Petronius Arbiter was a Roman writer condemned to death by Nero who held a party for his friends while committing suicide by opening his veins in a bath of hot water. The poem is slightly marred by Yeats's scorn for what he calls 'a common unreckonable race' in section v, but this vice of arrogance occurs continually in his poetry, and is perhaps the inevitable concomitant of its passionate involvement with aristocratic ceremony.

EASTER 1916. Celebrates the Easter Rising of 1916, in which a group of Irish insurgents captured the General Post Office in Dublin and held out for several days before surrendering. Sixteen of them, including the two leaders, Pearse and Connolly, were executed. Yeats was clearly fascinated and at the same time troubled by this heroic and yet in some ways pointless sacrifice. He later returned to the theme in poem after poem. This early treatment of it written shortly after the event is an excellent example of one of his favourite metres, of the swinging three stress line rhyming in an *ab ab* pattern. Green was the colour of the insurgent army.

THE SECOND COMING. This strange visionary poem seems to anticipate the terrible history of coming violence which was to culminate with the German concentration camps in the Second World War. The 'rough beast' referred to in the second last line of the poem might almost literally be identified with Hitler, whose career in politics was just beginning at the time the poem was written. See also following note.

SAILING TO BYZANTIUM. Published in *The Tower* in 1928, this poem inaugurates Yeats's third period, when he was concerned to explore and express the intricacies of a private mythology. The details of this have foxed many commentators, but need worry no sensible ordinary reader. Yeats read philosophy late in life with an imperfect understanding of what it was all about, and his ideas form a confused hotchpotch of idealist thinking from Plato onwards. The amazing thing is that this rather ridiculous substructure enabled him to enrich and deepen his response to experience in his later poems. In particular, the myth of Byzantium as a magical city where life was entirely transmuted into art inspired Yeats to some of his finest poetic flights. The idea of life as art was originally part of the common vocabulary of the decadence in the late nineteenth century, but Yeats gave it a new twist and a new meaning. He seems to give life after death, or life beyond this world, a special sort of concrete grace and ceremony. Eternity has rarely seemed so attractive as it sometimes does in Yeats's later poems. The irritating word 'gyre' which occurs in the third section of this poem is a favourite of Yeats's in his later work (cp. 'The Second Coming'). It means literally 'spiral' as in a tower staircase, but its full associations depend on the philosophy which he outlines in his prose book *A Vision*.

THE ROAD AT MY DOOR. Part of a sequence called 'Meditations in Time of Civil War', which was clearly written during the troubles in the early 1920s. The strength of the poem comes from its ability to contrast stability with adventure through the image of the moorhen's chicks in the last stanza. Yeats sees his involvement with these, as a man living at peace in the country, as some compensation for not taking part in the excitements of the war.

LEDA AND THE SWAN. A great and complex sonnet, probably based on a Michelangelo painting. The quality of violent sexual passion is forcefully conveyed in the poem. At the same time the Greek myth is effectively used to pose an important question about the frequently alleged cleansing and reviving power of revolution and violence. The fall of Troy is referred to in the sextet because, after her rape by Zeus, Leda gave birth to Helen.

AMONG SCHOOL CHILDREN. This enormously ambitious and widely praised poem is a product of Yeats's experience as an Irish senator making an official visit to a church school. The poem moves from a direct consideration of the children he is meeting to a long section of recollection about his early love, Maud Gonne, and then to a passionate philosophical conclusion in which all of Yeats's platonic thinking blends into an exalted hymn of praise to the glory and the puzzle of human existence. The word 'Ledaean' refers to Leda. Yeats is comparing Maud Gonne's beauty with Helen's. The 'King of Kings' referred to in section VI is Alexander the Great, whose tutor was the Greek philosopher Aristotle. Yeats, like other poets who began writing in the 1890s, was very interested in dancing and his image of the dance was rooted in performances he had seen by Loie Fuller and others.

DEATH. This little poem effectively contrives to present a recommendation as a statement of fact. Its nobility of tone is in no way weakened by its probable falsity.

FOR ANNE GREGORY. A straightforward ironical love poem for two voices.

BYZANTIUM. Perhaps the most extreme example of Yeats's third period, a masterpiece of density and evocative but mysterious detail. References to the history of the Holy Roman Empire blend with aspects of Yeats's own philosophy in a glittering, intense traffic jam of brilliant ideas. In essence, the poem is an ecstatic vision of the spontaneous creation of spirits in what Yeats seems to see as the furnace of heaven. The dolphin was the Byzantine guide to the other world. The idea of 'handiwork' in the poem is a common one in Yeats's later work (cp. 'Sailing to Byzantium' and 'Lapis Lazuli').

OLD TOM AGAIN. This again is about the intimate links between life and art. It hymns the praises of pure unexplained and unthinking creativity. Technically, the poem is beautifully neat and its conclusion ingeniously suggests a connection between ship's tackle and the paraphernalia of birth and death.

LAPIS LAZULI. Very unusual, and strangely satisfying, this poem seems to identify desirable happiness with the power to retain one's gaiety in spite of adverse circumstances such as war, tragic ill-fortune and old age. Gaiety for Yeats seems to imply continuing vitality as well as simply good spirits. The central image of the Chinese carving in lapis lazuli is beautifully described. Yeats's power to bring works of art to life in words is one of his most attractive and individual accomplishments.

WHAT THEN? The refrain is used to make an ominous and in some ways bitter comment on the ideas contained in each stanza. And though the poem is written in the third person the man described is obviously Yeats himself. The poem forms a short synopsis of his life together with a comment on it in a mood of disenchantment.

BEAUTIFUL LOFTY THINGS. One of Yeats's very few poems, perhaps the only one, written in an attempt at free verse, though there is an underlying six stress pattern. It may show some direct influence of T. S. Eliot. Yeats is known to have been indirectly influenced strongly by Eliot's friend Ezra Pound, but there is little direct evidence of Pound's rhythms or phrasing in his poetry. The people referred to here are all friends of Yeats's whom he sees as in some way heroic. The phrase 'all the Olympians' presents them as classical gods.

ROGER CASEMENT. After the Easter Rising in 1916, Sir Roger Casement was executed by the English as a traitor, because he had been negotiating with Germany for the sale of rifles to the Irish insurgents. 'Some amends' were made when the bones of Casement were returned to Ireland in 1964 and reburied in Dublin.

THE SPUR. A famous epigram, often quoted in discussion about the sex and violence of Yeats's last poems. A physiological explanation for this may be sought in the monkey glands operation which Yeats underwent to renew his virility.

LONG-LEGGED FLY. This might be called a poem in praise of quietness. The poem suggests how three sorts of people, the conqueror exemplified by Caesar, the lover exemplified by Helen of Troy and the artist exemplified by 'Michael Angelo', all need silence to do their work. Michael Angelo painted the ceiling of the Sistine Chapel while lying on his back in a specially rigged scaffolding.

JOHN KINSELLA'S LAMENT FOR MRS MARY MOORE. A splendid elegy which has something of the bawdy joy immortalised by Villon in his ballades. The poem was much admired by Dylan Thomas who made it part of his regular reading repertoire.

D. H. Lawrence

D. H. Lawrence was born in Nottingham in 1885 and died in the South of France in 1930. Like Hardy before him and Roy Fuller after him, Lawrence achieved an equal reputation as a poet and a novelist. Much of his reputation among the illiterate has been due to the legend of his free treatment of sex, and in particular his use of the so-called 'four letter word'. Lawrence has in fact been presented by Philip Rieff as a key figure in twentieth century thought because of his special relationship to Freud, whom he severely criticised. Lawrence treated sex as a dark and mysterious power to be apprehended by the blood; Freud sometimes seemed to treat it as an ailment to be recognised by a number of symptoms and restrained or cured. At a time when more and more contemporary literature, particularly in America, seems to be aiming at an increasingly frank and detailed treatment of sexual subject matter, Lawrence's reputation is bound to go up still further. The real interest of his work, however, lies in its concern for energy rather than for sex as such. All his best poetry is about the living but non-human world. The influence of his writing about animals and flowers on the work of younger writers such as Ted Hughes has been deep, and in some ways surprising. Ten years ago, when the work of Movement poets like Larkin was in vogue, the poetry of Lawrence would seem to have had no influence at all on the future course of English poetry. His loose, rugged style was entirely out of fashion. Today, however, there are half a dozen important writers who stand directly in line from him. Another reason for Lawrence's success has been the Butler Education Act of 1944. For the first time in the mid-1950s working-class writers began to come to the fore in sufficiently large numbers to form a group with its own power to impose standards and create a climate of opinion. All earlier working-class writers in England, including Lawrence himself, had been outsiders, tolerated or admired by the ruling upper-middle-class élite but not affecting or changing its standards. The position in which he found himself seems to me to have seriously affected Lawrence's power to write with sustained insight about people in their social relationships. Everything that is good in his work turns into a free play of energies below the social level at which the distinctions of class operate.

Bat

At evening, sitting on this terrace,
When the sun from the west, beyond Pisa, beyond the
    mountains of Carrara
Departs, and the world is taken by surprise . . .

When the tired flower of Florence is in gloom beneath the
    glowing
Brown hills surrounding . . .

When under the arches of the Ponte Vecchio
A green light enters against stream, flush from the west,
Against the current of obscure Arno . . .

Look up, and you see things flying
Between the day and the night;
Swallows with spools of dark thread sewing the shadows
    together.

A circle swoop, and a quick parabola under the bridge arches
Where light pushes through;
A sudden turning upon itself of a thing in the air.
A dip to the water.

And you think:
'The swallows are flying so late!'

Swallows?

Dark air-life looping
Yet missing the pure loop . . .
A twitch, a twitter, an elastic shudder in flight
And serrated wings against the sky,
Like a glove, a black glove thrown up at the light,
And falling back.

Never swallows!
Bats!
The swallows are gone.

At a wavering instant the swallows gave way to bats
By the Ponte Vecchio . . .
Changing guard.

Bats, and an uneasy creeping in one's scalp
As the bats swoop overhead!
Flying madly.

Pipistrello!
Black piper on an infinitesimal pipe.
Little lumps that fly in air and have voices indefinite, wildly
    vindictive;

Wings like bits of umbrella.

Bats!

Creatures that hang themselves up like an old rag, to
    sleep;
And disgustingly upside down.
Hanging upside down like rows of disgusting old rags
And grinning in their sleep.
Bats!

In China the bat is symbol of happiness

Not for me!

Snake

A snake came to my water-trough
On a hot, hot day, and I in pyjamas for the heat,
To drink there.

In the deep, strange-scented shade of the great dark carob-
    tree
I came down the steps with my pitcher
And must wait, must stand and wait, for there he was at the
    trough before me.

39

He reached down from a fissure in the earth-wall in the gloom
And trailed his yellow-brown slackness soft-bellied down, over
the edge of the stone trough
And rested his throat upon the stone bottom,
And where the water had dripped from the tap, in a small
clearness,
He sipped with his straight mouth,
Softly drank through his straight gums, into his slack long
body,
Silently.

Someone was before me at my water-trough,
And I, like a second comer, waiting.

He lifted his head from his drinking, as cattle do,
And looked at me vaguely, as drinking cattle do,
And flickered his two-forked tongue from his lips, and mused
a moment,
And stooped and drank a little more,
Being earth-brown, earth-golden from the burning bowels of
the earth
On the day of Sicilian July, with Etna smoking.

The voice of my education said to me
He must be killed,
For in Sicily the black, black snakes are innocent, the gold are
venomous.

And voices in me said, If you were a man
You would take a stick and break him now, and finish him off.

But must I confess how I liked him,
How glad I was he had come like a guest in quiet, to drink at
my water-trough
And depart peaceful, pacified, and thankless,
Into the burning bowels of this earth?

Was it cowardice, that I dared not kill him?
Was it perversity, that I longed to talk to him?

Was it humility, to feel so honoured?
I felt so honoured.

And yet those voices:
If you were not afraid, you would kill him!

And truly I was afraid, I was most afraid,
But even so, honoured still more
That he should seek my hospitality
From out the dark door of the secret earth.

He drank enough
And lifted his head, dreamily, as one who has drunken,
And flickered his tongue like a forked night on the air, so
    black,
Seeming to lick his lips,
And looked around like a god, unseeing, into the air,
And slowly turned his head,
And slowly, very slowly, as if thrice adream,
Proceeded to draw his slow length curving round
And climb again the broken bank of my wall-face.

And as he put his head into that dreadful hole,
And as he slowly drew up, snake-easing his shoulders, and
    entered farther,
A sort of horror, a sort of protest against his withdrawing into
    that horrid black hole,
Deliberately going into the blackness, and slowly drawing
    himself after,
Overcame me now his back was turned.

I looked round, I put down my pitcher,
I picked up a clumsy log
And threw it at the water-trough with a clatter.

I think it did not hit him,
But suddenly that part of him that was left behind convulsed
    in undignified haste,

Writhed like lightning, and was gone
Into the black hole, the earth-lipped fissure in the wall-front,
At which, in the intense still noon, I stared with fascination.
And immediately I regretted it.
I thought how paltry, how vulgar, what a mean act!
I despised myself and the voices of my accursed human
    education.

And I thought of the albatross,
And I wished he would come back, my snake.

For he seemed to me again like a king,
Like a king in exile, uncrowned in the underworld,
Now due to be crowned again.

And so, I missed my chance with one of the lords
Of life.
And I have something to expiate;
A pettiness.

Taormina

Tortoise Shout

I thought he was dumb,
I said he was dumb,
Yet I've heard him cry.

First faint scream,
Out of life's unfathomable dawn,
Far off, so far, like a madness, under the horizon's dawning rim,
Far, far off, far scream.

Tortoise *in extremis*.

Why were we crucified into sex?
Why were we not left rounded off, and finished in ourselves,
As we began,
As he certainly began, so perfectly alone?

A far, was-it-audible scream,
Or did it sound on the plasm direct?

Worse than the cry of the new-born,
A scream,
A yell,
A shout,
A pæan,
A death-agony,
A birth-cry,
A submission,
All tiny, tiny, far away, reptile under the first dawn.
War-cry, triumph, acute-delight, death-scream reptilian,
Why was the veil torn?
The silken shriek of the soul's torn membrane?
The male soul's membrane
Torn with a shriek half music, half horror.

Crucifixion.
Male tortoise, cleaving behind the hovel-wall of that dense
    female,
Mounted and tense, spread-eagle, out-reaching out of the shell
In tortoise-nakedness,
Long neck, and long vulnerable limbs extruded, spread-eagle
    over her house-roof,
And the deep, secret, all-penetrating tail curved beneath her
    walls,
Reaching and gripping tense, more reaching anguish in utter-
    most tension
Till suddenly, in the spasm of coition, tupping like a jerking
    leap, and oh!
Opening its clenched face from his outstretched neck
And giving that fragile yell, that scream,
Super-audible,
From his pink, cleft, old-man's mouth,
Giving up the ghost,
Or screaming in Pentecost, receiving the ghost.

His scream, and his moment's subsidence,
The moment of eternal silence,
Yet unreleased, and after the moment, the sudden, startling
   jerk of coition, and at once
The inexpressible faint yell –
And so on, till the last plasm of my body was melted back
To the primeval rudiments of life, and the secret.

So he tups, and screams
Time after time that frail, torn scream
After each jerk, the longish interval,
The tortoise eternity,
Age-long, reptilian persistence,
Heart-throb, slow heart-throb, persistent for the next spasm.

I remember, when I was a boy,
I heard the scream of a frog, which was caught with his foot
   in the mouth of an up-starting snake;
I remember when I first heard bull-frogs break into sound in
   the spring;
I remember hearing a wild goose out of the throat of night
Cry loudly, beyond the lake of waters;
I remember the first time, out of a bush in the darkness, a
   nightingale's piercing cries and gurgles startled the depths
   of my soul;
I remember the scream of a rabbit as I went through a wood at
   midnight;
I remember the heifer in her heat, blorting and blorting
   through the hours, persistent and irrepressible;
I remember my first terror hearing the howl of weird, amorous
   cats;
I remember the scream of a terrified, injured horse, the sheet-
   lightning,
And running away from the sound of a woman in labour,
   something like an owl whooing,
And listening inwardly to the first bleat of a lamb,
The first wail of an infant,
And my mother singing to herself,

44

And the first tenor singing of the passionate throat of a young
   collier, who has long' since drunk himself to death,
The first elements of foreign speech
On wild dark lips.

And more than all these,
And less than all these,
This last,
Strange, faint coition yell
Of the male tortoise at extremity,
Tiny from under the very edge of the farthest far-off horizon of
   life.

The cross,
The wheel on which our silence first is broken,
Sex, which breaks up our integrity, our single inviolability our
   deep silence
Tearing a cry from us.

Sex, which breaks us into voice, sets us calling across the
   deeps, calling, calling for the complement,
Singing, and calling, and singing again, being answered, having
   found.

Torn, to become whole again, after long seeking for what is
   lost,
The same cry from the tortoise as from Christ, the Osiris-cry
   of abandonment,
That which is whole, torn asunder,
That which is in part, finding its whole again throughout the
   universe.

Humming-bird

I can imagine, in some otherworld
Primeval-dumb, far back
In that most awful stillness, that only gasped and hummed,
Humming-birds raced down the avenues.

Before anything had a soul,
While life was a heave of Matter, half inanimate,
This little bit chipped off in brilliance
And went whizzing through the slow, vast, succulent stems.

I believe there were no flowers, then
In the world where the humming-bird flashed ahead of creation.
I believe he pierced the slow vegetable veins with his long
    beak.

Probably he was big
As mosses, and little lizards, they say were once big.
Probably he was a jabbing, terrifying monster.

We look at him through the wrong end of the long telescope
    of Time,
Luckily for us.

Española.

Kangaroo

In the northern hemisphere
Life seems to leap at the air, or skim under the wind
Like stags on rocky ground, or pawing horses, or springy
    scut-tailed rabbits.

Or else rush horizontal to charge at the sky's horizon,
Like bulls or bisons or wild pigs.

Or slip like water slippery towards its ends,
As foxes, stoats, and wolves, and prairie dogs.

Only mice, and moles, and rats, and badgers, and beavers,
    and perhaps bears
Seem belly-plumbed to the earth's mid-navel.
Or frogs that when they leap come flop, and flop to the centre
    of the earth.

But the yellow antipodal Kangaroo, when she sits up,
Who can unseat her, like a liquid drop that is heavy, and just
  touches earth.

The downward drip.
The down-urge,
So much denser than cold-blooded frogs.

Delicate mother Kangaroo
Sitting up there rabbit-wise, but huge, plumb-weighted,
And lifting her beautiful slender face, oh! so much more gently
  and finely lined than a rabbit's, or than a hare's,
Lifting her face to nibble at a round white peppermint drop,
  which she loves, sensitive mother Kangaroo.

Her sensitive, long, pure-bred face.
Her full antipodal eyes, so dark,
So big and quiet and remote, having watched so many empty
  dawns in silent Australia.

Her little loose hands, and drooping Victorian shoulders.
And then her great weight below the waist, her vast pale belly
With a thin young yellow little paw hanging out, and straggle
  of a long thin ear, like ribbon,
Like a funny trimming to the middle of her belly, thin little
  dangle of an immature paw, and one thin ear.

Her belly, her big haunches
And in addition, the great muscular python-stretch of her tail.

There, she shan't have any more peppermint drops.
So she wistfully, sensitively sniffs the air, and then turns, goes
  off in slow sad leaps.

On the long flat skis of her legs,
Steered and propelled by that steel-strong snake of a tail.

Stops again, half turns, inquisitive to look back.
While something stirs quickly in her belly, and a lean little face
    comes out, as from a window,
Peaked and a bit dismayed,
Only to disappear again quickly away from the sight of the
    world, to snuggle down in the warmth,
Leaving the trail of a different paw hanging out.

Still she watches with eternal, cocked wistfulness!
How full her eyes are, like the full, fathomless, shining eyes of
    an Australian black-boy.
Who has been lost so many centuries on the margins of
    existence!

She watches with insatiable wistfulness.
Untold centuries of watching for something to come,
For a new signal from life, in that silent lost land of the South.

Where nothing bites but insects and snakes and the sun, small
    life.
Where no bull roared, no cow ever lowed, no stag cried, no
    leopard screeched, no lion coughed, no dog barked,
But all was silent save for parrots occasionally, in the haunted
    blue bush.

Wistfully watching, with wonderful liquid eyes.
And all her weight, all her blood, dripping sack-wise down
    towards the earth's centre,
And the live little one taking in its paw at the door of her belly.

Leap then, and come down on the line that draws to the
    earth's deep, heavy centre.

Sydney

48

Bavarian Gentians

Not every man has gentians in his house
in Soft September, at slow, Sad Michaelmas.

Bavarian gentians, big and dark, only dark
darkening the day-time torch-like with the smoking blueness of
    Pluto's gloom,
ribbed and torch-like, with their blaze of darkness spread blue
down flattening into points, flattened under the sweep of white
    day
torch-flower of the blue-smoking darkness, Pluto's dark-blue
    daze,
black lamps from the halls of Dis, burning dark blue,
giving off darkness, blue darkness, as Demeter's pale lamps give
    off light,
lead me then, lead me the way.

Reach me a gentian, give me a torch
let me guide myself with the blue, forked torch of this flower
down the darker and darker stairs, where blue is darkened on
    blueness.
even where Persephone goes, just now, from the frosted Sep-
    tember
to the sightless realm where darkness is awake upon the dark
and Persephone herself is but a voice
or a darkness invisible enfolded in the deeper dark
of the arms of Plutonic, and pierced with the passion of dense
    gloom,
among the splendour of torches of darkness, shedding dark-
    ness on the lost bride and her groom.

Notes

BAT. This poem very effectively creates a sense of the agility and weirdness of bats. The metre is Lawrence's usual form of free verse – a mixture of short and long lines governed by repetition and rhythm with no regular metrical principle. This kind of free verse writing, which does not ultimately owe its connections to Jacobean drama but rather to the Bible and Whitman, depends on great skill in the making of phrases and constant rhythmical vigilance, as Kenneth Allott has pointed out in *The Penguin Book of Contemporary Verse*. The Ponte Vecchio is a bridge across the Arno in Florence much frequented by bats at nightfall. Lawrence has another poem about trying to get a bat out of his bedroom after it had suddenly flown in through an open window, and he seems to have been mildly obsessed by the oddity and broken-down quality of the beast, which repelled him and made him think of it as something unclean.

SNAKE. Perhaps Lawrence's most famous and certainly most frequently anthologised animal poem. It marvellously conveys his sense of the innate glory of wild beasts and the comparative vulgarity and pettiness of human beings. This is not a philosophy widely to be recommended for ordinary life but it works well as the basis for a poem about a snake. At the same time Lawrence manages to say a good deal about himself in describing the snake – his reliance on traditional views, his timorousness and his indecisiveness. It is also a very effective poem about the nature of life in a Mediterranean country (in this case Sicily) in the summer. The heat and the inevitable consequent slothfulness are beautifully conveyed by the undulating rhythm of the free verse, which is also a natural mime for the movement of the coiling snake. The poem exhibits Lawrence's tendency to rely on repetitions in thought and phrasing to keep his free verse 'alive'. This device works well here but can sometimes degenerate into a boring trick.

TORTOISE SHOUT. One of Lawrence's most powerful poems, and an energetic enactment of many of his views about the nature of sexual energy. Very few writers have conveyed so urgently the mingled ecstasy and violence of the sexual act as Lawrence does here. The poem is the culminating one in a series of six about tortoises. Three of them are exquisitely delicate descriptions of a baby tortoise and its place in the universe. The remaining two serve as an introduction to this final poem by describing the male and female adult tortoises and their courtship. The enormous skill and sincerity of Lawrence is borne out by his power to bring his whole philosophy to bear on such a superficially narrow area of experience. Such sustained concentration on detail had scarcely ever before been attempted in English poetry.

HUMMING-BIRD. Humming birds are native to Central America. The Aztecs believed that the souls of dead soldiers who were killed in battle entered into humming birds and there enjoyed eternal life. Lawrence lived for a number of years in Mexico and responded with great excitement to its whole landscape. The conception of the humming bird here as a dazzling fragment is brilliantly successful. Almost all Lawrence's poems about birds and beasts, unlike those of Ted Hughes, for example, are about exotic creatures in foreign countries he was touring through or visiting. The amazing thing is that he always avoids the sense that the poems are being written casually like picture postcards. Penetration in depth seems to come to Lawrence far quicker than to most people in new places.

KANGAROO. Written in Sydney and a product of Lawrence's involvement with Australia. The continuous excellence of the description, combined with an insight into the fundamental nature of life in Australia, gives the poem both accuracy and resonance.

BAVARIAN GENTIANS. The best of Lawrence's poems about flowers. It reveals the compulsive power of these dark gloomy flowers and develops the idea of them as 'torches of darkness' with great subtlety. The third last line seems to have had a direct influence on Ted Hughes in the last stanza of his poem

'Pike' (p. 324). Persephone was a Greek girl, daughter of Demeter, who was captured by the god of the underworld while picking flowers and taken down to his realm. Dis or Pluto was the king of the underworld.

Andrew Young

Andrew Young was born in Scotland in 1885, the same year as D. H. Lawrence. He is the oldest living British poet of outstanding quality, and perhaps the most neglected. His work began to be published before the First World War but it was not until the 1930s, when he heavily revised and cut some of his earlier poems, that his characteristic excellence began to emerge. Like John Betjeman, his work most immediately suggests parallels with an earlier age – in Andrew Young's case, with the Metaphysical poetry of the seventeenth century, particularly the work of Andrew Marvell. In some ways, Andrew Young has been unfortunate in his advocates; because he writes about the countryside, about birds and flowers, his work appeals to those with a taste for the worst kind of 'Georgian' poetry, and he was liable to be dismissed by serious critics who didn't read him carefully, as a sort of surviving John Drinkwater or, at best, Edward Thomas. Young's poetry, however, is (with the exception of Eliot's) the most ambitious and consistent religious poetry of our time, and his reputation is certain to increase.

A Dead Mole

Strong-shouldered mole,
That so much lived below the ground,
Dug, fought and loved, hunted and fed,
For you to raise a mound
Was as for us to make a hole;
What wonder now that being dead
Your body lies here stout and square
Buried within the blue vault of the air?

Cuckoos

When coltsfoot withers and begins to wear
Long silver locks instead of golden hair,
And fat red catkins from black poplars fall
And on the ground like caterpillars crawl,
And bracken lifts up slender arms and wrists
And stretches them, unfolding sleepy fists,
The cuckoos in a few well-chosen words
Tell they give Easter eggs to the small birds.

The Fear

How often I turn round
To face the beast that bound by bound
Leaps on me from behind,
Only to see a bough that heaves
With sudden gust of wind
Or blackbird raking withered leaves.

A dog may find me out
Or badger toss a white-lined snout;

And one day as I softly trod
Looking for nothing stranger than
A fox or stoat I met a man
And even that seemed not too odd.

And yet in any place I go
I watch and listen as all creatures do
For what I cannot see or hear,
For something warns me everywhere
That even in my land of birth
I trespass on the earth.

Passing the Graveyard

I see you did not try to save
The bouquet of white flowers I gave;
So fast they wither on your grave.

Why does it hurt the heart to think
Of that most bitter abrupt brink
Where the low-shouldered coffins sink?

These living bodies that we wear
So change by every seventh year
That in a new dress we appear;

Limbs, spongy brain and slogging heart,
No part remains the selfsame part;
Like streams they stay and still depart.

You slipped slow bodies in the past;
Then why should we be so aghast
You flung off the whole flesh at last?

Let him who loves you think instead
That like a woman who has wed
You undressed first and went to bed.

1 The Funeral

One midnight in the Paris Underground
Walking along the tunnel to a train,
I saw a man leaning against the wall,
Eyes shut, head sunk on chest; selling newspapers
He had fallen asleep, but still stood on his feet.
Just so I must have stood,
When drowsily I heard, as from a distance,
Forasmuch – Almighty God – unto himself
The soul of our dear brother here departed,
We therefore commit his body to the ground;
Earth to earth, ashes to ashes – Half-asleep,
My mind took time to gather in the meaning;
Then I began to wonder, and awoke.

By an open grave
Lined with the undertaker's verdant grass,
Their backs toward me, priest and people stood.
The verger, who dropped the clods, dusting his hands,
Why, it was Fred! And this was Stonegate Church!
These were my friends, the priest the Rural Dean;
Did they think I lay ill in the vicarage,
Too ill to bury a parishioner?
Could they not see me standing in the road?
But when I saw the Three,
Who after the priest's '*I heard a voice from heaven*'
Drew closer to the grave's brink and gazed down,
I gasped and cried, 'Stop! there is some mistake;
You cannot bury me; I am not dead'.
But no one turned, for no one heard my cry.
Terrified by the silence of my own voice,
I sank down with a shudder by the lych-gate.

3 The Body

I had seen a tree-trunk,
That hurt the ground with its dead weight, sprout leaves
Not knowing it was dead; I had caught fish,
Flounders that flapped, eels tying and untying
Slippery knots, slow to drown in our air;
Was I too living out my life's last remnant,
Not living, only lasting? Was Death a monster,
A cat that toyed with a mouse, caught but not killed?
The thought seized my brain, a fear so tumultuous
That, afraid of itself, it died in fascination,
A crouching, a yielding to the softened paw,
The sense I was safe – not to escape.

Or was I not yet myself,
Not recovered from my illness, cured by death,
Still convalescent? How had I died?
Had death come as a storm, tornado, razing
A tract of memory? There was a gap,
Days, weeks and months torn from the almanac.
I remembered my father's death;
How I had watched the hard, humiliating struggle,
That made me half ashamed that I, his son,
Spied on his weakness. I remembered her,
Who held her son's last letter in her hand
Like a passport to heaven. I remembered too
Thinking that some time I should go their way;
But had I then believed it?

Why, even now
The sight and touch of my accustomed body
Compromised the truth. Here it was out of place,
An obvious mistake. Raising my hand,
I recognised a white scar on my wrist;
I felt my heart; shut in its cage of bones,
That songless lark kept time. But the funeral!
The coffin with its cargo! I was confused;

Were there two bodies, two scars, two bird-cages?
Paudricia in *Palmerin of England*
In place of her lover, still alive in prison,
Buried his effigy. Trust the undertaker
Not to bury a guy.

As I looked at my body,
It stared back with a strange impertinence,
Familiar, hostile, superfluous proof I was dead.
It, too, was make-believe, stuff of myself,
Old use and wont expected, therefore seen.
I was my own Pygmalion!
A fungoid outgrowth, it was not like that other
I left in the churchyard, that stiff, straight soldier
Who kept good guard in his fallen sentry-box.

I must not sleep again;
Nothing to hold it, my body would be gone,
And, body gone, should I not also go?
The thought alarmed me; it was high time to answer
The long-unanswered knocking at my mind's
Back-door. I had heard it since I first awoke,
Steady as a clocklike dripping in a crypt.
Now I bustled about and with shamefaced 'Welcome,
    stranger,
You should have come up by the garden path',
I greeted my terrific visitor,
The thought of God.

Notes

A DEAD MOLE. This is perhaps Andrew Young's best-known poem. The poem's sombre compassion for the dead mole is tempered by its wit and conceit. The topsy-turvy nature of the mole's life is beautifully conveyed by the image of it seeming to be buried above ground. At the same time, this diminishes the sense of finality in the mole's death and enables Young to convey a sense of its place in the eternal scheme of things. Young's power to see the ways of God in and through nature is as great in its own way as Wordsworth's. At the same time, he never 'makes a thing of it'. Religion seems to come as naturally to him as breathing, in a way that is ultimately perhaps medieval. Although the poem seems artless, its form is strict and ingenious: the syllable numbers of the lines are 4, 8, 8, 6, 8, 8, 8, 10.

CUCKOOS. An elegant little descriptive poem with a charming conceit at the end. Its grace and strength come from the transference of images from one kind of living matter to another. Everything for Young is equally alive in nature. The metre of the poem is ten-syllable heroic couplets.

THE FEAR. The sense of grim unease in this poem is a note which points forward to the macabre power of Andrew Young's longer poems. Once again, the identification of the poet with nature is made clear in the line 'I watch and listen as all creatures do'. The ominous mood is underlined by the varying length of the lines from stanza to stanza and by the varying rhyme schemes. This is worth analysing in full. In the first stanza the rhyme scheme is *aabcbc*, in the second stanza it is *aabccb*, and in the third stanza it is *aabbcc*. The number of syllables in the lines is as follows: in the first stanza it is 6, 8, 6, 8, 6, 8, in the second stanza it is 6, 8, 8, 8, 8, 8, and in the third stanza it is 8, 10, 8, 8, 8, 6. Few other poets in the twentieth century have so subtly calculated, or so ingeniously concealed their metrics as Andrew Young.

PASSING THE GRAVEYARD. The directly personal note in this poem is relatively uncommon in Young's work. The mixture of sadness, horror and resolution is characteristically metaphysical. The poem would have been greatly admired both for its formal grace and its moral fibre by any of the Cavalier poets of the second quarter of the seventeenth century. The last three lines are particularly moving, and I think not at all sentimental. The lines are all eight-syllable ones and the rhyme scheme is *aaa* in each stanza all the way through.

From INTO HADES. These two sections are from Andrew Young's most ambitious work, a long poem about his own imagined death and resurrection which deserves to be read in its entirety and is the most important long poem to appear in England since the Second World War. The poem displays an unforeseen breadth and grandeur of imagination in Young's work, while losing none of his accustomed precision and grace in detailed imagery. The mood varies from fear through disgust through irritation through sadness and amusement to wonder and humility. In the sections quoted, the macabre note is perhaps most evident in 'The Funeral'. Until his retirement recently, Andrew Young was Canon of Chichester Cathedral, but his parish church was Stonegate Church. The metre in the poem is traditional English blank verse, as used by Shakespeare, Milton and Tennyson. It is greatly to his credit that Young manages to avoid any echoes of his predecessors in this form. He manages to use what is normally a long, sweeping, rather free form as if it were a tight, short-breathed one. His device of breaking the long poem up into sections and breaking the ten-syllable lines with an occasional six-syllable one gives the poem an added originality and concision. The device of interrupting a long line throughout an epic poem by an occasional short one was first used by the Latin poet Virgil in *The Aeneid*. Young is a Latin scholar and may have had this precedent in mind. The end of 'The Body' reminds one of another seventeenth century poet, the clergyman George Herbert.

Edwin Muir

Edwin Muir was born in Scotland in 1887 and died in England in 1958. He was a relatively late developer and only came to real prominence with the publication of his book *The Labyrinth* in 1949. Many of the poems in that book were based on Muir's experiences while working for the British Council in Prague immediately after the war, and the book remains one of the most consistent and serious collections of poems to be published since 1945. Muir is a severe and very Scottish writer whose work sometimes seems marred by an excessive plainness of style, but his best work rises to a massive seriousness. With his wife Willa Muir he was the first to translate the writings of Kafka into English.

Horses

Those lumbering horses in the steady plough,
On the bare field – I wonder why, just now,
They seemed terrible, so wild and strange,
Like magic power on the stony grange.

Perhaps some childish hour has come again,
When I watched fearful, through the blackening rain,
Their hooves like pistons in an ancient mill
Move up and down, yet seem as standing still.

Their conquering hooves which trod the stubble down
Were ritual that turned the field to brown,
And their great hulks were seraphim of gold,
Or mute ecstatic monsters on the mould.

And oh the rapture, when, one furrow done,
They marched broad-breasted to the sinking sun!
The light flowed off their bossy sides in flakes;
The furrows rolled behind like struggling snakes.

But when at dusk with steaming nostrils home
They came, they seemed gigantic in the gloam,
And warm and glowing with mysterious fire
That lit their smouldering bodies in the mire.

Their eyes as brilliant and as wide as night
Gleamed with a cruel apocalyptic light.
Their manes the leaping ire of the wind
Lifted with rage invisible and blind.

Ah, now it fades! it fades! and I must pine
Again for that dread country crystalline,
Where the blank field and the still-standing tree
Were bright and fearful presences to me.

The Combat

It was not meant for human eyes,
That combat on the shabby patch
Of clods and trampled turf that lies
Somewhere beneath the sodden skies
For eye of toad or adder to catch.

And having seen it I accuse
The crested animal in his pride,
Arrayed in all the royal hues
Which hide the claws he well can use
To tear the heart out of the side.

Body of leopard, eagle's head
And whetted beak, and lion's mane,
And frost-grey hedge of feathers spread
Behind – he seemed of all things bred.
I shall not see his like again.

As for his enemy, there came in
A soft round beast as brown as clay;
All rent and patched his wretched skin;
A battered bag he might have been,
Some old used thing to throw away.

Yet he awaited face to face
The furious beast and the swift attack.
Soon over and done. That was no place
Or time for chivalry or for grace.
The fury had him on his back.

And two small paws like hands flew out
To right and left as the trees stood by.
One would have said beyond a doubt
This was the very end of the bout,
But that the creature would not die.

For ere the death-stroke he was gone,
Writhed, whirled, huddled into his den,
Safe somehow there. The fight was done,
And he had lost who had all but won.
But oh his deadly fury then.

A while the place lay blank, forlorn,
Drowsing as in relief from pain.
The cricket chirped, the grating thorn
Stirred, and a little sound was born.
The champions took their posts again.

And all began. The stealthy paw
Slashed out and in. Could nothing save
These rags and tatters from the claw?
Nothing. And yet I never saw
A beast so helpless and so brave.

And now, while the trees stand watching, still
The unequal battle rages there.
The killing beast that cannot kill
Swells and swells in his fury till
You'd almost think it was despair.

The Interrogation

We could have crossed the road but hesitated,
And then came the patrol:
The leader conscientious and intent,
The men surly, indifferent.
While we stood by and waited
The interrogation began. He says the whole
Must come out now, who, what we are,
Where we have come from, with what purpose, whose
Country or camp we plot for or betray.
Question on question.

We have stood and answered through the standing day
And watched across the road beyond the hedge
The careless lovers in pairs go by,
Hand linked in hand, wandering another star,
So near we could shout to them. We cannot choose
Answer or action here,
Though still the careless lovers saunter by
And the thoughtless field is near.
We are on the very edge,
Endurance almost done,
And still the interrogation is going on.

The Good Town

Look at it well. This was the good town once,
Known everywhere, with streets of friendly neighbours,
Street friend to street and house to house. In summer
All day the doors stood open; lock and key
Were quaint antiquities fit for museums
With gyves and rusty chains. The ivy grew
From post to post across the prison door.
The yard behind was sweet with grass and flowers,
A place where grave philosophers loved to walk.
Old Time that promises and keeps his promise
Was our sole lord indulgent and severe,
Who gave and took away with gradual hand
That never hurried, never tarried, still
Adding, subtracting. These our houses had
Long fallen into decay but that we knew
Kindness and courage can repair time's faults,
And serving him breeds patience and courtesy
In us, light sojourners and passing subjects.
There is a virtue in tranquillity
That makes all fitting, childhood and youth and age,
Each in its place.

Look well. These mounds of rubble,
And shattered piers, half-windows, broken arches
And groping arms were once inwoven in walls
Covered with saints and angels, bore the roof,
Shot up the towering spire. These gaping bridges
Once spanned the quiet river which you see
Beyond that patch of raw and angry earth
Where the new concrete houses sit and stare.
Walk with me by the river. See, the poplars
Still gather quiet gazing on the stream.
The white road winds across the small green hill
And then is lost. These few things still remain.
Some of our houses too, though not what once
Lived there and drew a strength from memory.
Our people have been scattered, or have come
As strangers back to mingle with the strangers
Who occupy our rooms where none can find
The place he knew but settles where he can.
No family now sits at the evening table;
Father and son, mother and child are *out*,
A quaint and obsolete fashion. In our houses
Invaders speak their foreign tongues, informers
Appear and disappear, chance whores, officials
Humble or high, frightened, obsequious,
Sit carefully in corners. My old friends
(Friends ere these great disasters) are dispersed
In parties, armies, camps, conspiracies.
We avoid each other. If you see a man
Who smiles good-day or waves a lordly greeting
Be sure he's a policeman or a spy.
We know them by their free and candid air.

It was not time that brought these things upon us,
But these two wars that trampled on us twice,
Advancing and withdrawing, like a herd
Of clumsy-footed beasts on a stupid errand
Unknown to them or us. Pure chance, pure malice,
Or so it seemed. And when, the first war over,

The armies left and our own men came back
From every point by many a turning road,
Maimed, crippled, changed in body or in mind,
It was a sight to see the cripples come
Out on the fields. The land looked all awry,
The roads ran crooked and the light fell wrong.
Our fields were like a pack of cheating cards
Dealt out at random – all we had to play
In the bad game for the good stake, our life.
We played; a little shrewdness scraped us through.
Then came the second war, passed and repassed,
And now you see our town, the fine new prison,
The house-doors shut and barred, the frightened faces
Peeping round corners, secret police, informers,
And all afraid of all.

How did it come?
From outside, so it seemed, an endless source,
Disorder inexhaustible, strange to us,
Incomprehensible. Yet sometimes now
We ask ourselves, we the old citizens:
'Could it have come from us? Was our peace peace?
Our goodness goodness? That old life was easy
And kind and comfortable; but evil is restless
And gives no rest to the cruel or the kind.
How could our town grow wicked in a moment?
What is the answer? Perhaps no more than this,
That once the good men swayed our lives, and those
Who copied them took a while the hue of goodness,
A passing loan; while now the bad are up,
And we, poor ordinary neutral stuff,
Not good nor bad, must ape them as we can,
In sullen rage or vile obsequiousness.
Say there's a balance between good and evil
In things, and it's so mathematical,
So finely reckoned that a jot of either,
A bare preponderance will do all you need,
Make a town good, or make it what you see.

67

But then, you'll say, only that jot is wanting,
That grain of virtue. No: when evil comes
All things turn adverse, and we must begin
At the beginning, heave the groaning world
Back in its place again, and clamp it there.
Then all is hard and hazardous. We have seen
Good men made evil wrangling with the evil,
Straight minds grown crooked fighting crooked minds.
Our peace betrayed us; we betrayed our peace.
Look at it well. This was the good town once.'

These thoughts we have, walking among our ruins.

The Horses

Barely a twelvemonth after
The seven days war that put the world to sleep,
Late in the evening the strange horses came.
By then we had made our covenant with silence,
But in the first few days it was so still
We listened to our breathing and were afraid.
On the second day
The radios failed; we turned the knobs; no answer.
On the third day a warship passed us, heading north,
Dead bodies piled on the deck. On the sixth day
A plane plunged over us into the sea. Thereafter
Nothing. The radios dumb;
And still they stand in corners of our kitchens,
And stand, perhaps, turned on, in a million rooms
All over the world. But now if they should speak,
If on a sudden they should speak again,
If on the stroke of noon a voice should speak,
We would not listen, we would not let it bring
That old bad world that swallowed its children quick
At one great gulp. We would not have it again.

Sometimes we think of the nations lying asleep,
Curled blindly in impenetrable sorrow,
And then the thought confounds us with its strangeness.
The tractors lie about our fields; at evening
They look like dank sea-monsters couched and waiting.
We leave them where they are and let them rust:
'They'll moulder away and be like other loam.'
We make our oxen drag our rusty ploughs,
Long laid aside. We have gone back
Far past our fathers' land.
                                        And then, that evening
Late in the summer the strange horses came.
We heard a distant tapping on the road,
A deepening drumming; it stopped, went on again
And at the corner changed to hollow thunder.
We saw the heads
Like a wild wave charging and were afraid.
We had sold our horses in our fathers' time
To buy new tractors. Now they were strange to us
As fabulous steeds set on an ancient shield
Or illustrations in a book of knights.
We did not dare go near them. Yet they waited,
Stubborn and shy, as if they had been sent
By an old command to find our whereabouts
And that long-lost archaic companionship.
In the first moment we had never a thought
That they were creatures to be owned and used.
Among them were some half-a-dozen colts
Dropped in some wilderness of the broken world,
Yet new as if they had come from their own Eden.
Since then they have pulled our ploughs and borne our
     loads,
But that free servitude still can pierce our hearts.
Our life is changed; their coming our beginning.

Notes

HORSES. This poem describes watching horses ploughing in the Orkneys, where Muir was born. His power to treat horses as creatures of mythical significance is one of Muir's most striking characteristics, and this poem should be compared with his later poem also called 'The Horses'. The subject matter of this poem, as of a number in Muir's opus, is treated in prose in his interesting autobiography.

THE COMBAT. A good example of Muir's power to raise an everyday, sordid incident to the status of myth. The poem may have begun as one about a fight between a cat and a mouse, but the two combatants in the finished version are entirely non-naturalistic: the poem might stand as an emblem for the German conquest of smaller European nations during the war. The poem is a tribute to the pathos and the glory of commonplace heroism.

THE INTERROGATION. This poem effectively conveys the help-lessness of civilians in the face of officialdom. This was one of Kafka's main themes, and one which Muir took over in his postwar poems arising out of his experiences in eastern Europe. What gives the poem its quality is the way in which the situation seems neither completely real, nor completely imaginary. It may have begun as a personal experience with a frontier guard, but the purely irrelevant local details have all been pared away. In the days of the Berlin Wall the poem contains its contemporary relevance. It makes an interesting comparison for its intricacy of metre and rhyme with some of the poems of Muir's fellow countryman Andrew Young. The metre is a slightly resolved iambic line which varies in length from ten syllables to four and the rhyme scheme is: *abccabdefgfhi effijhgg*. The difference between this kind of intricacy and Andrew Young's is that there is no complete repetition of the pattern in later stanzas. The metre is effective, however, in miming the uncertainty of the people waiting and their sense that what is happening is going to continue for ever in the same rather pointless way.

THE GOOD TOWN. The best of Muir's longer poems in blank verse. Although 'the Good Town' is a mythical one, it is clearly based on Prague as Muir knew it. Czechoslovakia was a country created out of part of the Austro-Hungarian Empire in 1918. It was invaded and taken over by Nazi Germany in 1938, and a Communist coup in 1948 made it part of what seemed at the time Russia's Iron Curtain empire in eastern Europe. The poem is one of the most moving and instructive political ones to come out of the postwar world. Only George Orwell in his novel *1984* has equalled Muir in his analysis of the feelings of the cold war. Prague is the capital of Czechoslovakia.

THE HORSES. This magnificent poem takes Muir into the territory of writers of science fiction like John Wyndham and John Christopher. The terrifying picture of a world after a nuclear disaster painted in the opening section is beautifully contrasted with the arrival later of the mythical horses. They remind one a little of the white horses of the Camargue as they appear in a famous French slow-motion film, but in fact they are once again the farm horses which Muir remembered from his childhood in the Orkneys. This is perhaps the most movingly optimistic poem to have come out of the world of the hydrogen bomb.

T. S. Eliot

Thomas Stearns Eliot was born in the United States in 1888 and died in England in 1965. From 1915 he lived in England and in 1927 he became a naturalised British subject. As editor of the quarterly review *The Criterion*, and as a director of the publishing firm of Faber and Faber, he exerted an enormous influence over the writing of poetry in England for more than a generation. His many critical books, from the publication of *The Sacred Wood* in 1920 onwards, marked out a new tradition in English literature. What began as a revolution has for many years been an accepted orthodoxy. No other English writer of the century has done so much to stamp his own image on the writing of his time. Indeed, for many in England Eliot would rank with Stravinsky and Picasso as one of the three high priests of the modern movement. The paradox of Eliot's career lies in the skill with which an *avant-garde* poet turned himself into a pillar of the establishment. The transition really came with his conversion to Christianity in the late 1920s. Before this he seems to be the leader of a movement designed to uproot everything English society stood for: after, he seems to speak for all that is best in its entrenched Conservatism.

Re-reading his early poetry one notices the seeds of Eliot's later orthodoxy more clearly. Throughout his work he has been concerned with the problem of establishing stability after chaos. His early poetry mirrors the disintegration which his later poetry suggests a possible cure for. If the cool, classical, conservative tone of his later poetry seems too austere for many, at least it is the product of a thoroughly thought out and analysed literary position. From the point of view of its influence on other writing *The Waste Land* remains the single most important poem of the century. No poem written since – despite the passage of nearly fifty years since its first publication – strikes one as having made a more exciting and significant break with tradition.

The Love Song of J. Alfred Prufrock

S'io credessi che mia riposta fosse
a persona che mai tornasse al mondo,
questa fiamma staria senza più scosse.
Ma per ciò che giammai di questo fondo
non tornò vivo alcun, s'i'odo il vero,
senza tema d'infamia ti rispondo.

Let us go then, you and I,
When the evening is spread out against the sky
Like a patient etherised upon a table;
Let us go, through certain half-deserted streets,
The muttering retreats
Of restless nights in one-night cheap hotels
And sawdust restaurants with oyster-shells:
Streets that follow like a tedious argument
Of insidious intent
To lead you to an overwhelming question. . .
Oh, do not ask, 'What is it?'
Let us go and make our visit.

In the room the women come and go
Talking of Michelangelo.

The yellow fog that rubs its back upon the window-panes,
The yellow smoke that rubs its muzzle on the window-panes,
Licked its tongue into the corners of the evening,
Lingered upon the pools that stand in drains,
Let fall upon its back the soot that falls from chimneys,
Slipped by the terrace, made a sudden leap,
And seeing that it was a soft October night,
Curled once about the house, and fell asleep.

And indeed there will be time
For the yellow smoke that slides along the street
Rubbing its back upon the window-panes;
There will be time, there will be time
To prepare a face to meet the faces that you meet;

There will be time to murder and create,
And time for all the works and days of hands
That lift and drop a question on your plate;
Time for you and time for me,
And time yet for a hundred indecisions.
And for a hundred visions and revisions,
Before the taking of a toast and tea.

In the room the women come and go
Talking of Michelangelo.

And indeed there will be time
To wonder, 'Do I dare?' and, 'Do I dare?'
Time to turn back and descend the stair,
With a bald spot in the middle of my hair –
(They will say: 'How his hair is growing thin!')
My morning coat, my collar mounting firmly to the chin,
My necktie rich and modest, but asserted by a simple pin –
(They will say: 'But how his arms and legs are thin!')
Do I dare
Disturb the universe?
In a minute there is time
For decisions and revisions which a minute will reverse.

For I have known them all already, known them all –
Have known the evenings, mornings, afternoons,
I have measured out my life with coffee spoons;
I know the voices dying with a dying fall
Beneath the music from a farther room,
    So how should I presume?

And I have known the eyes already, known them all –
The eyes that fix you in a formulated phrase,
And when I am formulated, sprawling on a pin,
When I am pinned and wriggling on the wall,
Then how should I begin
To spit out all the butt-ends of my days and ways?
    And how should I presume?

And I have known the arms already, known them all –
Arms that are braceleted and white and bare
(But in the lamplight, downed with light brown hair!)
Is it perfume from a dress
That makes me so digress?
Arms that lie along a table, or wrap about a shawl.
    And should I then presume?
    And how should I begin?

        .   .   .   .   .   .

Shall I say, I have gone at dusk through narrow streets
And watched the smoke that rises from the pipes
Of lonely men in shirt-sleeves, leaning out of windows? ...

    I should have been a pair of ragged claws
Scuttling across the floors of silent seas.

        .   .   .   .   .   .

    And the afternoon, the evening, sleeps so peacefully!
Smoothed by long fingers,
Asleep ... tired ... or it malingers,
Stretched on the floor, here beside you and me.
Should I, after tea and cakes and ices,
Have the strength to force the moment to its crisis?
But though I have wept and fasted, wept and prayed,
Though I have seen my head (grown slightly bald)
        brought in upon a platter,
I am no prophet – and here's no great matter;
I have seen the moment of my greatness flicker,
And I have seen the eternal Footman hold my coat, and
        snicker,
And in short, I was afraid.

    And would it have been worth it, after all,
After the cups, the marmalade, the tea,
Among the porcelain, among some talk of you and me,
Would it have been worth while,
To have bitten off the matter with a smile,
To have squeezed the universe into a ball
To roll it towards some overwhelming question,

76

To say: 'I am Lazarus, come from the dead,
Come back to tell you all, I shall tell you all' –
If one, settling a pillow by her head,
    Should say: 'That is not what I meant at all.
    That is not it, at all.'

And would it have been worth it, after all,
Would it have been worth while,
After the sunsets and the dooryards and the sprinkled streets,
After the novels, after the teacups, after the skirts that trail
    along the floor –
And this, and so much more? –
It is impossible to say just what I mean!
But as if a magic lantern threw the nerves in patterns on a
    screen:
Would it have been worth while
If one, settling a pillow or throwing off a shawl,
And turning toward the window, should say:
    'That is not it at all,
    That is not what I meant, at all.'
                    .   .   .   .   .

No! I am not Prince Hamlet, nor was meant to be;
Am an attendant lord, one that will do
To swell a progress, start a scene or two,
Advise the prince; no doubt, an easy tool,
Deferential, glad to be of use,
Politic, cautious, and meticulous;
Full of high sentence, but a bit obtuse;
At times, indeed, almost ridiculous –
Almost, at times, the Fool.

    I grow old . . . I grow old . . .
I shall wear the bottoms of my trousers rolled.

    Shall I part my hair behind? Do I dare to eat a peach?
I shall wear white flannel trousers, and walk upon the beach.
I have heard the mermaids singing, each to each.

I do not think that they will sing to me.

I have seen them riding seaward on the waves
Combing the white hair of the waves blown back
When the wind blows the water white and black.

We have lingered in the chambers of the sea
By sea-girls wreathed with seaweed red and brown
Till human voices wake us, and we drown.

Preludes

I

The winter evening settles down
With smell of steaks in passageways.
Six o'clock.
The burnt-out ends of smoky days.
And now a gusty shower wraps
The grimy scraps
Of withered leaves about your feet
And newspapers from vacant lots;
The showers beat
On broken blinds and chimney-pots,
And at the corner of the street
A lonely cab-horse steams and stamps.

And then the lighting of the lamps.

II

The morning comes to consciousness
Of faint stale smells of beer
From the sawdust-trampled street
With all its muddy feet that press
To early coffee-stands.

With the other masquerades
That time resumes,
One thinks of all the hands

That are raising dingy shades
In a thousand furnished rooms.

III

You tossed a blanket from the bed,
You lay upon your back, and waited;
You dozed, and watched the night revealing
The thousand sordid images
Of which your soul was constituted;
They flickered against the ceiling.
And when all the world came back
And the light crept up between the shutters
And you heard the sparrows in the gutters,
You had such a vision of the street
As the street hardly understands;
Sitting along the bed's edge, where
You curled the papers from your hair,
Or clasped the yellow soles of feet
In the palms of both soiled hands.

IV

His soul stretched tight across the skies
That fade behind a city block,
Or trampled by insistent feet
At four and five and six o'clock;
And short square fingers stuffing pipes,
And evening newspapers, and eyes
Assured of certain certainties,
The conscience of a blackened street
Impatient to assume the world.

I am moved by fancies that are curled
Around these images, and cling:
The notion of some infinitely gentle
Infinitely suffering thing.

Wipe your hand across your mouth, and laugh;
The worlds revolve like ancient women
Gathering fuel in vacant lots.

Rhapsody on a Windy Night

Twelve o'clock.
Along the reaches of the street
Held in a lunar synthesis,
Whispering lunar incantations
Dissolve the floors of memory
And all its clear relations,
Its divisions and precisions.
Every street lamp that I pass
Beats like a fatalistic drum,
And through the spaces of the dark
Midnight shakes the memory
As a madman shakes a dead geranium.

Half-past one,
The street-lamp sputtered,
The street-lamp muttered,
The street-lamp said, 'Regard that woman
Who hesitates toward you in the light of the door
Which opens on her like a grin.
You see the border of her dress
Is torn and stained with sand,
And you see the corner of her eye
Twists like a crooked pin.'

The memory throws up high and dry
A crowd of twisted things;
A twisted branch upon the beach
Eaten smooth, and polished
As if the world gave up
The secret of its skeleton,
Stiff and white.
A broken spring in a factory yard,
Rust that clings to the form that the strength has left
Hard and curled and ready to snap.

Half-past two,
The street-lamp said,

'Remark the cat which flattens itself in the gutter,
Slips out its tongue
And devours a morsel of rancid butter.'
So the hand of the child, automatic,
Slipped out and pocketed a toy that was running along the quay.
I could see nothing behind that child's eye.
I have seen eyes in the street
Trying to peer through lighted shutters,
And a crab one afternoon in a pool,
An old crab with barnacles on his back,
Gripped the end of a stick which I held him.

Half-past three,
The lamp sputtered,
The lamp muttered in the dark.
The lamp hummed:
'Regard the moon,
La lune ne garde aucune rancune,
She winks a feeble eye,
She smiles into corners.
She smooths the hair of the grass.
The moon has lost her memory.
A washed-out smallpox cracks her face,
Her hand twists a paper rose,
That smells of dust and eau de Cologne,
She is alone
With all the old nocturnal smells
That cross and cross across her brain.'
The reminiscence comes
On sunless dry geraniums
And dust in crevices,
Smells of chestnuts in the streets,
And female smells in shuttered rooms,
And cigarettes in corridors
And cocktail smells in bars.

The lamp said,
'Four o'clock,

Here is the number on the door.
Memory!
You have the key,
The little lamp spreads a ring on the stair.
Mount.
The bed is open; the tooth-brush hangs on the wall,
Put your shoes at the door, sleep, prepare for life.'

The last twist of the knife.

Gerontion

Thou hast nor youth nor age
But as it were an after dinner sleep
Dreaming of both.

Here I am, an old man in a dry month,
Being read to by a boy, waiting for rain.
I was neither at the hot gates
Nor fought in the warm rain
Nor knee deep in the salt marsh, heaving a cutlass,
Bitten by flies, fought.
My house is a decayed house,
And the Jew squats on the window sill, the owner,
Spawned in some estaminet of Antwerp,
Blistered in Brussels, patched and peeled in London.
The goat coughs at night in the field overhead;
Rocks, moss, stonecrop, iron, merds.
The woman keeps the kitchen, makes tea,
Sneezes at evening, poking the peevish gutter.
                      I an old man,
A dull head among windy spaces.

Signs are taken for wonders. 'We would see a sign!'
The word within a word, unable to speak a word,

Swaddled with darkness. In the Juvescence of the year
Came Christ the tiger

In depraved May, dogwood and chestnut, flowering judas,
To be eaten, to be divided, to be drunk
Among whispers; by Mr Silvero
With caressing hands, at Limoges
Who walked all night in the next room;
By Hakagawa, bowing among the Titians;
By Madame de Tornquist, in the dark room
Shifting the candles; Fräulein von Kulp
Who turned in the hall, one hand on the door. Vacant shuttles
Weave the wind. I have no ghosts,
An old man in a draughty house
Under a windy knob.

After such knowledge, what forgiveness? Think now
History has many cunning passages, contrived corridors
And issues, deceives with whispering ambitions,
Guides us by vanities. Think now
She gives when our attention is distracted
And what she gives, gives with such supple confusions
That the giving famishes the craving. Gives too late
What's not believed in, or is still believed,
In memory only, reconsidered passion. Gives too soon
Into weak hands, what's thought can be dispensed with
Till the refusal propagates a fear. Think
Neither fear nor courage saves us. Unnatural vices
Are fathered by our heroism. Virtues
Are forced upon us by our impudent crimes.
These tears are shaken from the wrath-bearing tree.

The tiger springs in the new year. Us he devours. Think at last
We have not reached conclusion, when I
Stiffen in a rented house. Think at last
I have not made this show purposelessly
And it is not by any concitation
Of the backward devils.

I would meet you upon this honestly.
I that was near your heart was removed therefrom
To lose beauty in terror, terror in inquisition.
I have lost my passion: why should I need to keep it
Since what is kept must be adulterated?
I have lost my sight, smell, hearing, taste and touch:
How should I use them for your closer contact?

These with a thousand small deliberations
Protract the profit of their chilled delirium,
Excite the membrane, when the sense has cooled,
With pungent sauces, multiply variety
In a wilderness of mirrors. What will the spider do,
Suspend its operations, will the weevil
Delay? De Bailhache, Fresca, Mrs Cammell, whirled
Beyond the circuit of the shuddering Bear
In fractured atoms. Gull against the wind, in the windy straits
Of Belle Isle, or running on the Horn.
White feathers in the snow, the Gulf claims,
And an old man driven by the Trades
To a sleepy corner.

Tenants of the house,
Thoughts of a dry brain in a dry season.

Burbank with a Baedeker:
Bleistein with a Cigar

*Tra-la-la-la-la-la-laire – nil nisi divinum stabile
est; caetera fumus – the gondola stopped, the old
palace was there, how charming its grey and pink –
goats and monkeys, with such hair too! – so the
countess passed on until she came through the little
park, where Niobe presented her with a cabinet, and
so departed.*

Burbank crossed a little bridge
    Descending at a small hotel;
Princess Volupine arrived,
    They were together, and he fell.

Defunctive music under sea
    Passed seaward with the passing bell
Slowly: the God Hercules
    Had left him, that had loved him well.

The horses, under the axletree
    Beat up the dawn from Istria
With even feet. Her shuttered barge
    Burned on the water all the day.

But this or such was Bleistein's way:
    A saggy bending of the knees
And elbows, with the palms turned out,
    Chicago Semite Viennese.

A lustreless protrusive eye
    Stares from the protozoic slime
At a perspective of Canaletto.
    The smoky candle end of time

Declines. On the Rialto once.
    The rats are underneath the piles.
The Jew is underneath the lot.
    Money in furs. The boatman smiles,

Princess Volupine extends
    A meagre, blue-nailed, phthisic hand
To climb the waterstair. Lights, lights,
    She entertains Sir Ferdinand

Klein. Who clipped the lion's wings
    And flea'd his rump and pared his claws?
Thought Burbank, meditating on
    Time's ruins, and the seven laws.

Whispers of Immortality

Webster was much possessed by death
And saw the skull beneath the skin;
And breastless creatures under ground
Leaned backward with a lipless grin.

Daffodil bulbs instead of balls
Stared from the sockets of the eyes!
He knew that thought clings round dead limbs
Tightening its lusts and luxuries.

Donne, I suppose, was such another
Who found no substitute for sense,
To seize and clutch and penetrate;
Expert beyond experience,

He knew the anguish of the marrow
The ague of the skeleton;
No contact possible to flesh
Allayed the fever of the bone.

.   .   .   .   .

Grishkin is nice: her Russian eye
Is underlined for emphasis;
Uncorseted, her friendly bust
Gives promise of pneumatic bliss.

The couched Brazilian jaguar
Compels the scampering marmoset
With subtle effluence of cat;
Grishkin has a maisonnette;

The sleek Brazilian jaguar
Does not in its arboreal gloom
Distil so rank a feline smell
As Grishkin in a drawing-room.

And even the Abstract Entities
Circumambulate her charm;
But our lot crawls between dry ribs
To keep our metaphysics warm.

From THE WASTE LAND

The Fire Sermon

The river's tent is broken; the last fingers of leaf
Clutch and sink into the wet bank. The wind
Crosses the brown land, unheard. The nymphs are departed.
Sweet Thames, run softly, till I end my song.
The river bears no empty bottles, sandwich papers,
Silk handkerchiefs, cardboard boxes, cigarette ends
Or other testimony of summer nights. The nymphs are
    departed.
And their friends, the loitering heirs of City directors;
Departed, have left no addresses.
By the waters of Leman I sat down and wept . . .
Sweet Thames, run softly till I end my song,
Sweet Thames, run softly, for I speak not loud or long.
But at my back in a cold blast I hear
The rattle of the bones, and chuckle spread from ear to ear.

A rat crept softly through the vegetation
Dragging its slimy belly on the bank
While I was fishing in the dull canal
On a winter evening round behind the gashouse
Musing upon the king my brother's wreck
And on the king my father's death before him.
White bodies naked on the low damp ground
And bones cast in a little low dry garrett,
Rattled by the rat's foot only, year to year.
But at my back from time to time I hear

The sound of horns and motors, which shall bring
Sweeney to Mrs Porter in the spring.
O the moon shone bright on Mrs Porter
And on her daughter
They wash their feet in soda water
Et O ces voix d'enfants, chantant dans la coupole!

Twit twit twit
Jug jug jug jug jug jug
So rudely forc'd.
Tereu

   Unreal City
Under the brown fog of a winter noon
Mr Eugenides, the Smyrna merchant
Unshaven, with a pocket full of currants
C.i.f. London: documents at sight,
Asked me in demotic French
To luncheon at the Cannon Street Hotel
Followed by a weekend at the Metropole.

   At the violet hour, when the eyes and back
Turn upward from the desk, when the human engine waits
Like a taxi throbbing waiting,
I Tiresias, though blind, throbbing between two lives,
Old man with wrinkled female breasts, can see
At the violet hour, the evening hour that strives
Homeward, and brings the sailor home from sea,
The typist home at teatime, clears her breakfast, lights
Her stove, and lays out food in tins.
Out of the window perilously spread
Her drying combinations touched by the sun's last rays,
On the divan are piled (at night her bed)
Stockings, slippers, camisoles, and stays.
I Tiresias, old man with wrinkled dugs
Perceived the scene, and foretold the rest –
I too awaited the expected guest.

He, the young man carbuncular, arrives,
A small house agent's clerk, with one bold stare,
One of the low on whom assurance sits
As a silk hat on a Bradford millionaire.
The time is now propitious, as he guesses,
The meal is ended, she is bored and tired,
Endeavours to engage her in caresses
Which still are unreproved, if undesired.
Flushed and decided, he assaults at once;
Exploring hands encounter no defence;
His vanity requires no response,
And makes a welcome of indifference.
(And I Tiresias have foresuffered all
Enacted on this same divan or bed;
I who have sat by Thebes below the wall
And walked among the lowest of the dead.)
Bestows one final patronising kiss,
And gropes his way, finding the stairs unlit . . .

    She turns and looks a moment in the glass,
Hardly aware of her departed lover;
Her brain allows one half-formed thought to pass:
'Well now that's done: and I'm glad it's over.'
When lovely woman stoops to folly and
Paces about her room again, alone,
She smoothes her hair with automatic hand,
And puts a record on the gramophone.

    'This music crept by me upon the waters'
And along the Strand, up Queen Victoria Street.
O City city, I can sometimes hear
Beside a public bar in Lower Thames Street,
The pleasant whining of a mandoline
And a clatter and a chatter from within
Where fishmen lounge at noon: where the walls
Of Magnus Martyr hold
Inexplicable splendour of Ionian white and gold.

The river sweats
Oil and tar
The barges drift
With the turning tide
Red sails
Wide
To leeward, swing on the heavy spar.
The barges wash
Drifting logs
Down Greenwich reach
Past the Isle of Dogs.
                    Weialala leia
                    Wallala leialala

Elizabeth and Leicester
Beating oars
The stern was formed
A gilded shell
Red and gold
The brisk swell
Rippled both shores
Southwest wind
Carried down stream
The peal of bells
White towers
                    Weialala leia
                    Wallala leialala

   'Trams and dusty trees.
Highbury bore me. Richmond and Kew
Undid me. By Richmond I raised my knees
Supine on the floor of a narrow canoe.'

'My feet are at Moorgate, and my heart
Under my feet. After the event
He wept. He promised "a new start".
I made no comment. What should I resent?'

'On Margate Sands.
I can connect
Nothing with nothing.
The broken fingernails of dirty hands.
My people humble people who expect
Nothing.'
            la la

To Carthage then I came

Burning burning burning burning
O Lord Thou pluckest me out
O Lord Thou pluckest

burning

The Hollow Men

A penny for the Old Guy

I

We are the hollow men
We are the stuffed men
Leaning together
Headpiece filled with straw. Alas!
Our dried voices, when
We whisper together
Are quiet and meaningless
As wind in dry grass
Or rats' feet over broken glass
In our dry cellar

Shape without form, shade without colour,
Paralysed force, gesture without motion;

Those who have crossed
With direct eyes, to death's other Kingdom
Remember us – if at all – not as lost
Violent souls, but only
As the hollow men
The stuffed men.

II

Eyes I dare not meet in dreams
In death's dream kingdom
These do not appear:
There, the eyes are
Sunlight on a broken column
There, is a tree swinging
And voices are
In the wind's singing
More distant and more solemn
Than a fading star.

Let me be no nearer
In death's dream kingdom
Let me also wear
Such deliberate disguises
Rat's coat, crowskin, crossed staves
In a field
Behaving as the wind behaves
No nearer –

Not that final meeting
In the twilight kingdom

III

This is the dead land
This is cactus land
Here the stone images
Are raised, here they receive
The supplication of a dead man's hand
Under the twinkle of a fading star.

Is it like this
In death's other kingdom
Waking alone
At the hour when we are
Trembling with tenderness
Lips that would kiss
Form prayers to broken stone.

IV

The eyes are not here
There are no eyes here
In this valley of dying stars
In this hollow valley
This broken jaw of our lost kingdoms

In this last of meeting places
We grope together
And avoid speech
Gathered on this beach of the tumid river

Sightless, unless
The eyes reappear
As the perpetual star
Multifoliate rose
Of death's twilight kingdom
The hope only
Of empty men.

V

Here we go round the prickly pear
Prickly pear prickly pear
Here we go round the prickly pear
At five o'clock in the morning.

Between the idea
And the reality
Between the motion
And the act
Falls the Shadow
                    For Thine is the Kingdom

Between the conception
And the creation
Between the emotion
And the response
Falls the Shadow

      Life is very long

Between the desire
And the spasm
Between the potency
And the existence
Between the essence
And the descent
Falls the Shadow

     For Thine is the Kingdom

For Thine is
Life is
For Thine is the

This is the way the world ends
This is the way the world ends
This is the way the world ends
Not with a bang but a whimper.

Little Gidding

I

Midwinter spring is its own season
Sempiternal though sodden towards sundown,
Suspended in time, between pole and tropic.
When the short day is brightest, with frost and fire,
The brief sun flames the ice, on pond and ditches,
In windless cold that is the heart's heat,
Reflecting in a watery mirror
A glare that is blindness in the early afternoon.

94

And glow more intense than blaze of branch, or brazier,
Stirs the dumb spirit: no wind, but pentecostal fire
In the dark time of the year. Between melting and freezing
The soul's sap quivers. There is no earth smell
Or smell of living thing. This is the spring time
But not in time's covenant. Now the hedgerow
Is blanched for an hour with transitory blossom
Of snow, a bloom more sudden
Than that of summer, neither budding nor fading.
Not in the scheme of generation.
Where is the summer, the unimaginable
Zero summer?

          If you came this way,
Taking the route you would be likely to take
From the place you would be likely to come from,
If you came this way in may time, you would find the hedges
White again, in May, with voluptuary sweetness.
It would be the same at the end of the journey,
If you came at night like a broken king,
If you came by day not knowing what you came for,
It would be the same, when you leave the rough road
And turn behind the pig-sty to the dull façade
And the tombstone. And what you thought you came for
Is only a shell, a husk of meaning
From which the purpose breaks only when it is fulfilled
If at all. Either you had no purpose
Or the purpose is beyond the end you figured
And is altered in fulfilment. There are other places
Which also are the world's end, some at the sea jaws,
Or over a dark lake, in a desert or a city –
But this is the nearest, in place and time,
Now and in England.

          If you came this way,
Taking any route, starting from anywhere,
At any time or at any season,
It would always be the same: you would have to put off

Sense and notion. You are not here to verify,
Instruct yourself, or inform curiosity
Or carry report. You are here to kneel
Where prayer has been valid. And prayer is more
Than an order of words, the conscious occupation
Of the praying mind, or the sound of the voice praying.
And what the dead had no speech for, when living,
They can tell you, being dead: the communication
Of the dead is tongued with fire beyond the language of the
        living.
Here, the intersection of the timeless moment
Is England and nowhere. Never and always.

II

Ash on an old man's sleeve
Is all the ash the burnt roses leave.
Dust in the air suspended
Marks the place where a story ended.
Dust inbreathed was a house –
The wall, the wainscot and the mouse.
The death of hope and despair,
    This is the death of air.

There are flood and drouth
Over the eyes and in the mouth,
Dead water and dead sand
Contending for the upper hand.
The parched eviscerate soil
Gapes at the vanity of toil,
Laughs without mirth.
    This is the death of earth.

Water and fire succeed
The town, the pasture and the weed.
Water and fire deride
The sacrifice that we denied.
Water and fire shall rot
The marred foundations we forgot.

Of sanctuary and choir.
    This is the death of water and fire.

In the uncertain hour before the morning
    Near the ending of interminable night
    At the recurrent end of the unending
After the dark dove with the flickering tongue
    Had passed below the horizon of his homing
    While the dead leaves still rattled on like tin
Over the asphalt where no other sound was
    Between three districts whence the smoke arose
    I met one walking, loitering and hurried
As if blown towards me like the metal leaves
    Before the urban dawn wind unresisting.
    And as I fixed upon the down-turned face
That pointed scrutiny with which we challenge
    The first-met stranger in the waning dusk
    I caught the sudden look of some dead master
Whom I had known, forgotten, half recalled
    Both one and many; in the brown baked features
    The eyes of a familiar compound ghost
Both intimate and unidentifiable.
    So I assumed a double part, and cried
    And heard another's voice cry: 'What! are *you* here?'
Although we were not. I was still the same,
    Knowing myself yet being someone other –
    And he a face still forming; yet the words sufficed
To compel the recognition they preceded.
    And so, compliant to the common wind,
    Too strange to each other for misunderstanding,
In concord at this intersection time
    Of meeting nowhere, no before and after,
    We trod the pavement in a dead patrol.
I said: 'The wonder that I feel is easy,
    Yet ease is cause of wonder. Therefore speak:
    I may not comprehend, may not remember.'
And he: 'I am not eager to rehearse
    My thought and theory which you have forgotten.

97

These things have served their purpose: let them be.
So with your own, and pray they be forgiven
   By others, as I pray you to forgive
   Both bad and good. Last season's fruit is eaten
And the fullfed beast shall kick the empty pail.
   For last year's words belong to last year's language
   And next year's words await another voice.
But, as the passage now presents no hindrance
   To the spirit unappeased and peregrine
   Between two worlds become much like each other,
So I find words I never thought to speak
   In streets I never thought I should revisit
   When I left my body on a distant shore.
Since our concern was speech, and speech impelled us
   To purify the dialect of the tribe
   And urge the mind to aftersight and foresight,
Let me disclose the gifts reserved for age
   To set a crown upon your lifetime's effort.
   First, the cold friction of expiring sense
Without enchantment, offering no promise
   But bitter tastelessness of shadow fruit
   As body and soul begin to fall asunder.
Second, the conscious impotence of rage
   At human folly, and the laceration
   Of laughter at what ceases to amuse.
And last, the rending pain of re-enactment
   Of all that you have done, and been; the shame
   Of motives late revealed, and the awareness
Of things ill done and done to others' harm
   Which once you took for exercise of virtue.
   Then fools' approval stings, and honour stains.
From wrong to wrong the exasperated spirit
   Proceeds, unless restored by that refining fire
   Where you must move in measure, like a dancer.'
The day was breaking. In the disfigured street
   He left me, with a kind of valediction,
   And faded on the blowing of the horn.

There are three conditions which often look alike
Yet differ completely, flourish in the same hedgerow:
Attachment to self and to things and to persons, detachment
From self and from things and from persons; and, growing
      between them, indifference
Which resembles the others as death resembles life,
Being between two lives – unflowering, between
The live and the dead nettle. This is the use of memory:
For liberation – not less of love but expanding
Of love beyond desire, and so liberation
From the future as well as the past. Thus, love of a country
Begins as attachment to our own field of action
And comes to find that action of little importance
Though never indifferent. History may be servitude,
History may be freedom. See, now they vanish,
The faces and places, with the self which, as it could, loved
      them,
To become renewed, transfigured, in another pattern.
Sin is Behovely, but
All shall be well, and
All manner of thing shall be well.
If I think, again, of this place,
And of people, not wholly commendable,
Of no immediate kin or kindness,
But some of peculiar genius,
All touched by a common genius,
United in the strife which divided them;
If I think of a king at nightfall,
Of three men, and more, on the scaffold
And a few who died forgotten
In other places, here and abroad,
And of one who died blind and quiet,
Why should we celebrate
These dead men more than the dying?
It is not to ring the bell backward
Nor is it an incantation
To summon the spectre of a Rose.

We cannot revive old factions
We cannot restore old policies
Or follow an antique drum.
These men, and those who opposed them
And those whom they opposed
Accept the constitution of silence
And are folded in a single party.
Whatever we inherit from the fortunate
We have taken from the defeated
What they had to leave us – a symbol:
A symbol perfected in death.
And all shall be well and
All manner of thing shall be well
By the purification of the motive
In the ground of our beseeching.

IV

The dove descending breaks the air
With flame of incandescent terror
Of which the tongues declare
The one discharge from sin and error.
The only hope, or else despair
   Lies in the choice of pyre or pyre –
   To be redeemed from fire by fire.

Who then devised the torment? Love.
Love is the unfamiliar Name
Behind the hands that wove
The intolerable shirt of flame
Which human power cannot remove.
   We only live, only suspire
   Consumed by either fire or fire.

V

What we call the beginning is often the end
And to make an end is to make a beginning.
The end is where we start from. And every phrase
And sentence that is right (where every word is at home,

Taking its place to support the others,
The word neither diffident nor ostentatious,
An easy commerce of the old and the new,
The common word exact without vulgarity,
The formal word precise but not pedantic,
The complete consort dancing together)
Every phrase and every sentence is an end and a beginning
Every poem an epitaph. And any action
Is a step to the block, to the fire, down the sea's throat
Or to an illegible stone: and that is where we start.
We die with the dying:
See, they depart, and we go with them.
We are born with the dead:
See, they return, and bring us with them.
The moment of the rose and the moment of the yew-tree
Are of equal duration. A people without history
Is not redeemed from time, for history is a pattern
Of timeless moments, So, while the light fails
On a winter's afternoon, in a secluded chapel
History is now and England.

With the drawing of this Love and the voice of this Calling

We shall not cease from exploration
And the end of all our exploring
Will be to arrive where we started
And know the place for the first time.
Through the unknown, remembered gate
When the last of earth left to discover
Is that which was the beginning;
At the source of the longest river
The voice of the hidden waterfall
And the children in the apple-tree
Not known, because not looked for
But heard, half-heard, in the stillness
Between two waves of the sea.
Quick now, here, now, always –

A condition of complete simplicity
(Costing not less than everything)
And all shall be well and
All manner of thing shall be well
When the tongues of flame are in-folded
Into the crowned knot of fire
And the fire and the rose are one.

Notes

THE LOVE SONG OF J. ALFRED PRUFROCK. At first reading this great poem may strike one as a mixture of evocative but disconnected fragments. The difficulty in sorting out the central point of the poem lies in Eliot's use of what Hugh Kenner has called 'a central consciousness' rather than a recognisable, individualised speaker. In a dramatic monologue a nineteenth-century poet such as Robert Browning would have welded together the elements of his poem by the speaking style of the character he was creating. When Caliban in Browning's poem 'Caliban upon Setebos' speaks in a curiously broken, disrupted style we accept this because he is being presented as a primitive and sub-normal personality. Moreover, the central situation is clear; Caliban is lying on his belly in mud, as Browning tells us, imagining the nature of his God, Setebos. The rapid transitions in his thought are all related to his described circumstances. In 'The Love Song of J. Alfred Prufrock' Eliot makes a number of breaks with the tradition of the dramatic monologue as used by Browning, but at the same time draws on some of its familiar devices. Prufrock is being presented as a mentally enervated, middle-aged, frustrated man thinking about his present life and the current state of the world and carving his thoughts into the form of a love song. The difficulty is that we do not know exactly where he is supposed to be speaking, nor indeed many practical facts about him, beyond what he looks like. This means that he comes across more as an atmosphere, a consciousness, than as a character or a personality. He seems in a way to be a group of thoughts connected in mood and rhythm though not by a narrative thread or an underlying personality. The poem appears now very much as a *fin-de-siècle* one which owes a debt to Laforgue and other French and English poets of the 1890s. The mood is that of the man of sensibility who has exhausted all his pleasures and is exquisitely bored with the world. At the same time the poem cuts below the surface of this mood to a much deeper feeling about the meaning of things. As always with Eliot, the phrasing is perfect. Many lines and sentences lodge themselves in the mind with the power of mysterious aphorisms. The nine lines from 'No! I am not Prince Hamlet' are a beautiful imitation of a speech from a Jacobean drama. They already hint at the pre-occupation with drama which was to remain with Eliot throughout his life both in his criticism and in his poetry.

PRELUDES. These poems form a group of four portraits – two of places and two of people. Despite their inclusive title, which suggests the preoccupation with musical form that was to stay with Eliot until he wrote the *Four Quartets* towards the end of his career, one is immediately struck by their vividness as sketches. Each seems to suggest the material for a painting by a French artist at the turn of the century. Eliot has been wittily charged with writing the best French poetry in the English language and although the landscape of these poems seems to be that of Edwardian New York it is seen as if through the eyes of the French poet Paul Verlaine.

RHAPSODY ON A WINDY NIGHT. A poem conceived through the heightened sensibility of a man in a highly nervous condition going for a walk by himself in the middle of the night. Given these basic clues, which Eliot does little to make clear, the weird bitter flavour of the poem begins to make sense. Many of the details reveal that power of poetry to 'communicate before it is understood' to which Eliot himself drew attention. The syncopated, fevered rhythms are easy to pick up without being easy to analyse. The way in which the street lamp and the moon become sinister anthropomorphic personalities effectively conveys the working of a diseased imagination. The poem is a thoroughly 'sick' one and a masterpiece of its kind. It is also very French – even its words 'regard' and 'remark' take on their French overtones in the context.

GERONTION. The overall situation and mood of this poem is (unusually for Eliot) made clear in its first two lines. We are told who is talking and where. The difficulty begins to come with the details which proliferate in a fascinating but puzzling confusion in the way we are soon to be familiar with in *The Waste Land*. Indeed Hugh Kenner tells us in his book *The Invisible Poet* that Eliot at one time wrote this poem as part of *The Waste Land*, from which it was detached as one of Ezra Pound's many suggested emendations to that poem. It does indeed now seem too self-contained and perhaps too explicit in its overall structure to form an appropriate part of the longer poem, although it shares a preoccupation with disconnection and incapacity. The poem shows Eliot's power to invent melodious and evocative imaginary names. It also begins to foreshadow some of the preoccupations of his later poetry, beginning in the section 'The word within a word' with its use of the imagery of Christian theology. The apparent anti-semitism of the passage about the Jew has been used to accuse Eliot of latent emotional Fascism, but in fact this kind of reference is frequent and casual in the writing of the period and no more significant or dishonourable than similar ones in *The Merchant of Venice*.

BURBANK WITH A BAEDEKER: BLEISTEIN WITH A CIGAR. This is a kind of literary collage, or paste-up, which has some analogies with early Cubist paintings. The poem is made out of bits from familiar classics (e.g. 'Lights, Lights' from *Hamlet*) interspersed with original additions. The rhythmical breaks in the quatrains are arranged to produce a violently disruptive and switchback effect. The poem is 'modern' to its fingertips: memorable, showy and dated. If Eliot had written nothing else he could reasonably be charged, as he once was, with producing nothing but *vers de société*, a kind of jazzed-up Americanised version of the Victorian parlour verse which was done so well by writers like Austin Dobson and Frederick Locker-Lampson.

WHISPERS OF IMMORTALITY. This seems to be a poem of witty sexual bitterness. The link between the two early seventeenth-century poets, Webster and Donne, and the woman Grishkin, works through the dwelling on flesh and bone. The poem is richly morbid, with a nice blending of intellect and passion, in a way the seventeenth-century poets Eliot admired would have approved. The sense of smell is subtly used to bring home the poet's blend of lust and disgust for the woman's body.

THE FIRE SERMON. This is the third section of Eliot's poem *The Waste Land*, which can justly be called the most important poem of the century. The main defence of this great work, so long discussed and fought over by critics and commentators, and in no way simplified or explained by Eliot's own notes, is that it never fails to make an immediate and lasting impact on readers attuned to the specific pleasures which poetry can offer. Line by line it excites, moves and remains memorable in the way that all great poetry has done since Homer. Indeed, so effective is the poem in detail that one is sometimes disinclined to bother about its overall tenor and intention. This is a pity. Basically, the poem is doing two things at the same time: it is a record of the experience of one man, or one consciousness, on the edge of a period of mental crisis verging on nervous breakdown, and at the same time an account of a sensitive man's response to what he sees as the crack-up of western civilisation after the First World War. Everything in the poem has 'gone to pieces' and this accounts for its characteristic fragmentary structure. Justifications can easily be found outside literature in the art of collage in painting and montage, the building up of continuity by placing one shot against another in the cinema. *The Waste Land* would indeed lend itself to presentation either as a fresco or a film. It has also been presented on stage and on the radio as a play for a number of voices. This helps to emphasise the way in which, unlike a dramatic monologue by a Victorian writer, it presents a personality as a composite colony of cells rather than a single self. The necessity of emphasising the fragmentary nature of the material was seized on by Ezra Pound when he was shown an earlier and longer version of the poem. This no longer survives. In this version it appears likely that Eliot had included a larger proportion of explanatory linking material than Pound thought necessary. In a certain sense, therefore, the form of *The Waste Land* as we know it is due to Pound's accentuation of Eliot's original script. It in no way detracts from Eliot's originality or right to unique authorship of the poem. The overriding theme of 'The Fire Sermon' is the river Thames and its effect on the life of London through which it flows. The central event of this section of the poem, the seduction of the typist by her boy friend, is played out against a backcloth of past and present London life on the river and in the streets round about it. The section in short lines at the end brings in reminiscences of the Rhine Maidens from Wagner's opera cycle *The Ring*.

THE HOLLOW MEN. This poem takes up the mood of *The Waste Land* but presents it in a plain style which begins to foreshadow the characteristic style of Eliot's later poetry. The poem is one of despair and frustration, but it comes out of an extreme situation which seems already to envisage the hope of something better. This kind of nihilism has to draw on the vocabulary of religion to make its message clear and some parts of the italicised section of the poem build up a liturgical tone which is characteristically high Church of England. The central image of the poem, that human beings are all empty 'guys' stuffed with straw, was suggested to Eliot by the English celebrations for Guy Fawkes day, which, as an American new to them, perhaps struck him with unusual horror.

LITTLE GIDDING. Like *The Waste Land* Eliot's last great sequence of poems, *Four Quartets* needs to be read in its entirety to reveal its full power and importance. To admirers of his later poetry these poems represent the full flowering and final development of his genius. Despite their immense technical control and originality of thought, they do present severe obstacles to the reader not already committed to their point of view. Their subject is Time, and the effect of Time on human affairs, and the argument is often conducted at a highly cerebral and abstract level. The poem can sometimes sound like a sermon preached in St Paul's Cathedral by a latter-day Launcelot Andrewes. The poems were written over a period of several years and were concluded against the background of the Second World War. In 'Little Gidding' – which concludes the sequence – the merger of past and present is perhaps most violent and striking. The poem begins with a free verse section pin-pointing the soul's journey in the chapel of Little Gidding. Little Gidding, a small village in Huntingdonshire, associated with both Royalism and High Anglicanism, Eliot's strongest loves, in the time of the Civil War. The phrase 'you are here to kneel/where prayer has been valid' is an effectively modest claim pointing forward to the tone of Larkin's 'Church Going'. The major strength of the poem, however, comes in the second part of the second section. This is clearly affected by the experience of the German blitz on London in 1940. It manages the incredibly difficult feat of conveying the sense of this contemporary event and at the same time rising above it to speak with the dignity and ceremony of Dante. Although it doesn't rhyme, this section is based on the *terza rima* of Dante's metre in the *Divina Commedia*. Eliot has preserved the flavour of the Italian by contrasting eleven syllable with ten syllable lines all the way through. The 'familiar compound ghost' whom the poet meets is perhaps partly Dante himself. 'The blowing of the horn' is a reference to the all-clear on the siren. 'The dark dove' at the beginning of the poem refers to a Nazi bomber. The dove image is taken up again in the rhymed lyric of the fourth section. The fifth section brings the whole poem, and the sequence, to an end in the uniting symbol of the merged fire and rose.

The reader will find more detailed commentary than is possible to give here in Helen Gardner's *The Art of T. S. Eliot*.

Wilfred Owen

Wilfred Owen was born in 1893 and died in action in 1918. Owen stands as a moral exemplar for the younger poets of the 1960s. He was a man of great sensitivity, and an intellectual, plunged against his will into the holocaust of an atrocious war. He responded to the war, which horrified and disgusted him, in a way which was never simple. In one letter he wrote 'my senses are charred' but there is certainly no evidence in his surviving poetry that they were numbed. Despite his hatred of the war, Owen was not a pacifist; he was awarded the Military Cross for bravery, and seems to have done his duty as an infantry officer in a way that would have been approved of by Kipling. Owen came to see the war, not as a disease to be cured by purely political action, nor as a crusade against evil, but as a major tragedy to which the only appropriate response was compassion. 'The poetry is in the pity,' he said in the much-quoted introduction he had prepared for his first book of poems before his death. Owen's poetry is always likely to be overvalued at a time when men are preoccupied with violence. In his best poems, however, he writes not only about war but about war as a metaphor for the human condition. This gives his best work a far-reaching gravity and moral force which will never date and which makes his poems applicable to any situation in which people must suffer and die.

Exposure

Our brains ache, in the merciless iced east winds that knive
    us . . .
Wearied we keep awake because the night is silent . . .
Low, drooping flares confuse our memory of the salient . . .
Worried by silence, sentries whisper, curious, nervous,
       But nothing happens.

Watching, we hear the mad gusts tugging on the wire,
Like twitching agonies of men among its brambles.
Northward, incessantly, the flickering gunnery rumbles,
Far off, like a dull rumour of some other war.
       What are we doing here?

The poignant misery of dawn begins to grow . . .
We only know war lasts, rain soaks, and clouds sag stormy.
Dawn massing in the east her melancholy army
Attacks once more in ranks on shivering ranks of gray,
       But nothing happens.

Sudden successive flights of bullets streak the silence.
Less deadly than the air that shudders black with snow,
With sidelong flowing flakes that flock, pause, and renew,
We watch them wandering up and down the wind's nonchalance,
       But nothing happens.

Pale flakes with fingering stealth come feeling for our faces –
We cringe in holes, back on forgotten dreams, and stare,
    snow-dazed,
Deep into grassier ditches. So we drowse, sun-dozed,
Littered with blossoms trickling where the blackbird fusses.
       Is it that we are dying?

Slowly our ghosts drag home: glimpsing the sunk fires, glozed
With crusted dark-red jewels; crickets jingle there;
For hours the innocent mice rejoice: the house is theirs;
Shutters and doors, all closed: on us the doors are closed, –
       We turn back to our dying.

Since we believe not otherwise can kind fires burn;
Nor ever suns smile true on child, or field, or fruit.
For God's invincible spring our love is made afraid;
Therefore, not loath, we lie out here; therefore were born,
　　　For love of God seems dying.

To-night, His frost will fasten on this mud and us,
Shrivelling many hands, puckering foreheads crisp.
The burying-party, picks and shovels in their shaking grasp,
Pause over half-known faces. All their eyes are ice,
　　　But nothing happens.

Arms and the Boy

Let the boy try along this bayonet-blade
How cold steel is, and keen with hunger of blood;
Blue with all malice, like a madman's flash;
And thinly drawn with famishing for flesh.

Lend him to stroke these blind, blunt bullet-heads
Which long to nuzzle in the hearts of lads,
Or give him cartridges of fine zinc teeth,
Sharp with the sharpness of grief and death.

For his teeth seem for laughing round an apple.
There lurk no claws behind his fingers supple;
And god will grow no talons at his heels,
Nor antlers through the thickness of his curls.

The Show

We have fallen in the dreams the ever-living
Breathe on the tarnished mirror of the world,
And then smooth out with ivory hands and sigh.
                                                    W. B. Yeats

My soul looked down from a vague height with Death,
As unremembering how I rose or why,
And saw a sad land, weak with sweats of dearth,
Gray, cratered like the moon with hollow woe,
And pitted with great pocks and scabs of plagues.

Across its beard, that horror of harsh wire,
There moved thin caterpillars, slowly uncoiled.
It seemed they pushed themselves to be as plugs
Of ditches, where they writhed and shrivelled, killed.

By them had slimy paths been trailed and scraped
Round myriad warts that might be little hills.

From gloom's last dregs these long-strung creatures crept,
And vanished out of dawn down hidden holes.

(And smell came up from those foul openings
As out of mouths, or deep wounds deepening.)

On dithering feet upgathered, more and more,
Brown strings, towards strings of gray, with bristling spines,
All migrants from green fields, intent on mire.

Those that were gray, of more abundant spawns,
Ramped on the rest and ate them and were eaten.

I saw their bitten backs curve, loop, and straighten,
I watched those agonies curl, lift, and flatten.

Whereat, in terror what that sight might mean,
I reeled and shivered earthward like a feather.

And Death fell with me, like a deepening moan.
And He, picking a manner of worm, which half had hid
Its bruises in the earth, but crawled no further,
Showed me its feet, the feet of many men,
And the fresh-severed head of it, my head.

Insensibility

I

Happy are men who yet before they are killed
Can let their veins run cold.
Whom no compassion fleers
Or makes their feet
Sore on the alleys cobbled with their brothers.
The front line withers,
But they are troops who fade, not flowers,
For poets' tearful fooling:
Men, gaps for filling:
Losses who might have fought
Longer, but no one bothers.

II

And some cease feeling
Even themselves or for themselves.
Dullness best solves
The tease and doubt of shelling,
And Chance's strange arithmetic
Comes simpler than the reckoning of their shilling.
They keep no check on armies' decimation.

III

Happy are these who lose imagination:
They have enough to carry with ammunition.
Their spirit drags no pack,
Their old wounds save with cold can not more ache.

Having seen all things red,
Their eyes are rid
Of the hurt of the colour of blood for ever.
And terror's first constriction over,
Their hearts remain small-drawn.
Their senses in some scorching cautery of battle
Now long since ironed,
Can laugh among the dying, unconcerned.

IV

Happy the soldier home, with not a notion
How somewhere, every dawn, some men attack,
And many sighs are drained.
Happy the lad whose mind was never trained:
His days are worth forgetting more than not.
He sings along the march
Which we march taciturn, because of dusk,
The long, forlorn, relentless trend
From larger day to huger night.

V

We wise, who with a thought besmirch
Blood over all our soul,
How should we see our task
But through his blunt and lashless eyes?
Alive, he is not vital overmuch;
Dying, not mortal overmuch;
Nor sad, nor proud,
Nor curious at all.
He cannot tell
Old men's placidity from his.

VI

But cursed are dullards whom no cannon stuns,
That they should be as stones;
Wretched are they, and mean
With paucity that never was simplicity.

By choice they made themselves immune
To pity and whatever moans in man
Before the last sea and the hapless stars;
Whatever mourns when many leave these shores,
Whatever shares
The eternal reciprocity of tears.

Dulce et Decorum Est

Bent double, like old beggars under sacks,
Knock-kneed, coughing like hags, we cursed through sludge,
Till on the haunting flares we turned our backs,
And towards our distant rest began to trudge.
Men marched asleep. Many had lost their boots,
But limped on, blood-shod. All went lame, all blind;
Drunk with fatigue; deaf even to the hoots
Of gas-shells dropping softly behind.

Gas! GAS! Quick, boys! – An ecstasy of fumbling,
Fitting the clumsy helmets just in time,
But someone still was yelling out and stumbling
And floundering like a man in fire or lime. –
Dim through the misty panes and thick green light,
As under a green sea, I saw him drowning.

In all my dreams before my helpless sight
He plunges at me, guttering, choking, drowning.

If in some smothering dreams, you too could pace
Behind the wagon that we flung him in,
And watch the white eyes writhing in his face,
His hanging face, like a devil's sick of sin;
If you could hear, at every jolt, the blood
Come gargling from the froth-corrupted lungs,
Bitter as the cud
Of vile, incurable sores on innocent tongues, –

My friend, you would not tell with such high zest
To children ardent for some desperate glory,
The old Lie: Dulce et decorum est
Pro patria mori.

Futility

Move him into the sun –
Gently its touch awoke him once,
At home, whispering of fields unsown.
Always it woke him, even in France,
Until this morning and this snow.
If anything might rouse him now
The kind old sun will know.

Think how it wakes the seeds, –
Woke, once, the clays of a cold star.
Are limbs, so dear-achieved, are sides,
Full-nerved – still warm – too hard to stir?
Was it for this the clay grew tall?
– O what made fatuous sunbeams toil
To break earth's sleep at all?

Anthem for Doomed Youth

What passing-bells for these who die as cattle?
   Only the monstrous anger of the guns.
   Only the stuttering rifles' rapid rattle
Can patter out their hasty orisons.
No mockeries for them from prayers or bells,
   Nor any voice of mourning save the choirs, –
The shrill, demented choirs of wailing shells;
   And bugles calling for them from sad shires.

What candles may be held to speed them all?
  Not in the hands of boys, but in their eyes
Shall shine the holy glimmers of good-byes.
  The pallor of girls' brows shall be their pall;
Their flowers the tenderness of silent minds,
And each slow dusk a drawing-down of blinds.

Apologia pro Poemate Meo

I, too, saw God through mud –
  The mud that cracked on cheeks when wretches smiled.
War brought more glory to their eyes than blood,
  And gave their laughs more glee than shakes a child.

Merry it was to laugh there –
  Where death becomes absurd and life absurder.
For power was on us as we slashed bones bare
  Not to feel sickness or remorse of murder.

I, too have dropped off fear –
  Behind the barrage, dead as my platoon,
And sailed my spirit surging, light and clear
  Past the entanglement where hopes lay strewn;

And witnessed exultation –
  Faces that used to curse me, scowl for scowl,
Shine and lift up with passion of oblation,
  Seraphic for an hour; though they were foul.

I have made fellowships –
  Untold of happy lovers in old song.
For love is not the binding of fair lips
  With the soft silk of eyes that look and long,

By Joy, whose ribbon slips, –
  But wound with war's hard wire whose stakes are strong;
Bound with the bandage of the arm that drips;
  Knit in the webbing of the rifle-thong.

I have perceived much beauty
    In the hoarse oaths that kept our courage straight;
    Heard music in the silentness of duty;
    Found peace where shell-storms spouted reddest spate.

Nevertheless, except you share
    With them in hell the sorrowful dark of hell,
    Whose world is but the trembling of a flare,
    And heaven but as the highway for a shell,

You shall not hear their mirth:
    You shall not come to think them well content
    By any jest of mine. These men are worth
    Your tears. You are not worth their merriment.

November 1917.

The Sentry

We'd found an old Boche dug-out, and he knew,
And gave us hell, for shell on frantic shell
Hammered on top, but never quite burst through.
Rain, guttering down in waterfalls of slime
Kept slush waist-high that, rising hour by hour,
Choked up the steps too thick with clay to climb.
What murk of air remained stank old, and sour
With fumes of whizz-bangs, and the smell of men
Who'd lived there years, and left their curse in the den,
If not their corpses. . . .
              There we herded from the blast
Of whizz-bangs, but one found our door at last, –
Buffeting eyes and breath, snuffing the candles.
And thud! flump! thud! down the steep steps came thumping
And splashing in the flood, deluging muck –
The sentry's body; then, his rifle, handles
Of old Boche bombs, and mud in ruck on ruck.

We dredged him up, for killed, until he whined
'O sir, my eyes – I'm blind – I'm blind, I'm blind!'
Coaxing, I held a flame against his lids
And said if he could see the last blurred light
He was not blind; in time he'd get all right.
'I can't,' he sobbed. Eyeballs, huge-bulged like squids',
Watch my dreams still; but I forgot him there
In posting next for duty, and sending a scout
To beg a stretcher somewhere, and floundering about
To other posts under the shrieking air.

    .   .   .   .   .

Those other wretches, how they bled and spewed,
And one who would have drowned himself for good, –
I try not to remember these things now.
Let dread hark back for one word only: how
Half listening to that sentry's moans and jumps,
And the wild chattering of his broken teeth,
Renewed most horribly whenever crumps
Pummelled the roof and slogged the air beneath –
Through the dense din, I say, we heard him shout
'I see your lights!' But ours had long died out.

Strange Meeting

It seemed that out of battle I escaped
Down some profound dull tunnel, long since scooped
Through granites which titanic wars had groined.
Yet also there encumbered sleepers groaned,
Too fast in thought or death to be bestirred.
Then, as I probed them, one sprang up, and stared
With piteous recognition in fixed eyes,
Lifting distressful hands as if to bless.
And by his smile, I knew that sullen hall,
By his dead smile I knew we stood in Hell.
With a thousand pains that vision's face was grained;

Yet no blood reached there from the upper ground,
And no guns thumped, or down the flues made moan.
'Strange friend,' I said, 'here is no cause to mourn.'
'None,' said the other, 'save the undone years,
The hopelessness. Whatever hope is yours,
Was my life also; I went hunting wild
After the wildest beauty in the world,
Which lies not calm in eyes, or braided hair,
But mocks the steady running of the hour,
And if it grieves, grieves richlier than here.
For by my glee might many men have laughed,
And of my weeping something had been left,
Which must die now. I mean the truth untold,
The pity of war, the pity war distilled.
Now men will go content with what we spoiled.
Or, discontent, boil bloody, and be spilled.
They will be swift with swiftness of the tigress,
None will break ranks, though nations trek from progress.
Courage was mine, and I had mystery,
Wisdom was mine, and I had mastery;
To miss the march of this retreating world
Into vain citadels that are not walled.
Then, when much blood had clogged their chariot-wheels
I would go up and wash them from sweet wells,
Even with truths that lie too deep for taint.
I would have poured my spirit without stint
But not through wounds; not on the cess of war.
Foreheads of men have bled where no wounds were.
I am the enemy you killed, my friend.
I knew you in this dark; for so you frowned
Yesterday through me as you jabbed and killed.
I parried; but my hands were loath and cold.
Let us sleep now. . . .'

Notes

EXPOSURE. Mainly written in very long twelve- and thirteen-syllable lines, which emphasise the unending boredom and weariness of the exposed troops in the trenches. The effect is underlined by Owen's characteristic and most famous technical device, the para-rhyme. In a normal rhyme, such as 'boys' and 'toys', the initial consonants change but the vowel and end consonants remain the same. In a para-rhyme the initial and end consonants remain the same but the vowel sound changes. Thus, in this poem 'burn' rhymes with 'born'. It seems likely that Owen derived this kind of rhyme from some French source. Its application in English has secured him a permanent place in the history of English metrics.

ARMS AND THE BOY. There is perhaps a hint of morbidity in this poem about a young soldier and his weapons. The sensuous vividness of the description almost tips over into lushness. The poem has sometimes been interpreted as a protest against the cruel ruthlessness of weapons. They could, however, be represented as necessary defences for the boy who has no weapons actually on his body, as a hawk or a stag has. This ambivalence is common in Owen and gives his poems their enduring strength. They rarely come down to simply outbursts of protest. The title of the poem was perhaps suggested by Shaw's play *Arms and the Man*.

THE SHOW. A poem rich with controlled disgust and horror. The filth and mindless violence of trench warfare has never been so brutally conveyed as here. What gives realism and effectiveness to the poem is that although it adopts the convention of being a dream or a vision, it could also be taken as a literal aerial photograph of what the Western Front looked like from a reconnaissance plane.

INSENSIBILITY. This is Owen's greatest poem and one of the great poems of the century. The argument is complex and ambivalent. It seems to distinguish between the necessary insensitivity of men who have to survive in conditions so appalling that they might go mad, and the unawakened insensibility of people who have never been confronted with the hard facts of what war is really like. Owen recognises and gives full value to the toughness and self-control of the soldier who has lived through the horror and found some means of withstanding its full impact on his senses. At the same time he sees the pity of this. Nevertheless, he knows that he as a naturally over-sensitive man can only do his job properly in the war if he too can get a grip on himself. To be able to feel compassion, and yet not be overcome to it, seemed to Owen the great virtue in the war and by implication the great virtue in human affairs. Like Keats, who wanted to be a surgeon, Owen honoured and admired the infantry officer who had the insight to feel and at the same time the will power to control his feelings in the interest of his men. Part of the poem's power comes from its amazing simplicity and abstraction. We seem to be reading not about the problems of English soldiers on the Western Front in 1917 but about the problems of the damned in hell.

DULCE ET DECORUM EST. The title is meant to imply an ironical comment on the famous line by the Latin poet Horace 'Dulce et decorum est pro patria mori'. Owen suggests that far from it being pleasant and honourable to die for one's country it is in fact disgusting and painful. The poem is an excellent example of the horror in which gas warfare was held. As so often, Owen seems in this poem to have taken over some of the vocabulary and imagery of late nineteenth-century poetry and injected a new realism into it. It reminds us that some of the public horror of the First World War had already been experienced and predicted by the agonies and breakdowns of decadent poets from Baudelaire onwards.

FUTILITY. A moving exploitation of the familiar conceit that death is a form of sleep. The dead soldier in the snow looks as if the sun could wake him.

ANTHEM FOR DOOMED YOUTH. This fine sonnet is the sort of poem that one might have imagined Rupert Brooke writing if he had lived a little longer. It contrasts the violence of life on the Western Front with the quiet rituals of home life in England.

APOLOGIA PRO POEMATE MEO. The title might be translated 'In Defence of My Verse'. The poem vividly expresses Owen's sense of comradeship with the soldiers in the trenches, and at the same time his understanding of how the violence of war could enter into one and become exciting. The poem should be read with 'Insensibility' as a good example of the 'sheep and goats' division of the world to which Owen was sometimes led: those who knew what suffering was about at first hand, and those who lived at home and did not. The difference between Owen and his admired friend and fellow poet Siegfried Sassoon, is that in Owen his positive faith in his fellow soldiers is the strongest feeling, whereas in Sassoon it is his indignation at the complacency of the profiteers at home which is stronger. If he had lived, Owen might perhaps have written a more directly involved poetry about the problems of the working classes in the 1920s and 1930s than did Auden or his contemporaries.

THE SENTRY. A description of a real incident referred to in one of Owen's surviving letters. It movingly expresses the problems and the philosophy of an infantry officer faced with the difficulties of keeping a platoon together under heavy bombardment. The tragedy of the soldier who was blinded is balanced against the tragedy of the young officer who has no time to do anything about it. Few poems have ever confronted the problem of survival in the extreme situation more directly. This is normally the material of great prose but the density of Owen's language and the energy of his rhythm give this poem a sustained power which no prose could equal.

STRANGE MEETING. This poem has been justly admired for its compassion and anonymity. It seems to me, however, in its middle section to become too journalistic in its explicit forecasts about the future, and its language is imperfectly controlled. It is interesting to compare 'Strange Meeting' with Eliot's Dantesque section in 'Little Gidding (p. 94). The combination of the para-rhyme with the heroic couplet form emphasises the remoteness and weird other-worldly quality of the meeting between the two soldiers. Indeed, it has been suggested by D. S. R. Welland that the two men are, in fact, one man and his double or *doppelgänger*.

Robert Graves

Robert Graves was born in 1895. He was officially reported died of wounds on his twenty-first birthday in the First World War, but he is still alive and writing. Since the 1930s he has lived in Majorca from where he periodically visits London, Oxford and New York to lecture, broadcast or record poems. Many critics would regard Graves as the greatest English poet now living and his reputation has steadily increased throughout his lifetime. I personally regard this judgement as too high, though his poetry is certainly important for its independence, consistency and formal variety. The key concept in Graves's recent thinking is his dedication to the White Goddess, a symbolic and dangerous female figure who makes life worth living and poetry worth writing. The hard core of Graves's poetry is, in fact, still about Love although he is now seventy. What is ultimately worrying about it is perhaps its absence of enough clues to its origins in his own life – there is something one feels a little *too* gentlemanly and civilised about his concealment of his tracks. Nevertheless, Graves has pursued his career as a poet over more years with more integrity and purpose than perhaps any other living English poet, and the attempt alone is an inspiration and an example.

Ulysses

To the much-tossed Ulysses, never done
   With woman whether gowned as wife or whore,
Penelope and Circe seemed as one:
She like a whore made his lewd fancies run,
   And wifely she a hero to him bore.

Their counter-changings terrified his way:
   They were the clashing rocks, Symplegades,
Scylla and Charybdis too were they;
Now angry storms frosting the sea with spray
   And now the lotus island's drunken ease.

They multiplied into the Sirens' throng,
   Forewarned by fear of whom he stood bound fast
Hand and foot helpless to the vessel's mast,
Yet would not stop his ears: daring their song
   He groaned and sweated till that shore was past.

One, two and many: flesh had made him blind,
   Flesh had one pleasure only in the act,
Flesh set one purpose only in the mind –
Triumph of flesh and afterwards to find
   Still those same terrors wherewith flesh was racked.

His wiles were witty and his fame far known,
Every king's daughter sought him for her own,
   Yet he was nothing to be won or lost.
   All lands to him were Ithaca: love-tossed
He loathed the fraud, yet would not bed alone.

Welsh Incident

'But that was nothing to what things came out
From the sea-caves of Criccieth yonder.'
'What were they? Mermaids? dragons? ghosts?'
'Nothing at all of any things like that.'
'What were they, then?'

      'All sorts of queer things,
Things never seen or heard or written about,
Very strange, un-Welsh, utterly peculiar
Things. Oh, solid enough they seemed to touch,
Had anyone dared it. Marvellous creation,
All various shapes and sizes, and no sizes,
All new, each perfectly unlike his neighbour,
Though all came moving slowly out together.'
'Describe just one of them.'

        'I am unable.'
'What were their colours?'

       'Mostly nameless colours,
Colours you'd like to see; but one was puce
Or perhaps more like crimson, but not purplish.
Some had no colour.'

       'Tell me, had they legs?'
'Not a leg nor foot among them that I saw.'
'But did these things come out in any order?
What o'clock was it? What was the day of the week?
Who else was present? How was the weather?'
'I was coming to that. It was half-past three
On Easter Tuesday last. The sun was shining.
The Harlech Silver Band played *Marchog Jesu*
On thirty-seven shimmering instruments,
Collecting for Caernarvon's (Fever) Hospital Fund.
The populations of Pwllheli, Criccieth,
Portmadoc, Borth, Tremadoc, Penrhyndeudraeth,
Were all assembled. Criccieth's mayor addressed them
First in good Welsh and then in fluent English,
Twisting his fingers in his chain of office,
Welcoming the things. They came out on the sand,

Not keeping time to the band, moving seaward
Silently at a snail's pace. But at last
The most odd, indescribable thing of all,
Which hardly one man there could see for wonder,
Did something recognisably a something.'
'Well, what?'
                    'It made a noise.'
                                        'A frightening noise?'
'No, no.'
              'A musical noise? A noise of scuffling?'
'No, but a very loud, respectable noise –
Like groaning to oneself on Sunday morning
In Chapel, close before the second psalm.'
'What did the mayor do?'
                              'I was coming to that.'

Ogres and Pygmies

Those famous men of old, the Ogres –
They had long beards and stinking arm-pits,
They were wide-mouthed, long-yarded and great-bellied
Yet not of taller stature, Sirs, than you.
They lived on Ogre-Strand, which was no place
But the churl's terror of their vast extent,
Where every foot was three-and-thirty inches
And every penny bought a whole hog.
Now of their company none survive, not one,
The times being, thank God, unfavourable
To all but nightmare shadows of their fame;
Their images stand howling on the hill
(The winds enforced against those wide mouths),
Whose granite haunches country-folk salute
With May Day kisses, and whose knobbed knees.

So many feats they did to admiration:
With their enormous throats they sang louder

Than ten cathedral choirs, with their grand yards
Stormed the most rare and obstinate maidenheads,
With their strong-gutted and capacious bellies
Digested stones and glass like ostriches.
They dug great pits and heaped huge mounds,
Deflected rivers, wrestled with the bear
And hammered judgements for posterity –
For the sweet-cupid-lipped and tassel-yarded
Delicate-stomached dwellers
In Pygmy Alley, where with brooding on them
A foot is shrunk to seven inches
And twelve-pence will not buy a spare rib.
And who would judge between Ogres and Pygmies –
The thundering text, the snivelling commentary –
Reading between such covers he will marvel
How his own members bloat and shrink again.

The Cloak

Into exile with only a few shirts,
Some gold coin and the necessary papers.
But winds are contrary: the Channel packet
Time after time returns the sea-sick peer
To Sandwich, Deal or Rye. He does not land,
But keeps his cabin; so at last we find him
In humble lodgings maybe at Dieppe,
His shirts unpacked, his night-cap on a peg,
Passing the day at cards and swordsmanship
Or merry passages with chambermaids,
By night at his old work. And all is well –
The country wine wholesome although so sharp,
And French his second tongue; a faithful valet
Brushes his hat and brings him newspapers.
This nobleman is at home anywhere,
His castle being, the valet says, his title.

The cares of an estate would incommode
Such tasks as now his Lordship has in hand.
His Lordship, says the valet, contemplates
A profitable absence of some years.
Has he no friend at Court to intercede?
He wants none: exile's but another name
For an old habit of non-residence
In all but the recesses of his cloak.
It was this angered a great personage.

With Her Lips Only

This honest wife, challenged at dusk
At the garden gate, under a moon perhaps,
In scent of honeysuckle, dared to deny
Love to an urgent lover: with her lips only,
Not with her heart. It was no assignation;
Taken aback, what could she say else?
For the children's sake, the lie was venial;
'For the children's sake', she argued with her conscience.

Yet a mortal lie must follow before dawn:
Challenged as usual in her own bed,
She protests love to an urgent husband,
Not with her heart but with her lips only;
'For the children's sake', she argues with her conscience.
'For the children' – turning suddenly cold towards them.

Lollocks

By sloth on sorrow fathered,
These dusty-featured Lollocks
Have their nativity in all disordered
Backs of cupboard drawers.

They play hide and seek
Among collars and novels
And empty medicine bottles,
And letters from abroad
That never will be answered.

Every sultry night
They plague little children,
Gurgling from the cistern,
Humming from the air,
Skewing up the bed-clothes,
Twitching the blind.

When the imbecile agèd
Are over-long in dying
And the nurse drowses,
Lollocks come skipping
Up the tattered stairs
And are nasty together
In the bed's shadow.

The signs of their presence
Are boils on the neck,
Dreams of vexation suddenly recalled
In the middle of the morning,
Languor after food.

Men cannot see them,
Men cannot hear them,
Do not believe in them –
But suffer the more
Both in neck and belly.

Women can see them –
O those naughty wives
Who sit by the fireside
Munching bread and honey,

Watching them in mischief
From corners of their eyes,
Slily allowing them to lick
Honey-sticky fingers.

Sovereign against Lollocks
Are hard broom and soft broom,
To well comb the hair,
To well brush the shoe,
And to pay every debt
As it falls due.

The Persian Version

Truth-loving Persians do not dwell upon
The trivial skirmish fought near Marathon.
As for the Greek theatrical tradition
Which represents that summer's expedition
Not as a mere reconnaissance in force
By three brigades of foot and one of horse
(Their left flank covered by some obsolete
Light craft detached from the main Persian fleet)
But as a grandiose, ill-starred attempt
To conquer Greece – they treat it with contempt;
And only incidentally refute
Major Greek claims, by stressing what repute
The Persian monarch and the Persian nation
Won by this salutary demonstration:
Despite a strong defence and adverse weather
All arms combined magnificently together.

The Face in the Mirror

Grey haunted eyes, absent-mindedly glaring
From wide, uneven orbits; one brow drooping
Somewhat over the eye
Because of a missile fragment still inhering,
Skin deep, as a foolish record of old-world fighting.

Crookedly broken nose – low tackling caused it;
Cheeks, furrowed; coarse grey hair, flying frenetic;
Forehead, wrinkled and high;
Jowls, prominent; ears, large; jaw, pugilistic;
Teeth, few; lips, full and ruddy; mouth, ascetic.

I pause with razor poised, scowling derision
At the mirrored man whose beard needs my attention,
And once more ask him why
He still stands ready, with a boy's presumption,
To court the queen in her high silk pavilion.

Surgical Ward: Men

Something occurred after the operation
To scare the surgeons (though no fault of theirs),
Whose reassurance did not fool me long.
Beyond the shy, concerned faces of nurses
A single white-hot eye, focusing on me,
Forced sweat in rivers down from scalp to belly.
I whistled, gasped or sang, with blanching knuckles
Clutched at my bed-grip almost till it cracked:
Too proud, still, to let loose Bedlamite screeches
And bring the charge-nurse scuttling down the aisle
With morphia-needle levelled. . . .

                              Lady Morphia –

Her scorpion kiss and dark gyrating dreams –
She in mistrust of whom I dared out-dare,
Two minutes longer than seemed possible,
Pain, that unpurposed, matchless elemental
Stronger than fear or grief, stranger than love.

Not at Home

Her house loomed at the end of a Berkshire lane,
Tall but retired. She was expecting me;
And I approached with light heart and quick tread,
Having already seen from the garden gate
How bright her knocker shone – in readiness
For my confident rap? – and the steps holystoned.
I ran the last few paces, rapped and listened
Intently for the rustle of her approach. . . .

No reply, no movement. I waited three long minutes,
Then, in surprise, went down the path again
To observe the chimney stacks. No smoke from either.
And the curtains: were they drawn against the sun?
Or against what, then? I glanced over a wall
At her well-tended orchard, heavy with bloom
(Easter fell late that year, Spring had come early),
And found the gardener, bent over cold frames.

'Her ladyship is not at home?'
                              'No, sir.'
'She was expecting me. My name is Lion.
Did she leave a note?'
                        'No, sir, she left no note.'
'I trust nothing has happened. . .?'
                                    'No, sir, nothing. . .
And yet she seemed preoccupied: we guess
Some family reason.'

'*Has* she a family?'
'That, sir, I could not say. . . . She seemed distressed –
Not quite herself, if I may venture so.'
'But she left no note?'
                          'Only a verbal message:
Her ladyship will be away some weeks
Or months, hopes to return before midsummer,
And, please, you are not to communicate.
There was something else: about the need for patience.'

The sun went in, a bleak wind shook the blossom,
Dust flew, the windows glared in a blank row. . . .
And yet I felt, when I turned slowly away,
Her eyes boring my back, as it might be posted
Behind a curtain slit, and still in love.

Notes

ULYSSES. A good example of Graves's use of myth to express his personal philosophy of love. Penelope was the wife of Ulysses who stayed at home while he went to the Trojan war and Circe was the beautiful witch who turned his men into swine and with whom he slept. The poem is a robust masculine defence of unfaithfulness. The concluding sentence, 'love-tossed he loathed the fraud, yet would not bed alone', well expresses the view of a sensitive philanderer. Wrapping this up as a pursuit of the White Goddess, is perhaps a harmless, but certainly an obvious, piece of deception.

WELSH INCIDENT. A splendid fantasy, which well conveys a sense of the oddity and garrulousness of a certain kind of Welshman. One could imagine the poem well read by Emlyn Williams. Graves has always been interested in monsters in his lighter poems and his success here largely depends on the skill with which the monsters are *not* described but left as vague presences. The poem is never sinister but continuously cheerful and amusing.

OGRES AND PYGMIES. This poem shows Graves's forceful diction to advantage. His use of hyphenated adjectives reminds one a little of the later Yeats, a poet for whom he has no respect. The clue to the poem is perhaps the third last line 'The thundering text, the snivelling commentary', which suggests that Graves is really comparing contemporary writings, or criticism, with the writing of the past. His own critical writings in prose are eccentric to a degree, though frequently full of interesting insights. His main fault as a critic is a forthright, though in some ways an engaging, tendency to dislike all the established writers of the twentieth century, including his contemporaries and juniors.

THE CLOAK. This is about a sort of eighteenth-century James Bond, a secret agent whose work seems to involve travelling on the Continent. This character is a symbol, however, for the spirit of ruthlessness and adventure (compare his 'Ulysses') which leads men to dislike the ordinary routines of everyday life. One is reminded of Graves's thirty year voluntary exile in Majorca.

WITH HER LIPS ONLY. This unrhymed sonnet is another of Graves's poems about the problem of Love; the words of Love may not always be sincere, and the pleasures of loyalty can sometimes lead to hatred.

LOLLOCKS. One of Graves most charming – and at the same time sinister – poems for children. It suggests an excellent moral lesson without in any way being pompous or adult about it. The invention of the creatures called 'Lollocks' is an inspired creation for the products of carelessness and untidiness. The poem might be taken as a sort of cautionary bedtime story for a child.

THE PERSIAN VERSION. This seems to me a major light poem. It strikingly expresses the views of a 1960s generation which is no longer prepared to accept the conventional view about the First or Second World Wars. In fact, this poem was written in the 1930s and probably arose out of Graves's natural independence of mind and perversity about accepted opinions. The usual view about the battle of Marathon, fought in 495 B.C. by the Greeks against the Persians, is that a small Greek force heroically met and defeated an enormous Persian one whose object was to invade their country.

FACE IN THE MIRROR. This much-imitated poem (notably and well by Anthony Thwaite) sums up Graves's career as an athlete and a First World War soldier and later lover through an honest description of his face seen in the mirror. 'The Queen in her high silk pavilion' refers to the White Goddess.

SURGICAL WARD: MEN. A powerful, honest poem, and a good example of how Graves manages to elevate a real experience into a near mythical one without losing, as he sometimes does, the original starting point of the poem.

NOT AT HOME. One of Graves's later love poems. It creates what Eliot would have called 'an objective correlative' for the sense of sudden pain and loss felt by someone deserted by the person he loves. The doctrine of the objective correlative suggested that emotions, to be communicable, had to be embedded in a concrete situation to give them weight and clarity. As often with Graves's later love poems, one feels here that the actual incident which gave rise to the poem has been deliberately disguised and omitted. The emotion still comes through in the fictional treatment Graves uses here, but it might have been even stronger if the original experience had been allowed to remain. The poem should be read in relation to the last sentence of Graves's introduction to the 1965 edition of his *Collected Poems*: 'My main theme was always the practical impossibility, transcended only by a belief in miracle, of absolute love continuing between man and woman.'

John Betjeman

John Betjeman was born in 1906. He is the best-known and the best-selling English poet now living. These two facts have unfortunately combined to diminish his reputation among poets and critics, although Philip Larkin regards him as the best English poet now writing and Edmund Wilson picked him out before the war with Dylan Thomas and Auden as one of the three most significant poets of his generation. Betjeman is in my own view a major poet, but perhaps in the last analysis a rather specialised taste. He might well be described as the last great Victorian and he would surely cherish this description himself, since he is an authority on Victorian taste. Apart from his reputation as a poet, Betjeman is known as a leading authority on Victorian architecture, who has done more than anyone else to revive interest in, and prevent the destruction of, many beautiful and important buildings of the nineteenth century. The most obvious central characteristic of his work is its humour, but this should deceive no one into thinking that he is a writer of light verse, or that what he is doing is trivial or easy. He has an eye for ephemeral visual detail which would be the envy of the late Ian Fleming, and an ear for the nuance of passing jargon which would be the envy of Joyce Grenfell. His huge public is right to support and enjoy Betjeman for these surface excellences, and the future will return to him, as it sometimes returns to Pope and Austin Dobson, as a brilliant social historian and a master of *vers de société*.

Pot Pourri from a Surrey Garden

Miles of pram in the wind and Pam in the gorse track,
  Coco-nut smell of the broom, and a packet of Weights
Press'd in the sand. The thud of a hoof on a horse-track –
    A horse-riding horse for a horse-track –
    Conifer county of Surrey approached
  Through remarkable wrought-iron gates.

Over your boundary now, I wash my face in a bird-bath,
  Then which path shall I take? that over there by the pram?
Down by the pond! or – yes, I will take the slippery third path,
    Trodden away with gym shoes,
    Beautiful fir-dry alley that leads
  To the bountiful body of Pam.

Pam, I adore you, Pam, you great big mountainous sports girl,
  Whizzing them over the net, full of the strength of five:
That old Malvernian brother, you zephyr and khaki shorts girl,
    Although he's playing for Woking,
    Can't stand up
  To your wonderful backhand drive.

See the strength of her arm, as firm and hairy as Hendren's;
  See the size of her thighs, the pout of her lips as, cross,
And full of pent-up strength, she swipes at the rhododendrons,
    Lucky the rhododendrons,
    And flings her arrogant love-lock
  Back with a petulant toss.

Over the redolent pinewoods, in at the bathroom casement,
  One fine Saturday, Windlesham bells shall call:
Up the Butterfield aisle rich with Gothic enlacement,
    Licensed now for embracement,
    Pam and I, as the organ
  Thunders over you all.

A Subaltern's Love-song

Miss J. Hunter Dunn, Miss J. Hunter Dunn,
Furnish'd and burnish'd by Aldershot sun,
What strenuous singles we played after tea,
We in the tournament – you against me!

Love-thirty, love-forty, oh! weakness of joy,
The speed of a swallow, the grace of a boy,
With carefullest carelessness, gaily you won,
I am weak from your loveliness, Joan Hunter Dunn.

Miss Joan Hunter Dunn, Miss Joan Hunter Dunn,
How mad I am, sad I am, glad that you won.
The warm-handled racket is back in its press,
But my shock-headed victor, she loves me no less.

Her father's euonymus shines as we walk,
And swing past the summer-house, buried in talk,
And cool the verandah that welcomes us in
To the six-o'clock news and a lime-juice and gin.

The scent of the conifers, sound of the bath,
The view from my bedroom of moss-dappled path,
As I struggle with double-end evening tie,
For we dance at the Golf Club, my victor and I.

On the floor of her bedroom lie blazer and shorts
And the cream-coloured walls are be-trophied with sports,
And westering, questioning settles the sun
On your low-leaded window, Miss Joan Hunter Dunn.

The Hillman is waiting, the light's in the hall,
The pictures of Egypt are bright on the wall,
My sweet, I am standing beside the oak stair
And there on the landing's the light on your hair.

By roads 'not adopted', by woodlanded ways,
She drove to the club in the late summer haze,

Into nine-o'clock Camberley, heavy with bells
And mushroomy, pine-woody, evergreen smells.

Miss Joan Hunter Dunn, Miss Joan Hunter Dunn,
I can hear from the car-park the dance has begun.
Oh! full Surrey twilight! importunate band!
Oh! strongly adorable tennis-girl's hand!

Around us are Rovers and Austins afar,
Above us, the intimate roof of the car,
And here on my right is the girl of my choice,
With the tilt of her nose and the chime of her voice,

And the scent of her wrap, and the words never said,
And the ominous, ominous dancing ahead.
We sat in the car park till twenty to one
And now I'm engaged to Miss Joan Hunter Dunn.

Indoor Games near Newbury

In among the silver birches winding ways of tarmac wander
   And the signs to Bussock Bottom, Tussock Wood and
                                  Windy Brake,
Gabled lodges, tile-hung churches, catch the lights of our
                                  Lagonda
As we drive to Wendy's party, lemon curd and Christmas
                                  cake.
    Rich the makes of motor whirring,
    Past the pine-plantation purring
       Come up, Hupmobile, Delage!
    Short the way your chauffeurs travel,
    Crunching over private gravel
       Each from out his warm garáge.

Oh but Wendy, when the carpet yielded to my indoor pumps
    There you stood, your gold hair streaming,

Handsome in the hall-light gleaming
There you looked and there you led me off into the game of
clumps
Then the new Victrola playing
And your funny uncle saying
'Choose your partners for a fox-trot! Dance until its *tea* o'clock!
'Come on, young 'uns, foot it featly!'
Was it chance that paired us neatly,
I, who loved you so completely,
You, who pressed me closely to you, hard against your party
frock?

'Meet me when you've finished eating!' So we met and no one
found us.
Oh that dark and furry cupboard while the rest played hide
and seek!
Holding hands our two hearts beating in the bedroom silence
round us,
Holding hands and hardly hearing sudden footstep, thud
and shriek.
Love that lay too deep for kissing –
'Where *is* Wendy? Wendy's missing!'
Love so pure it *had* to end,
Love so strong that I was frighten'd
When you gripped my fingers tight and
Hugging, whispered 'I'm your friend.'

Good-bye Wendy! Send the fairies, pinewood elf and larch tree
gnome,
Spingle-spangled stars are peeping
At the lush Lagonda creeping
Down the winding ways of tarmac to the leaded lights of home.
There, among the silver birches,
All the bells of all the churches
Sounded in the bath-waste running out into the frosty air.
Wendy speeded my undressing,
Wendy is the sheet's caressing
Wendy bending gives a blessing.
Holds me as I drift to dreamland, safe inside my slumberwear.

Devonshire Street W.1

The heavy mahogany door with its wrought-iron screen
　　Shuts. And the sound is rich, sympathetic, discreet.
The sun still shines on this eighteenth-century scene
　　With Edwardian faience adornments – Devonshire Street.

No hope. And the X-ray photographs under his arm
　　Confirm the message. His wife stands timidly by.
The opposite brick-built house looks lofty and calm
　　Its chimney steady against a mackerel sky.

No hope. And the iron nob of this palisade
　　So cold to the touch, is luckier now than he
'Oh merciless, hurrying Londoners! Why was I made
　　For the long and the painful deathbed coming to me?'

She puts her fingers in his as, loving and silly,
　　At long-past Kensington dances she used to do
'It's cheaper to take the tube to Piccadilly
　　And then we can catch a nineteen or a twenty-two.'

from Summoned by Bells

　　　　　　Then I found
Second-hand bookshops in the Essex Road,
Stacked high with powdery leather flaked and dry,
Gilt letters on red labels – *Mason's Works*
(But volume II is missing), Young's *Night Thoughts*,
Falconer's *Shipwreck* and *The Grave* by Blair,
A row of Scott, for certain incomplete,
And always somewhere Barber's *Isle of Wight*;
The antiquarian works that no one reads –
Church Bells of Nottingham, Baptismal Fonts
('Scarce, 2s. 6d., a few plates slightly foxed').

Once on a stall in Farringdon Road I found
An atlas of great lithographs,
Views of Ionian Isles, flyleaf inscribed
By Edward Lear – and bought it for a bob.
Perhaps one day I'll find a 'first' of Keats,
Wedged between Goldsmith and *The Law of Torts*;
Perhaps – but that was not the reason why
Untidy bookshops gave me such delight.
It was the smell of books, the plates in them,
Tooled leather, marbled paper, gilded edge,
The armorial book-plate of some country squire,
From whose tall library windows spread his park
On which this polished spine may once have looked,
From whose twin candlesticks may once have shone
Soft beams upon the spacious title-page.
Forgotten poets, parsons with a taste
For picturesque descriptions of a hill
Or ruin in the parish, pleased me much;
But steel engravings pleased me most of all –
Volumes of London views or Liverpool,
Or Edinburgh, 'The Athens of the North'.
I read the prose descriptions, gazed and gazed
Deep in the plates, and heard again the roll
Of market-carts on cobbles, coach-doors slammed
Outside the posting inn; with couples walked
Toward the pillared entrance of the church
'Lately erected from designs by Smirke';
And sauntered in some newly planted square.
Outside the bookshop, treasure in my hands,
I scarcely saw the trams or heard the bus
Or noticed modern London: I was back
With George the Fourth, post-horns, street-cries and bells.
'More books,' my mother sighed as I returned;
My father, handing to me half-a-crown,
Said, 'If you must buy books, then buy the best.'

Notes

POT POURRI FROM A SURREY GARDEN. A charming celebration of decent lust in the Home Counties. The poem delightfully conveys the cosy, idyllic atmosphere of cricket and toast for tea which used to characterise pre-war middle-class life in the south of England. The sustained ecstatic lyricism, combined with the author's clear understanding that he is overdoing it, gives the poem its blend of conviction and humour. The rhythm is particularly unusual and attractive. It depends on a free variation of a basic dactylic pattern which veers between five and six stresses to the longer lines and four and three to the shorter ones. The poem is a good example of how force of emotion can create a varying rhythm even on a most unusual and apparently arbitrary metrical base. A dactyl is a foot consisting of one heavy stress followed by two light ones; the phrase 'over your boundary' in the first line of the second stanza of this poem consists of two dactyls with the heavy stresses on the first syllable of the word 'over' and the first syllable of the word 'boundary'.

A SUBALTERN'S LOVE-SONG. Perhaps the most famous of Betjeman's humorous love poems. It forms an interesting comparison with 'Pot Pourri from a Surrey Garden'. Once again the rhythm is bouncing and variable, but this time it depends on a mixture of iambs and anapaests. An anapaest is a foot in which two light syllables are followed by one heavily stressed one; in the eighth line of the poem 'I am weak' is an anapaest with the heavy stress falling on the word 'weak'. An article in the *Sunday Times* Colour Supplement revealed that Miss Joan Hunter-Dunn is in fact a real person. Nevertheless, this poem is an imaginary monologue and well conveys the attitudes of the sort of young army officer it presents as speaking. What gives it its personality is Betjeman's eye and ear for detail. One might add his tongue and his nose for detail, for, as often, the poem includes references to what life tastes and smells like as well as looks and sounds like. Despite the fun, the poem conveys all the excitement of a young man in love.

INDOOR GAMES NEAR NEWBURY. An evocation of childhood love at a Christmas party. It beautifully catches the life of a rich upper middle-class family in the 1930s. The metre is trochaic, based on a stressed syllable followed by an unstressed one in each foot, and is perhaps best known for its use by Longfellow in his poem *Hiawatha*. The associations of the Longfellow poem are subdued by variations in the length of the lines and by initially making each long line equal to two of the Longfellow ones. Lagonda, Hupmobile and Delage were all makes of motor-car, and Victrola a make of gramophone.

DEVONSHIRE STREET W.I. This is one of Betjeman's sombre poems about death. A real sense of compassion for the couple outside the doctor's door comes through. The metre is a mixture of iambs and anapaests. This helps to give the poem its mixture of conversational lightness and at the same time, its underlying sadness.

From SUMMONED BY BELLS. This extract is from Chapter VI, 'London', of Betjeman's autobiographical poem in blank verse *Summoned by Bells*. The poem begins with his early life in High-gate and takes us up to the end of his career at Oxford, where he was a contemporary of Auden and MacNeice, though he moved in other circles. This passage illustrates Betjeman's fascination with Victoriana and his taste for the byways of literature. The pleasure of looking for old books has never been caught more vividly, except possibly by Browning at the beginning of his long poem *The Ring and the Book*. The strength of Betjeman's autobiography is his mixture of candour and modesty, and the flat almost self-parodying manner of the blank verse style helps him to avoid pomposity and at the same time to send up the solemn exercises in this vein of earlier English poets, notably Wordsworth. The poem should be read like Pope's *The Rape of the Lock*, as a tribute to and a satire on a bygone literary genre.

William Empson

William Empson was born in Yorkshire in 1906. He read mathematics as well as literature at Cambridge and had already produced some of his best verse and criticism while still an undergraduate. Like Eliot before him and Donald Davie after him, Empson has an equal reputation as a poet and critic; like Davie, he is a university professor – at Sheffield. The passionate intelligence of his poetry has something in common with the work of the seventeenth-century poet John Donne, though Empson is more perversely obscure than Donne ever was and much less directly concerned – on the surface at least – with his own experience. Empson has himself spoken of the 'puzzle interest' of poetry, though one feels that this is in part said with his tongue in his cheek for the sake of shocking readers out of their preconceived ideas. Unlike Eliot's notes to *The Waste Land*, the notes which Empson prints in the back of his *Collected Poems* are of considerable value in elucidating the imagery and intention behind some of his poems.

In recent years Empson's reputation has come increasingly to depend on his tough-minded and yet not uninvolved attitude to life, which has begun to be felt as a sort of moral touchstone. This may in part be due to his open opposition to established Christianity. It is certainly also due to his (as it now seems) more perceptive attitude to the problems of the 1930s than the group of poets who centred round Auden. Empson was himself teaching in the Far East in the late 1930s and saw more of the upheaval caused by war than poets who seemed to write more directly about it in Europe. His work was a major influence on the counter-revolutionary poetry of The Movement in the 1950s. Indeed, John Wain, one of the impressarios of The Movement, once wittily claimed that he had 'invented' Empson. The stylistic viciousness of Empson's imitators is now clearly apparent but he is no more to blame for this than Milton was for the excesses of his imitators in the late eighteenth century. Empson has written no new poetry for twenty-five years, but he is still young enough to embark on a new period of creative activity.

The Ants

We tunnel through your noonday out to you.
We carry our tube's narrow darkness there
Where, nostrum-plastered, with prepared air,
With old men running and trains whining through

We ants may tap your aphids for your dew.
You may not wish their sucking or our care;
Our all-but freedom, too, your branch must bear,
High as roots' depth in earth, all earth to view.

No, by too much this station the air nears.
How small a chink lets in how dire a foe.
What though the garden is one glance appears?

Winter will come and all her leaves will go.
We do not know what skeleton endures.
Carry at least her parasites below.

To an Old Lady

Ripeness is all; her in her cooling planet
Revere; do not presume to think her wasted.
Project her no projectile, plan nor man it;
Gods cool in turn, by the sun long outlasted.

Our earth alone given no name of god
Gives, too, no hold for such a leap to aid her;
Landing, you break some palace and seem odd;
Bees sting their need, the keeper's queen invader.

No, to your telescope; spy out the land;
Watch while her ritual is still to see,
Still stand her temples emptying in the sand
Whose waves o'erthrew their crumbled tracery;

Still stand uncalled-on her soul's appanage;
Much social detail whose successor fades,
Wit used to run a house and to play Bridge,
And tragic fervour, to dismiss her maids.

Years her precession do not throw from gear.
She reads a compass certain of her pole;
Confident, finds no confines on her sphere,
Whose failing crops are in her sole control.

Stars how much further from me fill my night,
Strange that she too should be inaccessible,
Who shares my sun. He curtains her from sight,
And but in darkness is she visible.

Letter II

Searching the cave gallery of your face
My torch meets fresco after fresco ravishes
Rebegets me; it crumbles each; no trace
Stays to remind me what each heaven lavishes.

How judge their triumph, these primeval stocks,
When to the sketchbook nought but this remains,
A gleam where jellyfish have died on rocks,
Bare canvas that the golden frame disdains?

Glancing, walk on; there are portraits yet, untried,
Unbleached; the process, do not hope to change.
Let us mark in general terms their wealth, how wide
Their sense of character, their styles, their range.

Only walk on; the greater part have gone;
Whom lust, nor cash, nor habit join, are cold;
The sands are shifting as you walk; walk on,
The new is an emptier darkness than the old.

Crossing and doubling, many-fingered, hounded,
Those desperate stars, those worms dying in flower
Ashed paper holds, nose-sailing, search their bounded
Darkness for a last acre to devour.

This Last Pain

This last pain for the damned the Fathers found:
'They knew the bliss with which they were not crowned.'
   Such, but on earth, let me foretell,
   Is all, of heaven or of hell.

Man, as the prying housemaid of the soul,
May know her happiness by eye to hole:
   He's safe; the key is lost; he knows
   Door will not open, nor hole close.

'What is conceivable can happen too,'
Said Wittgenstein, who had not dreamt of you;
   But wisely; if we worked it long
   We should forget where it was wrong.

Those thorns are crowns which, woven into knots,
Crackle under and soon boil fool's pots;
   And no man's watching, wise and long,
   Would ever stare them into song.

Thorns burn to a consistent ash, like man;
A splendid cleanser for the frying-pan:
   And those who leap from pan to fire
   Should this brave opposite admire.

All those large dreams by which men long live well
Are magic-lanterned on the smoke of hell;
   This then is real, I have implied,
   A painted, small, transparent slide.

These the inventive can hand-paint at leisure,
Or most emporia would stock our measure;
  And feasting in their dappled shade
  We should forget how they were made.

Feign then what's by a decent tact believed
And act that state is only so conceived,
  And build an edifice of form
  For house where phantoms may keep warm.

Imagine, then, by miracle, with me,
(Ambiguous gifts, as what gods give must be)
  What could not possibly be there,
  And learn a style from a despair.

Note on Local Flora

There is a tree native in Turkestan,
Or further east towards the Tree of Heaven,
Whose hard cold cones, not being wards to time,
Will leave their mother only for good cause;
Will ripen only in a forest fire;
Wait, to be fathered as was Bacchus once,
Through men's long lives, that image of time's end.
I knew the Phoenix was a vegetable.
So Semele desired her deity
As this in Kew thirsts for the Red Dawn.

Aubade

Hours before dawn we were woken by the quake.
My house was on a cliff. The thing could take
Bookloads off shelves, break bottles in a row.
Then the long pause and then the bigger shake.
It seemed the best thing to be up and go.

And far too large for my feet to step by.
I hoped that various buildings were brought low.
The heart of standing is you cannot fly.

It seemed quite safe till she got up and dressed.
The guarded tourist makes the guide the test.
Then I said The Garden? Laughing she said No.
Taxi for her and for me healthy rest.
It seemed the best thing to be up and go.

The language problem but you have to try.
Some solid ground for lying could she show?
The heart of standing is you cannot fly.

None of these deaths were her point at all.
The thing was that being woken he would bawl
And finding her not in earshot he would know.
I tried saying Half an Hour to pay this call.
It seemed the best thing to be up and go.

I slept, and blank as that I would yet lie.
Till you have seen what a threat holds below,
The heart of standing is you cannot fly.

Tell me again about Europe and her pains,
Who's tortured by the drought, who by the rains.
Glut me with floods where only the swine can row
Who cuts his throat and let him count his gains.
It seemed the best thing to be up and go.

A bedshift flight to a Far Eastern sky.
Only the same war on a stronger toe.
The heart of standing is you cannot fly.

Tell me more quickly what I lost by this,
Or tell me with less drama what they miss
Who call no die a god for a good throw,
Who say after two aliens had one kiss
It seemed the best thing to be up and go.

But as to risings, I can tell you why.
It is on contradiction that they grow.
It seemed the best thing to be up and go.
Up was the heartening and the strong reply.
The heart of standing is we cannot fly.

Missing Dates

Slowly the poison the whole blood stream fills.
It is not the effort nor the failure tires.
The waste remains, the waste remains and kills.

It is not your system or clear sight that mills
Down small to the consequence a life requires;
Slowly the poison the whole blood stream fills.

They bled an old dog dry yet the exchange rills
Of young dog blood gave but a month's desires.
The waste remains, the waste remains and kills.

It is the Chinese tombs and the slag hills
Usurp the soil, and not the soil retires.
Slowly the poison the whole blood stream fills.

Not to have fire is to be a skin that shrills.
The complete fire is death. From partial fires
The waste remains, the waste remains and kills.

It is the poems you have lost, the ills
From missing dates, at which the heart expires.
Slowly the poison the whole blood stream fills.
The waste remains, the waste remains and kills.

Just a Smack at Auden

Waiting for the end, boys, waiting for the end.
What is there to be or do?
What's become of me or you?
Are we kind or are we true?
Sitting two and two, boys, waiting for the end.

Shall I build a tower, boys, knowing it will rend
Crack upon the hour, boys, waiting for the end?
Shall I pluck a flower, boys, shall I save or spend?
All turns sour, boys, waiting for the end.

Shall I send a wire, boys? Where is there to send?
All are under fire, boys, waiting for the end.
Shall I turn a sire, boys? Shall I choose a friend?
The fat is in the pyre, boys, waiting for the end.

Shall I make it clear, boys, for all to apprehend,
Those that will not hear, boys, waiting for the end,
Knowing it is near, boys, trying to pretend,
Sitting in cold fear, boys, waiting for the end?

Shall we send a cable, boys, accurately penned,
Knowing we are able, boys, waiting for the end,
Via the Tower of Babel, boys? Christ will not ascend.
He's hiding in his stable, boys, waiting for the end.

Shall we blow a bubble, boys, glittering to distend,
Hiding from our trouble, boys, waiting for the end?
When you build on rubble, boys, Nature will append
Double and re-double, boys, waiting for the end.

Shall we make a tale, boys, that things are sure to mend,
Playing bluff and hale, boys, waiting for the end?
It will be born stale, boys, stinking to offend,
Dying ere it fail, boys, waiting for the end.

Shall we go all wild, boys, waste and make them lend,
Playing at the child, boys, waiting for the end?
It has all been filed, boys, history has a trend,
Each of us enisled, boys, waiting for the end.

What was said by Marx, boys, what did he perpend?
No good being sparks, boys, waiting for the end.
Treason of the clerks, boys, curtains that descend,
Lights becoming darks, boys, waiting for the end.

Waiting for the end, boys, waiting for the end.
Not a chance of blend, boys, things have got to tend.
Think of those who vend, boys, think of how we wend,
Waiting for the end, boys, waiting for the end.

Let it Go

It is this deep blankness is the real thing strange.
   The more things happen to you the more you can't
     Tell or remember even what they were.

The contradictions cover such a range.
   The talk would talk and go so far aslant.
     You don't want madhouse and the whole thing there.

The Teasers

Not but they die, the teasers and the dreams,
Not but they die,
         and tell the careful flood
To give them what they clamour for and why.

You could not fancy where they rip to blood,
You could not fancy
                    nor that mud
I have heard speak that will not cake or dry.

Our claims to act appear so small to these,
Our claims to act
                    colder lunacies
That cheat the love, the moment, the small fact.

Make no escape because they flash and die,
Make no escape
                    build up your love,
Leave what you die for and be safe to die.

Notes

THE ANTS. An excellent example of Empson's gnomic early style. The tightness of the sonnet form, combined with the end stopping of single sentences, slows the rhythm of the poem and gives a great weight of authority to what is being said. Unfortunately, it is extremely difficult to know what this is. The poem seems, like Christopher Middleton's 'The Forenoon' (p. 293), to make a connection between ants and people, but the exact nature and purpose of this is unclear. Are the ants predators or healers, or in some ways both? As with Dylan Thomas, one is able to respond to the music and overall evocative power of the poem without feeling at all secure about its point. 'Aphids' are greenfly which ants use like cows to milk for sugar, which they particularly enjoy.

TO AN OLD LADY. One of Empson's least impenetrable early poems. The old lady whom the poem describes is Empson's mother and she is being used to suggest what the poet sees as the admirable rhythms and rituals of a stable society. The central image of the poem presents the old woman as a planet. This is a very seventeenth-century sort of conceit, and if treated in purely visual terms becomes faintly ridiculous. The poem is not meant, however, to create a kind of surrealist portrait, and the details should be intellectually conceived rather than literally envisaged. The poem has an undercurrent of strong feeling which carries and sometimes breaks through the odd apparatus of imagery.

LETTER II. A love poem which suggests something of the fierce urge two people can feel to know everything about each other. The tortuous horror of the last stanza is very powerful, despite its extreme density. The syntax of the second and third line should be paraphrased as 'which ravages and rebegets me'. This missing out of simple connective words was a device taken from the nineteenth-century poet Gerard Manley Hopkins and very popular in the 1930s. To my mind it leads to ugliness as well as obscurity.

THIS LAST PAIN. A witty, ironic and abstract poem, instinct with strong feeling, about how one might cope with extreme situations. The end of the poem, particularly the last line, suggests a comparison with Hemingway in his definition of courage as 'grace under pressure'. The first line of the fifth stanza is a terrifying anticipation of the Nazi concentration camps, although it was written sometime before the war. As always with Empson, the argument is extremely intricate and difficult, but here the tone of voice is consistent and clear – the poem is against violence and is against illusions. Nevertheless, the poem has an air of being hermetically sealed and it would be a brave man who would accept a challenge to paraphrase it.

NOTE ON LOCAL FLORA. The trees described are in the Botanical Gardens at Kew. The 'Red Dawn' perhaps refers both to the possibility of a Communist revolution and to the familiar country saying 'a red sky in the morning is the shepherd's warning'. Bacchus was the god of wine and Semele a Greek maiden visited by Zeus in a thunderbolt. Once again, the poem seems to be an oblique, ironic comment on contemporary politics and the possibility of violence. It is worth remembering that the title of Empson's second book, published in 1940, was *The Gathering Storm*. This title was later used by Sir Winston Churchill for the first volume of his History of the Second World War.

AUBADE. A good example of Empson's later, more relaxed and plain style. The poem is about his travels in the Far East shortly before the outbreak of war. The seventh line, 'I hoped that various buildings were brought low', has the kind of aristocratic, fastidious distaste and wit which a writer like Oscar Wilde would have admired. Empson's attitudes often manage to combine the insight and facetiousness of the academic with the coolness of the man of action. The combination is unusual and attractive.

MISSING DATES. This villanelle makes an interesting comparison with Dylan Thomas's 'Do Not Go Gentle into that Good Night' (p. 244). My note on that poem explains the nature of the form. The poem is one of Empson's most characteristic and severely powerful ones. Whether one takes it as mainly about politics, or mainly about private life, it conveys a kind of doomed grandeur. Even the inversion in the first of the two refrain lines seems unobtrusive in the context of the whole poem's even, dignified delivery.

JUST A SMACK AT AUDEN. A gay, satirical squib directed against the sort of 1930s poem which was always going on about the way the world was going from bad to worse. In fact Empson admires the poetry of Auden and has repeatedly and most generously said in public that he regards Auden's poetry as more important than his own. Nevertheless, he aptly hits on and hits at the unearned gloom which was the stock-in-trade of Auden when writing below his best. The poem is all written on one rhyme with the exception of lines two, three and four. This effectively conveys the boring repetition and tediousness of the kind of poem it is satirising. There is also in each stanza an internal rhyme in each line. In the second stanza for example this is 'tower', 'hour', 'flower' and 'sour'.

LET IT GO. One of Empson's very few post-war poems. It has an air of great poignancy. In a way it could be read as his apology for not writing more poetry.

THE TEASERS. It was this poem, analysed by John Wain in *Penguin New Writing* in 1950, which gave rise to the Empson revival. The poem is a slight one compared to some of Empson's other pieces in this vein, but it has a musical quality and is able to make abstraction sound mysterious and sinister. The central point of the poem is hard to fix on, but it may be about the puncturing of illusions and the wastage of effort.

W. H. Auden

Wystan Hugh Auden was born in England in 1907. He went to the United States in 1940 and is now an American citizen, though he lives in Austria. His work falls into two periods. During the 1930s he established himself as the most brilliant and original poet of his generation, whose influence on the thinking of intellectuals went far beyond normal readers of poetry. He was once, in fact, called the 'Kipling of the Left', though his poetry was never to be interpreted simply in terms of one political commitment and indeed its flavour in his early 'Cops and Robbers' period is arguably more right wing than left. The truth of the matter is that Auden responded with a uniquely various sensitivity to all the political and social pressures of the 1930s. His poems seem to predict and prepare for the Second World War even from *The Orators* in 1932. Hindsight suggests, however, that this narrowly political view of

Auden was a mistake. His departure for America in 1940 was certainly not a matter of chickening out of his responsibilities. His reasons for going were no doubt as complex and cogent as Eliot's reasons for coming to England had been before. The superficial difference between Auden's work in his second, or American, period and his pre-war political one is that he now seems to have become more absorbed with the problems of a middle-aged man in a stable society, and, indeed, he has repudiated a number of his pre-war poems. The religious flavour of his later poems is, I think, much less significant than in the case of Eliot. His main concern increasingly appears as a warm, unbuttoned response to life in all its variety and richness as seen from the standpoint of an intelligent, playful, domestic-minded, music-loving, and last but not least tremendously creative man. The sheer bulk of Auden's poetic output is in the last analysis perhaps the most remarkable thing about him. No other modern English poet has even tried to do half the things which Auden has done, and he matches Tennyson in the range of his forms and metres from drama and narrative verse to sonnets, songs and prose poems. He has always remained true to the craft of poetry as a marvellous game and one has a sense that he may still undertake quite new kinds of poem which he has so far not attempted.

Musée des Beaux Arts

About suffering they were never wrong,
The Old Masters: how well they understood
Its human position; how it takes place
While someone else is eating or opening a window or just
    walking dully along;
How, when the aged are reverently, passionately waiting
For the miraculous birth, there always must be
Children who did not specially want it to happen, skating
On a pond at the edge of the wood:
They never forgot
That even the dreadful martyrdom must run its course
Anyhow in a corner, some untidy spot
Where the dogs go on with their doggy life and the torturer's
    horse
Scratches its innocent behind on a tree.

In Brueghel's *Icarus*, for instance: how everything turns away
Quite leisurely from the disaster; the ploughman may
Have heard the splash, the forsaken cry.
But for him it was not an important failure; the sun shone
As it had to on the white legs disappearing into the green
Water; and the expensive delicate ship that must have seen
Something amazing, a boy falling out of the sky,
Had somewhere to get to and sailed calmly on.

Gare du Midi

A nondescript express in from the South,
Crowds round the ticket barrier, a face
To welcome which the mayor has not contrived
Bugles or braid: something about the mouth
Distracts the stray look with alarm and pity.
Snow is falling. Clutching a little case,
He walks out briskly to infect a city
Whose terrible future may have just arrived.

Who's Who

A shilling life will give you all the facts:
How Father beat him, how he ran away,
What were the struggles of his youth, what acts
Made him the greatest figure of his day:
Of how he fought, fished, hunted, worked all night,
Though giddy, climbed new mountains; named a sea:
Some of the last researchers even write
Love made him weep pints like you and me.

With all his honours on, he sighed for one
Who, say astonished critics, lived at home;
Did little jobs about the house with skill
And nothing else; could whistle; would sit still
Or potter round the garden; answered some
Of his long marvellous letters but kept none.

Consider

Consider this and in our time
As the hawk sees it or the helmeted airman:
The clouds rift suddenly – look there
At cigarette-end smouldering on a border
At the first garden party of the year.
Pass on, admire the view of the massif
Through plate-glass windows of the Sport Hotel;
Join there the insufficient units
Dangerous, easy, in furs, in uniform
And constellated at reserved tables
Supplied with feelings by an efficient band,
Relayed elsewhere to farmers and their dogs
Sitting in kitchens in the stormy fens.

Long ago, supreme Antagonist,
More powerful than the great northern whale,

Ancient and sorry at life's limiting defect,
In Cornwall, Mendip, or the Pennine moor
Your comments on the highborn mining-captains,
Found they no answer, made them wish to die
– Lie since in barrows out of harm.
You talk to your admirers every day
By silted harbours, derelict works,
In strangled orchards, and a silent comb
Where dogs have worried or a bird was shot.
Order the ill that they attack at once:
Visit the ports and, interrupting
The leisurely conversation in the bar
Within a stone's throw of the sunlit water,
Beckon your chosen out. Summon
Those handsome and diseased youngsters, those women
Your solitary agents in the country parishes;
And mobilise the powerful forces latent
In soils that make the farmer brutal
In the infected sinus, and the eyes of stoats,
Then, ready, start your rumour, soft
But horrifying in its capacity to disgust
Which, spreading magnified, shall come to be
A polar peril, a prodigious alarm,
Scattering the people, as torn-up paper
Rags and utensils in a sudden gust,
Seized with immeasurable neurotic dread.

Seekers after happiness, all who follow
The convolutions of your simple wish,
It is later than you think; nearer that day
Far other than that distant afternoon
Amid rustle of frocks and stamping feet
They gave the prizes to the ruined boys.
You cannot be away, then, no
Not though you pack to leave within an hour,
Escaping humming down arterial roads:
The date was yours; the prey to fugues,
Irregular breathing and alternate ascendancies

165

After some haunted migratory years
To disintegrate on an instant in the explosion of mania
Or lapse for ever into a classic fatigue.

The Novelist

Encased in talent like a uniform,
The rank of every poet is well known;
They can amaze us like a thunderstorm,
Or die so young, or live for years alone.

They can dash forward like hussars: but he
Must struggle out of his boyish gift and learn
How to be plain and awkward, how to be
One after whom none think it worth to turn.

For, to achieve his lightest wish, he must
Become the whole of boredom, subject to
Vulgar complaints like love, among the Just

Be just, among the Filthy filthy too,
And in his own weak person, if he can,
Dully put up with all the wrongs of Man.

Missing

From scars where kestrels hover,
The leader looking over
Into the happy valley,
Orchard and curving river,

May turn away to see
The slow fastidious line
That disciplines the fell,
Hear curlew's creaking call
From angles unforeseen,
The drumming of a snipe
Surprise where driven sleet
Had scalded to the bone
And streams are acrid yet
To an unaccustomed lip;
The tall unwounded leader
Of doomed companions, all
Whose voices in the rock
Are now perpetual,
Fighters for no one's sake,
Who died beyond the border.

Heroes are buried who
Did not believe in death,
And bravery is now,
Not in the dying breath
But resisting the temptations
To skyline operations.
Yet glory is not new;
The summer visitors
Still come from far and wide,
Choosing their spots to view
The prize competitors,
Each thinking that he will
Find heroes in the wood,
Far from the capital,
Where lights and wine are set
For supper by the lake,
But leaders must migrate:
'Leave for Cape Wrath to-night,'
And the host after waiting
Must quench the lamps and pass
Alive into the house.

Edward Lear

Left by his friend to breakfast alone on the white
Italian shore, his Terrible Demon arose
Over his shoulder; he wept to himself in the night,
A dirty landscape-painter who hated his nose.

The legions of cruel inquisitive They
Were so many and big like dogs; he was upset
By Germans and boats; affection was miles away:
But guided by tears he successfully reached his Regret.

How prodigious the welcome was. Flowers took his hat
And bore him off to introduce him to the tongs;
The demon's false nose made the table laugh; a cat
Soon had him waltzing madly, let him squeeze her hand;
Words pushed him to the piano to sing comic songs;

And children swarmed to him like settlers. He became a land.

Epitaph on a Tyrant

Perfection, of a kind, was what he was after,
And the poetry he invented was easy to understand;
He knew human folly like the back of his hand,
And was greatly interested in armies and fleets;
When he laughed, respectable senators burst with laughter,
And when he cried the little children died in the streets.

Rimbaud

The nights, the railway-arches, the bad sky,
His horrible companions did not know it;
But in that child the rhetorician's lie
Burst like a pipe: the cold had made a poet.

Drinks bought him by his weak and lyric friend
His five wits systematically deranged,
To all accustomed nonsense put an end;
Till he from lyre and weakness was estranged.

Verse was a special illness of the ear;
Integrity was not enough; that seemed
The hell of childhood: he must try again.

Now, galloping through Africa, he dreamed
Of a new self, a son, an engineer,
His truth acceptable to lying men.

·

From The Witnesses

You are the town and We are the clock.
We are the guardians of the gate in the rock,
   The Two.
On your left and on your right,
In the day and in the night,
   We are watching you.

Wiser not to ask just what has occurred
To them who disobeyed our word;
   To those
We were the whirlpool, we were the reef,
We were the formal nightmare, grief
   And the unlucky rose.

Climb up the crane, learn the sailor's words
When the ships from the islands laden with birds
   Come in;
Tell your stories of fishing and other men's wives,
The expansive dreams of constricted lives,
   In the lighted inn.

But do not imagine We do not know,
Or that what you hide with such care won't show
    At a glance:
Nothing is done, nothing is said,
But don't make the mistake of believing us dead;
    I shouldn't dance.

We're afraid in that case you'll have a fall;
We've been watching you over the garden wall
    For hours:
The sky is darkening like a stain;
Something is going to fall like rain,
    And it won't be flowers.

When the green field comes off like a lid,
Revealing what was much better hid –
    Unpleasant:
And look, behind you without a sound
The woods have come up and are standing round
    In deadly crescent.

The bolt is sliding in its groove;
Outside the window is the black remov-
    -er's van:
And now with sudden swift emergence
Come the hooded women, the hump-backed surgeons,
    And the Scissor Man.

This might happen any day;
So be careful what you say
    And do:
Be clean, be tidy, oil the lock,
Weed the garden, wind the clock;
    Remember the Two.

Dear, Though the Night is Gone

Dear, though the night is gone,
Its dream still haunts to-day,
That brought us to a room
Cavernous, lofty as
A railway terminus,
And crowded in that gloom
Were beds, and we in one
In a far corner lay.

Our whisper woke no clocks,
We kissed and I was glad
At everything you did,
Indifferent to those
Who sat with hostile eyes
In pairs on every bed,
Arms round each other's neck,
Inert and vaguely sad.

What hidden worm of guilt
Or what malignant doubt
Am I the victim of,
That you then, unabashed,
Did what I never wished,
Confessed another love;
And I, submissive, felt
Unwanted and went out?

Miss Gee

(Tune: St James's Infirmary)

Let me tell you a little story
  About Miss Edith Gee;
She lived in Clevedon Terrace
  At Number 83.

She'd a slight squint in her left eye,
    Her lips they were thin and small,
She had narrow sloping shoulders
    And she had no bust at all.

She'd a velvet hat with trimmings,
    And a dark grey serge costume;
She lived in Clevedon Terrace
    In a small bed-sitting room.

She'd a purple mac for wet days,
    A green umbrella too to take,
She'd a bicycle with shopping basket
    And a harsh back-pedal brake.

The Church of Saint Aloysius
    Was not so very far;
She did a lot of knitting,
    Knitting for that Church Bazaar.

Miss Gee looked up at the starlight
    And said, 'Does anyone care
That I live in Clevedon Terrace
    On one hundred pounds a year?'

She dreamed a dream one evening
    That she was the Queen of France
And the Vicar of Saint Aloysius
    Asked Her Majesty to dance.

But a storm blew down the palace,
    She was biking through a field of corn,
And a bull with the face of the Vicar
    Was charging with lowered horn.

She could feel his hot breath behind her,
    He was going to overtake;
And the bicycle went slower and slower
    Because of that back-pedal brake.

Summer made the trees a picture,
   Winter made them a wreck;
She bicycled to the evening service
   With her clothes buttoned up to her neck.

She passed by the loving couples,
   She turned her head away;
She passed by the loving couples
   And they didn't ask her to stay.

Miss Gee sat down in the side-aisle,
   She heard the organ play;
And the choir it sang so sweetly
   At the ending of the day,

Miss Gee knelt down in the side-aisle,
   She knelt down on her knees;
'Lead me not into temptation
   But make me a good girl, please.'

The days and nights went by her
   Like waves round a Cornish wreck;
She bicycled down to the doctor
   With her clothes buttoned up to her neck.

She bicycled down to the doctor,
   And rang the surgery bell;
'O, doctor, I've a pain inside me,
   And I don't feel very well.'

Doctor Thomas looked her over,
   And then he looked some more;
Walked over to his wash-basin,
   Said, 'Why didn't you come before?'

Doctor Thomas sat over his dinner,
   Though his wife was waiting to ring,
Rolling his bread into pellets;
   Said, 'Cancer's a funny thing.

'Nobody knows what the cause is,
    Though some pretend they do;
It's like some hidden assassin
    Waiting to strike at you.

'Childless women get it,
    And men when they retire;
It's as if there had to be some outlet
    For their foiled creative fire.'

His wife she rang for the servant,
    Said, 'Don't be so morbid, dear';
He said: 'I saw Miss Gee this evening
    And she's a goner, I fear.'

They took Miss Gee to the hospital,
    She lay there a total wreck,
Lay in the ward for women
    With the bedclothes right up to her neck.

They laid her on the table,
    The students began to laugh;
And Mr Rose the surgeon
    He cut Miss Gee in half.

Mr Rose he turned to his students,
    Said, 'Gentlemen, if you please,
We seldom see a sarcoma
    As far advanced as this.'

They took her off the table,
    They wheeled away Miss Gee
Down to another department
    Where they study Anatomy.

They hung her from the ceiling,
    Yes, they hung up Miss Gee;
And a couple of Oxford Groupers
    Carefully dissected her knee.

From The Orators

Not, Father, further do prolong
   Our necessary defeat;
Spare us the numbing zero-hour,
   The desert-long retreat.

Against Your direct light, displayed,
   Regardant, absolute,
In person stubborn and oblique
   We set our maddened foot.

These nissen huts, if hide we could
   Your eye inseeing from,
Firm fenders were, but lo! to us
   Your loosened angers come.

Against Your accusations
   Though ready wit devise,
Nor magic countersigns prevail
   Nor airy sacrifice.

Weaker we are, and strict within
   Your organised blockade,
And from our desperate shore the last
   Few pallid youngsters fade.

Be not another than our hope;
   Expect we routed shall
Upon your peace; with ray disarm,
   Illumine, and not kill.

O What is That Sound

O what is that sound which so thrills the ear
   Down in the valley, drumming, drumming?
Only the scarlet soldiers, dear,
   The soldiers coming.

O what is that light I see flashing so clear
    Over the distance brightly, brightly?
Only the sun on their weapons, dear,
    As they step lightly.

O what are they doing with all that gear,
    What are they doing this morning, this morning?
Only their usual manoeuvres, dear,
    Or perhaps a warning.

O why have they left the road down there,
    Why are they suddenly wheeling, wheeling?
Perhaps a change in their orders, dear.
    Why are you kneeling?

O haven't they stopped for the doctor's care,
    Haven't they reined their horses, their horses?
Why, they are none of them wounded, dear,
    None of these forces.

O is it the parson they want, with white hair,
    Is it the parson, is it, is it?
No, they are passing his gateway dear,
    Without a visit.

O it must be the farmer who lives so near.
    It must be the farmer so cunning, so cunning?
They have passed the farmyard already, dear,
    And now they are running.

O where are you going? Stay with me here!
    Were the vows you swore deceiving, deceiving?
No, I promised to love you, dear,
    But I must be leaving.

O it's broken the lock and splintered the door,
    O it's the gate where they're turning, turning;
Their boots are heavy on the floor
    And their eyes are burning.

176

The Managers

In the bad old days it was not so bad:
     The top of the ladder
Was an amusing place to sit; success
     Meant quite a lot – leisure
And huge meals, more palaces filled with more
     Objects, books, girls, horses
Than one would ever get round to, and to be
     Carried uphill while seeing
Others walk. To rule was a pleasure when
     One wrote a death-sentence
On the back of the Ace of Spades and played on
     With a new deck. Honours
Are not so physical or jolly now,
     For the species of Powers
We are used to are not like that. Could one of them
     Be said to resemble
The Tragic Hero, the Platonic Saint,
     Or would any painter
Portray one rising triumphant from a lake
     On a dolphin, naked,
Protected by an umbrella of cherubs? Can
     They so much as manage
To behave like genuine Caesars when alone
     Or drinking with cronies,
To let their hair down and be frank about
     The world? It is doubtful.
The last word on how we may live or die
     Rests today with such quiet
Men, working too hard in rooms that are too big,
     Reducing to figures
What is the matter, what is to be done.
     A neat little luncheon
Of sandwiches is brought to each on a tray,
     Nourishment they are able
To take with one hand without looking up
     From papers a couple

Of secretaries are needed to file,
  From problems no smiling
Can dismiss. The typewriters never stop
  But whirr like grasshoppers
In the silent siesta heat as, frivolous
  Across their discussions,
From woods unaltered by our wars and our vows
  There drift the scents of flowers
And the songs of birds who will never vote
  Or bother to notice
Those distinguishing marks a lover sees
  By instinct and policemen
Can be trained to observe. Far into the night
  Their windows burn brightly
And, behind their backs bent over some report,
  On every quarter,
For ever like a god or a disease
  There on the earth the reason
In all its aspects why they are tired, the weak,
  The inattentive, seeking
Someone to blame. If, to recuperate
  They go a-playing, their greatness
Encounters the bow of the chef or the glance
  Of the ballet-dancer
Who cannot be ruined by any master's fall.
  To rule must be a calling,
It seems, like surgery or sculpture; the fun
  Neither love nor money
But taking necessary risks, the test
  Of one's skill, the question,
If difficult, their own reward. But then
  Perhaps one should mention
Also what must be a comfort as they guess
  In times like the present
When guesses can prove so fatally wrong,
  The fact of belonging
To the very select indeed, to those
  For whom, just supposing

They do, there will be places on the last
   Plane out of disaster.
No; no one is really sorry for their
   Heavy gait and careworn
Look, nor would they thank you if you said you were.

Lakes

(*for Isaiah Berlin*)

A lake allows an average father, walking slowly,
   To circumvent it in an afternoon,
And any healthy mother to halloo the children
   Back to her bedtime from their games across:
(Anything bigger than that, like Michigan or Baikal,
   Though potable, is an 'estranging sea').

Lake-folk require no fiend to keep them on their toes;
   They leave aggression to ill-bred romantics
Who duel with their shadows over blasted heaths:
   A month in a lacustrine atmosphere
Would find the fluvial rivals waltzing not exchanging
   The rhyming insults of their great-great-uncles.

No wonder Christendom did not get really started
   Till, scarred by torture, white from caves and jails,
Her pensive chiefs converged on the Ascanian Lake
   And by that stork-infested shore invented
The life of Godhead, making catholic the figure
   Of three small fishes in a triangle.

Sly Foreign Ministers should always meet beside one,
   For, whether they walk widdershins or deasil,
The path will yoke their shoulders to one liquid centre
   Like two old donkeys pumping as they plod;
Such physical compassion may not guarantee
   A marriage for their armies, but it helps.

Only a very wicked or conceited man,
  About to sink somewhere in mid-Atlantic,
Could think Poseidon's frown was meant for him in person,
  But it is only human to believe
The little lady of the glacier lake has fallen
  In love with the rare bather whom she drowns.

The drinking water of the city where one panics
  At nothing noticing how real one is
May come from reservoirs whose guards are all too conscious
  Of being followed: Webster's cardinal
Saw in a fish-pool something horrid with a hay-rake;
  I know a Sussex hammer-pond like that.

A haunted lake is sick, though; normally, they doctor
  Our tactile fevers with a visual world
Where beaks are dumb like boughs and faces calm like houses;
  The water-scorpion finds it quite unticklish,
And, if it shudder slightly when caressed by boats,
  It never asks for water or a loan.

Liking one's Nature, as lake-lovers do, benign
  Goes with a wish for savage dogs and man-traps:
One Fall, one dispossession, is enough, I'm sorry;
  Why should I give Lake Eden to the Nation
Just because every mortal Jack and Jill has been
  The genius of some amniotic mere?

It is unlikely I shall ever keep a swan
  Or build a tower on any small tombolo,
But that's not going to stop me wondering what sort
  Of lake I would decide on if I should.
Moraine, pot, oxbow, glint, sink, crater, piedmont, dimple...?
  Just reeling off their names is ever so comfy.

Vespers

If the hill overlooking our city has always been known as Adam's Grave, only at dusk can you see the recumbent giant, his head turned to the west, his right arm resting for ever on Eve's haunch,

can you learn, from the way he looks up at the scandalous pair, what a citizen really thinks of his citizenship,

just as now you can hear in a drunkard's caterwaul his rebel sorrows crying for a parental discipline, in lustful eyes perceive a disconsolate soul,

scanning with desperation all passing limbs for some vestige of her faceless angel who in that long ago when wishing was a help mounted her once and vanished:

For Sun and Moon supply their conforming masks, but in this hour of civil twilight all must wear their own faces.

And it is now that our two paths cross.

Both simultaneously recognise his Anti-type: that I am an Arcadian, that he is a Utopian.

He notes, with contempt, my Aquarian belly: I note, with alarm, his Scorpion's mouth.

He would like to see me cleaning latrines: I would like to see him removed to some other planet.

Neither speaks. What experience could we possibly share?

Glancing at a lampshade in a store window, I observe it is too hideous for anyone in their senses to buy: He observes it is too expensive for a peasant to buy.

Passing a slum child with rickets, I look the other way: He looks the other way if he passes a chubby one.

I hope our senators will behave like saints, provided they don't reform me: He hopes they will behave like *baritoni cattivi*, and, when lights burn late in the Citadel,

I (who have never seen the inside of a police station) am shocked and think: 'Were the city as free as they say, after sundown all her bureaus would be huge black stones.':

He (who has been beaten up several times) is not shocked at all but thinks 'One fine night our boys will be working up there.'

You can see, then, why, between my Eden and his New Jerusalem, no treaty is negotiable.

In my Eden a person who dislikes Bellini has the good manners not to get born: In his New Jerusalem a person who dislikes work will be very sorry he was born.

In my Eden we have a few beam-engines, saddle-tank loco-motives, overshot waterwheels and other beautiful pieces of obsolete machinery to play with: In his New Jerusalem even chefs will be cucumber-cool machine minders.

In my Eden our only source of political news is gossip: In his New Jerusalem there will be a special daily in simplified spelling for non-verbal types.

In my Eden each observes his compulsive rituals and super-stitious tabus but we have no morals; In his New Jerusalem the temples will be empty but all will practise the rational virtues.

One reason for his contempt is that I have only to close my eyes, cross the iron footbridge to the tow-path, take the barge through the short brick tunnel and there I stand in Eden again, welcomed back by the krum-horns, doppions, sordumes of jolly miners and a bob major from the Cathedral (romanesque) of St Sophie (*Die Kalte*):

One reason for my alarm is that, when he closes his eyes, he arrives, not in New Jerusalem, but on some august day of outrage when hellikins cavort through ruined drawing-rooms and fish-wives intervene in the Chamber or

some autumn night of delations and noyades, when the unrepentant thieves (including me) are sequestered and those he hates shall hate themselves instead.

So with a passing glance we take the other's posture. Already our steps recede, heading, incorrigible each, towards his kind of meal and evening.

Was it (as it must look to any god of cross-roads) simply a fortuitous intersection of life-paths, loyal to different fibs?

Or also a rendezvous between two accomplices who, in spite of themselves, cannot resist meeting

to remind the other (do both, at bottom, desire truth?) of that half of their secret which he would most like to forget,

forcing us both, for a fraction of a second, to remember our victim (but for him I could forget the blood, but for me he could forget the innocence),

on whose immolation (call him Abel, Remus, whom you will, it is one Sin Offering) arcadias, utopias, our dear old bag of a democracy are alike founded:

For without a cement of blood (it must be human, it must be innocent) no secular wall will safely stand.

Notes

MUSÉE DES BEAUX ARTS. An excellent early example of the characteristic tone of Auden's later poetry. It stresses, like Brueghel's painting in the museum at Brussels, the importance of life's carrying on despite whatever appalling atrocities may be happening in some other part of the world. The poem is much looser and freer in rhythm than Auden normally allows himself to be, although it has a strict rhyme scheme. The phrase 'expensive delicate ship' is a good example of Auden's familiar contrasting of two kinds of adjective – a romantic, elegant one and a deflating, realistic one.

GARE DU MIDI. The power of this simple short poem about a French railway station rests almost entirely in the ominous word 'infect' in the second last line. It introduces Auden's characteristic link between political and physiological change.

WHO'S WHO. Auden is very fond of the sonnet form in his early poems and this is a good example of how its tightness helps him to keep his thinking concise and pithy. The poem is a brief psychological and sentimental biography of an imaginary and representative famous man of our time. Before the war critics would have emphasised the importance of a phrase like 'how father beat him', stressing its indebtedness to Auden's reading of Freud or some other writer on the importance of early training. Reading the poem now, it is the charm and humanity of the close relative described in the sextet which strikes one as most effective about the poem. There is a short epigraph by Auden to his long poem 'The Orators' which has often been quoted: 'Private faces in public places are wiser and nicer than public faces in private places.' This poem is about the niceness of private faces in private places.

CONSIDER. Perhaps the best of Auden's monitory pre-war poems. For once the paraphernalia of his secret agents and movements of armies seems to be magnetised in the interests of overall feeling. The poem conveys perfectly the sense of nervous excitement at anticipated coming trouble. The industrial landscape of the north of England, the military flamboyance of central Europe – and the atmosphere of a school speech day – are subtly fused and infected with the poem's pervading sense of crisis. The structural device of presenting the middle section as an address to the 'supreme Antagonist' helps to give it its elevated tone, its sense of being somewhere midway between a political speech and a prayer. The 'supreme Antagonist', of course, is not to be narrowly interpreted as a reference to Hitler, or the devil, or any other particular enemy. He is a sort of familiar compound evil.

THE NOVELIST. Another compact sonnet which neatly sums up the task of the novelist as Auden saw it. He has said that he regards novel-writing as ultimately a more important job than writing poetry, but perhaps his own example indicates how a poet can reclaim much of the territory ceded to the novelist by the Romantic Movement.

MISSING. One of the more obviously 'Fascist' of Auden's early poems. The obsession with hero worship which he never quite grew out of in his early work is here strongly to the fore. Nevertheless, the poem is elegantly written and has, for addicts of early Auden, the familiar ominous tone.

EDWARD LEAR. An example of Auden's power to bring to life the key characteristics of a famous personality or writer. Edward Lear was a Victorian writer of comic verse most famous for his revival of the limerick. He was also well known in his own lifetime as a landscape painter. Many of the characters in his limericks are persecuted by people frequently described as 'they'. The poem is a disguised sonnet written in a stress accent form with five main stresses to each line instead of the familiar five heavy beats of the regular iambic line in which most of Auden's sonnets are written.

EPITAPH ON A TYRANT. This short poem deploys its material as if it were really a concentrated version of one of Auden's sonnets. It presents its tyrant as a kind of artist. The second line is a good comment on what Hitler gave to the German people in his Nuremberg rallies.

RIMBAUD. Arthur Rimbaud was one of the great French poets of the late nineteenth century. All his verse was written between the ages of sixteen and nineteen. Although he lived on until he was thirty-eight the latter part of his life was spent as a trader and gun runner in Africa. The 'weak and lyric friend' to whom Auden refers is probably Paul Verlaine, who lived for some years with Rimbaud and was, when they were breaking up, shot and wounded by Rimbaud one day with a revolver. The poem is another of Auden's attempts at concise interpretive biography. The first line of the sestet is typically Audenesque.

From THE WITNESSES. The speakers in this poem are a jazzed-up version of the Furies who hounded the doomed in Greek tragedy. The poem is a good example of Auden's lighter vein at its most sinister. The metre effectively teeters on the edge of doggerel. The Witnesses become even more terrifying through their power to send themselves up by this oddly offhand way of talking in casual verse. Once again the serious point of the poem is the threat of coming war.

DEAR, THOUGH THE NIGHT IS GONE. This is one of Auden's best love poems. In his *Collected Poems* it is classified at the back of the book with the songs, though its tone is more that of the talking than the singing voice. The poem is written in six syllable, mainly iambic lines, with a loose off-rhyming scheme, in eight line stanzas.

MISS GEE. Auden made a number of attempts to revive the ballad form in twentieth-century terms, and this is perhaps the most famous and successful. The plain narrative style and irregular rhythm attempt to reproduce the effect of the anonymous ballads of the sixteenth-century and earlier. The irony and vitality of the poem's tone are also quite in keeping with this tradition. Whether or not the link between frustration and cancer which the poem suggests can be medically authenticated, it has a horrifying air of plausibility as a plot for a grim story.

From THE ORATORS. An attempt on Auden's part to use the form of the traditional hymn. The God of Wrath who is addressed in the poem through such disciplined and cold inversions seems to be a composite figure built out of the 'supreme Antagonist' and 'no man's enemy' of the two poems 'Consider' and 'Petition'. Taken together these poems go a long way towards explaining Auden's conversion and entry into the Christian church. The only explanation of the organised ill in the world had to be a divine power. It is interesting to note how strong feeling seems to come through in this poem despite its highly literary and conscious technique. It would have been easy for it to turn out a simple parody. More than any other poet of the twentieth century Auden has been able to draw on the resources and associations of traditional forms without either seeming old-fashioned or losing his own personality. Not even John Betjeman seriously rivals him in this.

O WHAT IS THAT SOUND. An attempt at a serious straight ballad very close to the manner of the anonymous traditional ones. It achieves a bare and simple style which is almost entirely free from Auden's characteristic personality. No one who came across it suddenly in a book without a name attached to it would think that the poem was by Auden. Nevertheless the poem conveys real feeling and is far more than an exercise.

THE MANAGERS. A good example of Auden's later full, elaborate, rather prosaic style. The measure of his success in moving from the pre-war to the post-war world (this poem was first published in *Nones* in 1952) is apparent in his power to grasp the essence of the new means of control in the affluent society. The poem is an effective portrait of the new managerial class, neither capitalists nor workers. Such people would have been unthinkable in Auden's pre-war poetry and yet their nature, problems and qualities are analysed with his familiar surgical exactness.

LAKES. Part of a sequence called *Bucolics*, about natural phenomena such as winds, islands, streams and so on. The interest lies in a civilised man's urbane response to the idea of lakes. The poem may be almost entirely intellectual but it contains far more local interest in its detail than most poems do. It works rather like a *Times* fourth leader. Its tone is that of a clever man speaking to clever men (it is dedicated to the philosopher Isaiah Berlin, after all) and its use of a number of unusual words emphasises this gracefully witty, high-brow quality. The last line deserves close attention. To my ear it has a faintly 'excruciating' flavour, but it may be that Auden is mimicking, perhaps in a rather snobbish way, the tone of voice of somebody to whom he feels slightly superior. Of course, in one way this makes it worse. On the other hand the candid admission, leaving aside the words in which it is expressed, engagingly deflates the high-flown language of some of the rest of the poem. It is as if Auden were saying 'I know and you know that I am really just playing'. For Auden, of course, playing is a serious business and one of the most sensible activities of civilised man.

VESPERS. One of Auden's relatively rare prose poems. It relies for its effect on a sustained antithesis between a portrait of himself as a comfort-loving empiricist and another figure whom he sees as a dangerous extremist. The *persona* Auden adopts here as elsewhere in his later poems, is very much that of a Roman country gentleman, like the Latin poet Horace, whose civilis-ation is threatened by barbarism. Despite its witty flavour, the poem concludes on an ominous and faintly prophetic note. The whole poem makes an interesting comparison with the *terza rima* section from Eliot's poem 'Little Gidding' (p. 94). Eliot there is writing very much like another slightly earlier Roman poet, Vergil. The contrast between Eliot and Auden, both of whom are in some ways very poised and classical poets in their later work, is often a contrast between the rather marmoreal epic style of Vergil and the more domestic sensuous one of Horace.

Louis MacNeice

Louis MacNeice was born in Northern Ireland in 1907 and died in 1964. He took a first in Greats at Oxford and later taught classics at the University of Birmingham. For the last twenty-four years of his life he worked for the B.B.C. as a writer and producer of feature programmes. MacNeice has seemed to a number of critics, notably G. S. Fraser, as a potential major poet who never quite made it. His work is often spoken of in the same breath as Auden's and he is now widely regarded as, after Auden, the most important poet of the 1930s. He is also thought to have consolidated his work in the post-war years more effectively than Auden has done. MacNeice's radio play *The Dark Tower* is in my view the best piece of writing ever done for radio. The range and variety of his work is outstanding, and perhaps no one has conveyed the surface of so many experiences so vividly in the twentieth century as MacNeice. The main worry about his poetry is its occasional lack of penetration and depth, although in his best work there is a piercing sweetness and melancholy.

Snow

The room was suddenly rich and the great bay-window was
Spawning snow and pink roses against it
Soundlessly collateral and incompatible:
World is suddener than we fancy it.

World is crazier and more of it than we think,
Incorrigibly plural. I peel and portion
A tangerine and spit the pips and feel
The drunkenness of things being various.

And the fire flames with a bubbling sound for world
Is more spiteful and gay than one supposes –
On the tongue on the eyes on the ears in the palms of one's
    hands –
There is more than glass between the snow and the huge
    roses.

The Sunlight on the Garden

The sunlight on the garden
Hardens and grows cold,
We cannot cage the minute
Within its nets of gold,
When all is told
We cannot beg for pardon.

Our freedom as free lances
Advances towards its end;
The earth compels, upon it
Sonnets and birds descend;
And soon, my friend,
We shall have no time for dances.

The sky was good for flying
Defying the church bells
And every evil iron
Siren and what it tells:
The earth compels,
We are dying, Egypt, dying

And not expecting pardon,
Hardened in heart anew,
But glad to have sat under
Thunder and rain with you,
And grateful too
For sunlight on the garden.

Bagpipe Music

It's no go the merrygoround, it's no go the rickshaw,
All we want is a limousine and a ticket for the peepshow.
Their knickers are made of crêpe-de-chine, their shoes are
    made of python,
Their halls are lined with tiger rugs and their walls with heads
    of bison.

John MacDonald found a corpse, put it under the sofa,
Waited till it came to life and hit it with a poker,
Sold its eyes for souvenirs, sold its blood for whiskey,
Kept its bones for dumb-bells to use when he was fifty.

It's no go the Yogi-Man, it's no go Blavatsky,
All we want is a bank balance and a bit of skirt in a taxi.

Annie MacDougall went to milk, caught her foot in the heather,
Woke to hear a dance record playing of Old Vienna.
It's no go your maidenheads, it's no go your culture,
All we want is a Dunlop tyre and the devil mend the puncture.

The Laird o' Phelps spent Hogmany declaring he was sober,
Counted his feet to prove the fact and found he had one foot
over.
Mrs Carmichael had her fifth, looked at the job with repulsion,
Said to the midwife 'Take it away; I'm through with over-
production'.

It's no go the gossip column, it's no go the Ceilidh,
All we want is a mother's help and a sugar-stick for the baby.

Willie Murray cut his thumb, couldn't count the damage,
Took the hide of an Ayrshire cow and used it for a bandage.
His brother caught three hundred cran when the seas were
lavish,
Threw the bleeders back in the sea and went upon the parish.

It's no go the Herring Board, it's no go the Bible,
All we want is a packet of fags when our hands are idle.

It's no go the picture palace, it's no go the stadium,
It's no go the country cot with a pot of pink geraniums,
It's no go the Government grants, it's no go the elections,
Sit on your arse for fifty years and hang your hat on a pension.

It's no go my honey love, it's no go my poppet;
Work your hands from day to day, the winds will blow the
profit,
The glass is falling hour by hour, the glass will fall for ever,
But if you break the bloody glass you won't hold up the
weather.

From Autumn Journal

August is nearly over, the people
  Back from holiday are tanned
With blistered thumbs and a wallet of snaps and a little
  Joie de vivre which is contraband;
Whose stamina is enough to face the annual
  Wait for the annual spree,
Whose memories are stamped with specks of sunshine
  Like faded *fleurs de lys.*
Now the till and the typewriter call the fingers,
  The workman gathers his tools
For the eight-hour day but after that the solace
  Of films or football pools
Or of the gossip or cuddle, the moments of self-glory
  Or self-indulgence, blinkers on the eyes of doubt,
The blue smoke rising and the brown lace sinking
  In the empty glass of stout.
Most are accepters, born and bred to harness,
  And take things as they come,
But some refusing harness and more who are refused it
  Would pray that another and a better Kingdom come,
Which now is sketched in the air or travestied in slogans
  Written in chalk or tar on stucco or plaster-board
But in time may find its body in men's bodies,
  Its law and order in their heart's accord,
Where skill will no longer languish nor energy be trammelled
  To competition and graft,
Exploited in subservience but not allegiance
  To an utterly lost and daft
System that gives a few at fancy prices
  Their fancy lives
While ninety-nine in the hundred who never attend the banquet
  Must wash the grease of ages off the knives.
And now the tempter whispers 'But you also
  Have the slave-owner's mind,
Would like to sleep on a mattress of easy profits,
  To snap your fingers or a whip and find

Servants or houris ready to wince and flatter
    And build with their degradation your self-esteem;
What you want is not a world of the free in function
    But a niche at the top, the skimmings of the cream.'
And I answer that that is largely so for habit makes me
    Think victory for one implies another's defeat,
That freedom means the power to order, and that in order
    To preserve the values to the élite
The élite must remain a few. It is so hard to imagine
    A world where the many would have their chance without
A fall in the standard of intellectual living
    And nothing left that the highbrow cared about.
Which fears must be suppressed. There is no reason for think-
      ing
    That, if you give a chance to people to think or live,
The arts of thought or life will suffer and become rougher
    And not return more than you could ever give.
And now I relapse to sleep, to dreams perhaps and reaction
    Where I shall play the gangster or the sheikh,
Kill for the love of killing, make the world my sofa,
    Unzip the women and insult the meek.
Which fantasies no doubt are due to my private history,
    Matter for the analyst,
But the final cure is not in his past-dissecting fingers
    But in a future of action, the will and fist
Of those who abjure the luxury of self-pity
    And prefer to risk a movement without being sure
If movement would be better or worse in a hundred
    Years or a thousand when their heart is pure.
None of our hearts are pure, we always have mixed motives,
    Are self deceivers, but the worst of all
Deceits is to murmur 'Lord, I am not worthy'
    And, lying easy, turn your face to the wall.
But may I cure that habit, look up and outwards
    And may my feet follow my wider glance
First no doubt to stumble, then to walk with the others
    And in the end – with time and luck – to dance.

Autobiography

In my childhood trees were green
And there was plenty to be seen.

Come back early or never come.

My father made the walls resound,
He wore his collar the wrong way round.

Come back early or never come.

My mother wore a yellow dress;
Gently, gently, gentleness.

Come back early or never come.

When I was five the black dreams came;
Nothing after was quite the same.

Come back early or never come.

The dark was talking to the dead;
The lamp was dark beside my bed.

Come back early or never come.

When I woke they did not care;
Nobody, nobody was there.

Come back early or never come.

When my silent terror cried,
Nobody, nobody replied.

Come back early or never come.

I got up; the chilly sun
Saw me walk away alone.

Come back early or never come.

Cradle Song for Eleanor

Sleep, my darling, sleep;
   The pity of it all
Is all we compass if
   We watch disaster fall.
Put off your twenty-odd
   Encumbered years and creep
Into the only heaven,
   The robbers' cave of sleep.

The wild grass will whisper,
   Lights of passing cars
Will streak across your dreams
   And fumble at the stars;
Life will tap the window
   Only too soon again,
Life will have her answer –
   Do not ask her when.

When the winsome bubble
   Shivers, when the bough
Breaks, will be the moment
   But not here or now.
Sleep and, asleep, forget
   The watchers on the wall
Awake all night who know
   The pity of it all.

Prayer Before Birth

I am not yet born; O hear me.
Let not the bloodsucking bat or the rat or the stoat or the club-
   footed ghoul come near me.

I am not yet born, console me.
I fear that the human race may with tall walls wall me,
   with strong drugs dope me, with wise lies lure me,
     on black racks rack me, in blood-baths roll me.

I am not yet born; provide me
With water to dandle me, grass to grow for me, trees to talk
    to me, sky to sing to me, birds and a white light
       in the back of my mind to guide me.

I am not yet born; forgive me
For the sins that in me the world shall commit, my words
    when they speak me, my thoughts when they think me,
      my treason engendered by traitors beyond me,
       my life when they murder by means of my
        hands, my death when they live me.

I am not yet born; rehearse me
In the parts I must play and the cues I must take when
    old men lecture me, bureaucrats hector me, mountains
      frown at me, lovers laugh at me, the white
       waves call me to folly and the desert calls
        me to doom and the beggar refuses
         my gift and my children curse me.

I am not yet born; O hear me,
Let not the man who is beast or who thinks he is God
    come near me.

I am not yet born; O fill me
With strength against those who would freeze my
    humanity, would dragoon me into a lethal automaton,
      would make me a cog in a machine, a thing with
       one face, a thing, and against all those
       who would dissipate my entirety, would
        blow me like thistledown hither and
         thither or hither and thither
          like water held in the
           hands would spill me.

Let them not make me a stone and let them not spill me.
Otherwise kill me.

Brother Fire

When our brother Fire was having his dog's day
Jumping the London streets with millions of tin cans
Clanking at his tail, we heard some shadow say
'Give the dog a bone' – and so we gave him ours;
Night after night we watched him slaver and crunch away
The beams of human life, the tops of topless towers.

Which gluttony of his for us was Lenten fare
Who mother-naked, suckled with sparks, were chill
Though cotted in a grill of sizzling air
Striped like a convict – black, yellow and red;
Thus were we weaned to knowledge of the Will
That wills the natural world but wills us dead.

O delicate walker, babbler, dialectician Fire,
O enemy and image of ourselves,
Did we not on those mornings after the All Clear,
When you were looting shops in elemental joy
And singing as you swarmed up city block and spire,
Echo your thought in ours? 'Destroy! Destroy!'

The Suicide

And this, ladies and gentlemen, whom I am not in fact
Conducting, was his office all those minutes ago,
This man you never heard of. There are the bills
In the intray, the ash in the ashtray, the grey memoranda
    stacked
Against him, the serried ranks of the box-files, the packed
Jury of his unanswered correspondence

Nodding under the paperweight in the breeze
From the window by which he left; and here is the cracked
Receiver that never got mended and here is the jotter
With his last doodle which might be his own digestive tract
Ulcer and all or might be the flowery maze
Through which he had wandered deliciously till he stumbled
Suddenly finally conscious of all he lacked
On a manhole under the hollyhocks. The pencil
Point had obviously broken, yet, when he left this room
By catdrop sleight-of-foot or simple vanishing act,
To those who knew him for all that mess in the street
This man with the shy smile has left behind
Something that was intact.

Notes

SNOW. The eighth line of this poem might well sum up the excitement of MacNeice's poetry as a whole. Unlike the other poets of the 1930s with whom he was first associated, MacNeice never unquestioningly accepted a political allegiance, and his appreciation of the incompatibilities of things is well brought out in this poem by the image of the snow and pink roses which would touch but for the glass between them. The poem is in a loosely used five-stress line which derives from the principles of Hopkins.

THE SUNLIGHT ON THE GARDEN. One of MacNeice's saddest and most beautiful lyrics. He once said that when forced to choose between sound and sense he would have a slight preference for the word whose sound was most apt to the required context. In this poem the sense seems to be conveyed *through* the music. The rhyme scheme is interesting because it involves both end rhymes and rhymes between the last word in one line and the first word in the next. Thus, in the first stanza 'Garden' rhymes with 'pardon' five lines below it and also with 'Hardens' in the line immediately next to it. This device has the effect of dovetailing the lines together and producing a constant sense of echo emphasising the lingering, fading quality of the joys of life which the poem is talking about. 'We are dying, Egypt, dying' refers to the last words of Antony in Shakespeare's play *Antony and Cleopatra*.

BAGPIPE MUSIC. This entertaining poem mimes the sound of Scottish pipe music. It really needs to be read in a sort of high-pitched wailing voice which will bring out the yearning, straining sound of the bagpipes. The metre is a syncopated version of a basic trochaic–dactylic pattern. Despite the bouncy excitement of the rhythm, the underlying mood of the poem is despairing and melancholy, as almost always in Mac-Neice's best work. The wit and irony of the last stanza is bitter and powerful.

From AUTUMN JOURNAL. This is the third section of a long poem in the form of a sort of day-to-day diary which MacNeice wrote in 1938. The poem is a fascinating record of one man's response to the problems of this crucial period on the brink of war. One is inclined to wonder whether 'the future of action' MacNeice refers to suggests a passing wish to throw in his lot with his friends already in the Communist party. The serious common sense of the attitudes earlier in the poem is very distinctive.

AUTOBIOGRAPHY. The syncopated, ballad rhythm of the couplets and the refrain would perhaps incline one to think of this poem as fictional; but from external evidence it seems that the autobiography referred to in the title is MacNeice's own. His father became a bishop and the fifth line is clearly a reference to this. The poem is a moving and frightening one. In 1965, a prose autobiography, *The Strings are False*, was published posthumously.

CRADLE SONG FOR ELEANOR. A beautiful lullaby for a child sleeping; 'the watchers on the wall' in the third last line are perhaps to be compared with 'the Two' in Auden's poem 'The Witnesses'.

PRAYER BEFORE BIRTH. A dramatic monologue spoken by an unborn child. This unusual device enables MacNeice to give great poignancy to his list of contemporary dangers which will threaten the child if it enters the world. The poem's headlong rhythm is unique in MacNeice's work. It helps to give the poem a liturgical quality, like a metrical psalm or a passage from the Bible. The form of the poem is strengthened by internal rhymes, such as 'bat' and 'rat' in the second line, by repetitions such as the word 'call' in line 22, and by repetitions with slight changes, all of which give the poem the effect of being a developing list.

BROTHER FIRE. A poem about the London blitz. Its suggestion that the destructive impulse is native to all of us is a surprisingly modern one to find in a poem of the 1940s. Once again it shows MacNeice's political sensitivity and independence of mind.

THE SUICIDE. This touching poem about a colleague who killed himself is a moving record of MacNeice's response to years of office life. The image of 'a manhole under the hollihocks' is an effective one for the sudden sense of a yawning void at one's feet which extreme depression can sometimes produce. The last two lines 'This man with the shy smile has left behind/ Something that was intact' might serve as an epitaph on MacNeice himself.

Roy Fuller

Roy Fuller was born in 1912, served throughout the war in the Royal Navy and is now solicitor to one of the Big Five building societies. He is the only writer now at work in England whose reputation seems secure both in poetry and prose fiction. Fuller came to fiction relatively late in life and the qualities which distinguish his novels were already present in his early poems – an interest in plot, accurate description, and a willingness to interpret individual experience in political and social terms. As a poet Fuller was unlucky in the date of his birth. He was just too young to become well known in the 1930s, he was not killed in the war, and so was never established as a legend, and is just too old to have received his full meed of praise in the 1950s. As a successful man of affairs, with a legal career as well as a literary one, he has the generosity and common sense to remain quite unaffected by this. He has steadily gone on writing, refining and consolidating his achievement to a point where he is perhaps with Graves the most admired living English poet of those who were already writing before the war.

War Poet

Swift had pains in his head.
Johnson dying in bed
Tapped the dropsy himself.
Blake saw a flea and an elf.
Tennyson could hear the shriek
Of a bat. Pope was a freak.
Emily Dickinson stayed
Indoors for a decade.
Water inflated the belly
Of Hart Crane, and of Shelley.
Coleridge was a dope.
Southwell died on a rope.
Byron had a round white foot.
Smart and Cowper were put
Away. Lawrence was a fidget.
Keats was almost a midget.
Donne, alive in his shroud,
Shakespeare, in the coil of a cloud,
Saw death very well as he
Came crab-wise, dark and massy.
I envy not only their talents
And fertile lack of balance
But the appearance of choice
In their sad and fatal voice.

The Image

A spider in the bath. The image noted:
Significant maybe but surely cryptic.
A creature motionless and rather bloated,
The barriers shining, vertical and white:
Passing concern, and pity mixed with spite.

Next day with some surprise one finds it there.
It seems to have moved an inch or two, perhaps.
It starts to take on that familiar air
Of prisoners for whom time is erratic:
The filthy aunt forgotten in the attic.

Quite obviously it came up through the waste,
Rejects through ignorance or apathy
That passage back. The problem must be faced;
And life go on though strange intruders stir
Among its ordinary furniture.

One jibs at murder, so a sheet of paper
Is slipped beneath the accommodating legs.
The bathroom window shows for the escaper
The lighted lanterns of laburnum hung
In copper beeches – on which scene it's flung.

We certainly would like thus easily
To cast out of the house all suffering things.
But sadness and responsibility
For our own kind lives in the image noted:
A half-loved creature, motionless and bloated.

Translation

Now that the barbarians have got as far as Picra,
And all the new music is written in the twelve-tone scale,
And I am anyway approaching my fortieth birthday,
     I will dissemble no longer.

I will stop expressing my belief in the rosy
Future of man, and accept the evidence
Of a couple of wretched wars and innumerable
     Abortive revolutions.

I will cease to blame the stupidity of the slaves
Upon their masters and nurture, and will say,
Plainly, that they are enemies to culture,
            Advancement and cleanliness.

From progressive organisations, from quarterlies
Devoted to daring verse, from membership of
Committees, from letters of various protest
            I shall withdraw forthwith.

When they call me reactionary I shall smile,
Secure in another dimension. When they say
'Cinna has ceased to matter' I shall know
            How well I reflect the times.

The ruling class will think I am on their side
And make friendly overtures, but I shall retire
To the side further from Picra and write some poems
            About the doom of the whole boiling.

Anyone happy in this age and place
Is daft or corrupt. Better to abdicate
From a material and spiritual terrain
            Fit only for barbarians.

From Mythological Sonnets

To My Son

I

Far out, the voyagers clove the lovat sea
Which fizzed a little round its oily calms,
Straw sun and bleached planks swinging, the
Gunwale ribbed with a score of tawny arms.
Nursing a bellyache, a rope-rubbed hand
Or a vague passion for the cabin boy,

Accustomed to the rarity of land
And water's ennui, these found all their joy
In seeing the hyphens of archipelagos
Or a green snake of coast rise and fall back.
And little they imagined that in those
Inlets and groves, stretched out as on the rack,
Their girls were ground under the enormous thews
Of visiting gods, watched by staid munching ewes.

II

There actually stood the fabled riders,
Their faces, to be truthful, far from white;
Their tongue incomprehensible, their height
Negligible: in a word, complete outsiders.

Why had they come? To wonder at the tarts,
Trade smelly hides, gawp at the statuary,
Copy our straddling posture and our arts?
How right that we had not thought fit to flee!

'Join us at cocktails, bathing?' No reply.
'Let's see your wild dances, hear your simple airs.'
No move save the shifting of a shifty eye.

Trailing great pizzles, their dun stallions
Huddled against the hedges while our mares
Cavorted on the grass, black, yellow, bronze.

From To X

The car arrived that brought you to the place:
As you got out I saw your very groin.
Thus goddesses, nude, upon a distant quoin
Reveal their chaste religion to the race.

The aged, usual guests who sit or pace,
By chance I casually wandered out to join:
The car arrived that brought you to the place;
As you got out I saw your very groin.

Later it seemed impossible to trace,
As you politely spooned your macedoine,
That I had known the dark skin near the loin;
Already in another time and space
The car arrived that brought you to the place.

.   .   .

The long road greyly striping scarp and vale
Ran from the city to our meeting place.
You came by quieter and more devious ways.
Like beasts, our two cars rested head to tail.

I left a lie behind to smudge the trail,
And, conjuring up your speculative embrace
(The long road greyly striping scarp and vale),
Ran from the city to our meeting place.

Whose lie it was that made the sunlight fail,
Who knows? It was a fairly equal case.
Rain started, as I set out to retrace
(Passing at first your face, returning, pale)
The long road, greyly striping scarp and vale.

.   .   .

I rediscovered during our affair
Perceptions that in my Dark Age had gone.
How, say, astonishingly high upon
The spine the fastening of a brassière.

That every trivial thing in earth and air
Can constitute a mysterious eidolon,
I rediscovered during our affair.
Perceptions that in my dark age had gone

(The prurient disproportion of the bare:
Pinks, so conceived of, nearer cinnamon),

But that the gift of the youthful simpleton
To make dearth richness was in disrepair,
I rediscovered during our affair.

From the great distance of the end of caring
I saw our weak attempt at happiness;
Of you recalled a certain buttoned dress,
Cringed at my characteristic lack of daring.

The tortuous machinery of pairing
In our case seemed of utter pointlessness
From the great distance of the end of caring.
I saw our weak attempt at happiness

Related only to the lust for sparing
Our lives the terror of complete success.
And gone the absorbing, vital kind of chess
I played to try to bring about your baring,
From the great distance of the end of caring.

Brahms Peruses
The Score of *Siegfried*

(*The photograph by von Eichholz*)

Enormous boots, thick-soled, elastic-sided,
Rest on a carpet shaggy as the pelt
                    Of a mountain beast – perhaps
                    Is precisely a mountain beast.

The chair adjoining, being unoccupied,
Reveals its antimacassar of scalloped lace
                    Like the lower half
                    Of a bikini of our day.

The frock-coat is disposed in folds as ample
As those of saints' robes in Renaissance painting:
　　　　The pants, large cylinders
　　　　Of a more recent art.

The background is a dark and shining wealth
Of gilt-tooled books, mahogany, and frames
　　　　For photographs – for this,
　　　　Eventually, no doubt.

The peering old man holds the little score so close
His white beard sweeps the page; but gives no sign
　　　　That he perceives – or smells –
　　　　Anything untoward.

He could not be expected to be thinking
That the legend of courage, kiss and sword arose
　　　　From those atrocious Huns
　　　　Who ruined an empire's comfort.

But how can he not be falling back aghast
At the chromatic spectrum of decay,
　　　　Starting to destroy already
　　　　His classical universe?

Notes

WAR POET. This is a good example of the journalistic list poem of the 1930s put to a new use. The tone and method were probably partly suggested by a well-known poem by the American writer John Crowe Ransom, 'Survey of Literature'. Fuller's originality lies in his ability to emphasise his own sense of being merely a cog in the military machine by his comment at the end of the poem. The tight, emphatic rhyming is already a mark of Fuller's concern with formal neatness. The phrase 'fertile lack of balance' expresses the quality which adverse critics of Fuller sometimes miss in his work.

THE IMAGE. In this post-war poem the domestic event of finding a spider in the bath and wanting to get rid of it but not wanting to kill it is used as the basis for a meditation on human irresponsibility. The line 'The filthy aunt forgotten in the attic' reminds one a little of Auden, whose work is the major influence on Fuller's style.

TRANSLATION. This reads like a translation from the work of the modern Greek poet Cavafy. Despite the title, it is not a translation: pretending that it is, is a device to give a distancing effect to the poem's message. Fuller has increasingly come to interest himself in history and myth, and his comparisons between life in England today and life in the Roman Empire form one point of comparison between his work and that of Peter Porter.

From MYTHOLOGICAL SONNETS. The sonnet form has always been one of Fuller's favourites. The strength of this sequence, of which these form the first two poems, is that it fertilises the tight, gnomic manner of the Audenesque sonnet with an injection of the harsh language and mythological apparatus of Robert Graves. As a whole the sequence is concerned with the relationships between sex, art and religion, and the poems effectively chart the insistence of an underlying middle-aged lustfulness. This increasingly becomes an important theme in Fuller's later work. The sequence is dedicated to his son, the poet John Fuller. In each of the two sonnets quoted, as in Graves's poem 'Ogres and Pygmies' (p. 127), the humour masks a serious preoccupation with the exaggeration of human vices and virtues to form the material for the divine attributes of legend.

From TO x. These poems are from a narrative sequence of twenty-one which describe, as a novel told in the first person might, the course of an affair between a middle-aged man and a younger married woman. The poems are rondels, a medieval French metre sometimes revived in the later nineteenth century by poets like Andrew Lang. The metre consists of thirteen ten-syllable iambic lines with the first line repeated twice as the seventh line and the thirteenth line, and the second line repeated once as the eighth line. The whole poem is written on two rhymes and the scheme is a *abba, abab, abbaa*. Normally this form is used for romantic love lyrics and hence there is an aptness in its application to a romantic theme here. Fuller's originality lies in his power to conceal the immense restrictiveness of the form and to move with ease through the plot of his story. In fact, however, the chiming echoes of the metre immensely strengthen the exquisite pathos of the poem, which seems to me Fuller's best and one of the best love poems of the century. It should essentially be read in its entirety but the first sections quoted convey something of its flavour.

BRAHMS PERUSES THE SCORE OF 'SIEGFRIED'. The poem describes Brahms as he appears in a nineteenth-century photograph. Brahms was a great classical composer and the exponent of traditional values against the revolutionary ideas brought in by Wagner, particularly in *The Ring of the Nibelungs*. The poem is a light-hearted one but it emphasises one of Fuller's main themes – the destruction of civilisation by barbarians. The poem is in the metre of the eighteenth-century poet William Collins's 'Ode to Evening'. All four lines in each stanza are resolved iambic, the first two usually having ten syllables and the last two six each. The poem is unrhymed.

Stevie Smith

The age of Miss Stevie Smith is not normally disclosed in books. She has lived for many years with an aged aunt, about whom she has written a book, *Novel on Yellow Paper*. She is perhaps the most eccentric and least easily classifiable poet now writing. Much of her artless verse looks at first sight, and indeed sounds at first hearing, like pure doggerel. It is, however, instinct with a most individual personality and is extremely difficult to imitate. In one sense she has done what has been claimed for Robert Graves: she has 'written the purest poetry of our time'. Several of her poems have a sort of grotesque anonymity which seems a sure mark of greatness. Her reputation over the last few years has greatly increased due to her success in public readings of her own poetry. Like John Betjeman, she has the power to amuse and entertain large audiences by sheer force of personality, and there is no doubt that the spirit of her poetry is in tune with the times. Apart from her total originality, which is always the first mark of an important poet, the noticeable features of Miss Smith's poetry are its combination of tenderness, humour and a sort of sustained running battle with Christianity. At her best she appears in her poems as a kind of good fairy, but one feels that, like a gamekeeper who was once a poacher, this good fairy has enjoyed an earlier career as a witch. Perhaps the role of sorceress, which in her very different way Stevie Smith shares with Sylvia Plath, is the most appropriate one for a woman poet in the mid-twentieth century.

Was he Married?

Was he married, did he try
To support as he grew less fond of them
Wife and family?

No,
He never suffered such a blow.

Did he feel pointless, feeble and distrait,
Unwanted by everyone and in the way?

From his cradle he was purposeful,
His bent strong and his mind full.

Did he love people very much
Yet find them die one day?

He did not love in the human way.

Did he ask how long it would go on,
Wonder if Death could be counted on for an end?

He did not feel like this,
He had a future of bliss.

Did he never feel strong
Pain for being wrong?

He was not wrong, he was right,
He suffered from others', not his own, spite.

But there *is* no suffering like having made a mistake
Because of being of an inferior make.

He was not inferior,
He was superior.

He knew then that power corrupts but some must govern?

His thoughts were different.

Did he lack friends? Worse,
Think it was for his fault, not theirs?

He did not lack friends,
He had disciples he moulded to his ends.

Did he feel over-handicapped sometimes, yet must draw even?

How could he feel like this? He was the King of Heaven.

. . . find a sudden brightness one day in everything
Because a mood had been conquered, or a sin?

I tell you, he did not sin.

Do only human beings suffer from the irritation
I have mentioned? learn too that being comical
Does not ameliorate the desperation?

Yes, only human beings feel this,
It is because they are so mixed.

All human beings should have a medal,
A god cannot carry it, he is not able.

A god is Man's doll, you ass,
He makes him up like this on purpose.

He might have made him up worse.

He often has, in the past.

To choose a god of love, as he did and does,
Is a little move then?

Yes, it is.

A larger one will be when men
Love love and hate hate but do not deify them?

It will be a larger one.

Poor Soul, Poor Girl!

(*A Debutante*)

I cannot imagine anything nicer
Than to be struck by lightning and killed suddenly crossing a
field
As if somebody cared.
Nobody cares whether I am alive or dead.

Not Waving but Drowning

Nobody heard him, the dead man,
But still he lay moaning:
I was much further out than you thought
And not waving but drowning.

Poor chap, he always loved larking
And now he's dead
It must have been too cold for him his heart gave way,
They said.

Oh, no no no, it was too cold always
(Still the dead one lay moaning)
I was much too far out all my life
And not waving but drowning.

Fafnir and the Knights

In the quiet waters
Of the forest pool
Fafnir the dragon
His tongue will cool

His tongue will cool
And his muzzle dip
Until the soft waters lave
His muzzle tip

Happy simple creature
In his coat of mail
With a mild bright eye
And a waving tail

Happy the dragon
In the days expended
Before the time had come for dragons
To be hounded

Delivered in their simplicity
To the Knights of the Advancing Band
Who seeing the simple dragon
Must kill him out of hand

The time has not come yet
But must come soon
Meanwhile happy Fafnir
Take thy rest in the afternoon

Take thy rest
Fafnir while thou mayest
In the long grass
Where thou liest

Happy knowing not
In thy simplicity
That the knights have come
To do away with thee.

When thy body shall be torn
And thy lofty spirit
Broken into pieces
For a knight's merit

When thy lifeblood shall be spilt
And thy Being mild
In torment and dismay
To death beguiled

Fafnir, I shall say then,
Thou art better dead
For the knights have burnt thy grass
And thou couldst not have fed.

The Jungle Husband

Dearest Evelyn, I often think of you
Out with the guns in the jungle stew
Yesterday I hittapotamus
I put the measurements down for you but they got lost in the
    fuss
It's not a good thing to drink out here
You know, I've practically given it up dear.
Tomorrow I am going alone a long way
Into the jungle. It is all grey
But green on top
Only sometimes when a tree has fallen
The sun comes down plop, it is quite appalling.

You never want to go in a jungle pool
In the hot sun, it would be the act of a fool
Because it's always full of anacondas, Evelyn, not looking ill-
    fed
I'll say. So no more now, from your loving husband, Wilfred.

I Remember

It was my bridal night I remember,
An old man of seventy-three
I lay with my young bride in my arms,
A girl with t.b.
It was wartime, and overhead
The Germans were making a particularly heavy raid on
    Hampstead.
What rendered the confusion worse, perversely
Our bombers had chosen that moment to set out for Germany.
Harry, do they ever collide?
I do not think it has ever happened,
Oh my bride, my bride.

Croft

Aloft,
In the loft,
Sits Croft;
He is soft.

Après la Politique, la Haine des Bourbons

Count Flanders
Was eaten up with pride;
His dog Sanders
Thought only of his inside.

They were a precious couple,
And let the people feed on straw and rubble.

Bitter was the weather,
Bitter the people,
When they flung Count Flanders
From the church steeple.
Bitter was the weather,
Iron the ground,
When Dog Sanders died of a stomach wound.

Notes

WAS HE MARRIED? This is a poem in the form of a dialogue about the life of Jesus Christ. The poem is an excellent example of Stevie Smith's love–hate relationship towards Christianity. The conclusion of the poem in the last six lines suggests that she is in favour of Christian moral principles but not Christian theology. Most of the poem, however, is a critique of the personality of Christ as a fundamentally remote, inhuman and rather pompous one. This bold, and to many people no doubt blasphemous, point of view is made more acceptable by the humour, oddity and good temper of the dialogue. One is inclined to treat the poem simply as a sort of joke, perhaps in rather bad taste: but it is really deeply felt, and is making a serious point.

POOR SOUL, POOR GIRL! A short dramatic monologue spoken by a lonely debutante. In Stevie Smith's *Selected Poems* there is a drawing of a rather aristocratic-looking girl sitting by herself on a chair to go with it. Once again, the poem looks like a sort of quickly written joke – a piece of doggerel. It *is* funny, of course, but its underlying purpose is to suggest that to somebody who feels lonely *anything* is better than indifference, even the most unpleasant kind of attention.

NOT WAVING BUT DROWNING. Once again this is a deeply felt and tragic poem posing as a lighthearted one. The idea of somebody's drowning struggle being mistaken in the distance for a friendly wave is a moving one in itself. Used as a metaphor for our failure to recognise other people's need for help, it takes on added power.

FAFNIR AND THE KNIGHTS. This has the childlike quality of a nursery song or an anonymous ballad. The central situation has the quality of a myth whose full relevance is not yielded in the poem. The rhythm has a sort of archaic ruggedness which adds to the legendary quality of the story. At the same time there is intensity of feeling on behalf of the dragon. Stevie Smith is often at her most touching in writing about animals. One of her most remarkable qualities, as in the fourth line of the first stanza, is to introduce sudden grammatical oddities and changes of tone which successfully convey the eccentricity of a childlike temperament. It would be very hard to get away with this sort of thing unless one could do it absolutely naturally, and for this reason Stevie Smith has had no imitators.

THE JUNGLE HUSBAND. A dramatic monologue in the form of a letter written to his wife by a drunken hunter somewhere in Africa. The poem is written with the directness and simplicity of a child's letter and this helps to give it charm as well as humour. The deliberately eccentric rhyming such as 'hitta-potamus' and 'fuss' and 'ill-fed' and 'Wilfred' underline the sophistication behind the simplicity. The poem is poking fun at the art of poetry with its familiar dependence on similarities of sound. It seems to be suggesting that if one *must* write in verse then verse is going to be pushed as far as it can to ac-commodate one's thought. Milder versions of this device were used by Byron and Browning and later by Hilaire Belloc.

I REMEMBER. This very strange poem is a difficult one to inter-pret. I think the idea of the bombers never colliding might be intended to suggest that two people are always too far apart to communicate with each other even when they are very much in love. The difference in their ages between the two lovers in the poem and the fact that the young girl is ill support this view. This kind of explanation, however, is un-important beside the queer sense of mystery and grandeur that the poem manages to convey.

CROFT. These nine words form the shortest poem in this book. In their weird combination of grimness and humour, they create the basis for a play worthy of Samuel Beckett. They also remind us of that stock figure in Victorian melodrama whom Roy Fuller once characterised as 'the filthy aunt forgotten in the attic'. By avoiding all comment, the poem forces us to make up our own minds about the plight of the mad boy. Do we think of him simply as a figure of fun or do we feel pity for him and rage at his situation?

APRÈS LA POLITIQUE, LA HAINE DES BOURBONS. ('After the statecraft the hatred of the Bourbons'.) Another grim ballad-like poem. One has the sense that a whole body of medieval legend has been compressed into a few lines. The poem is of course also making a moral point about the feudal system – the failure of lords to look after the material needs of their subjects.

R. S. Thomas

Ronald Stuart Thomas was born in Wales in 1913, a year before his namesake Dylan Thomas. He has lived his life as a clergyman, often in the remote country parishes whose landscape and people he has celebrated in his poems. Thomas's poetry seems at first sight a grim and forbidding body of work to approach. His tone of voice is almost invariably severe, his rhythm slow and heavy and his subject matter Man scratching a pitiful livelihood from a bare and inhospitable land. Thomas's poetry is narrow in range, but it seems sure to last for its depth and its honesty.

Evans

Evans? Yes, many a time
I came down his bare flight
Of stairs into the gaunt kitchen
With its wood fire, where crickets sang
Accompaniment to the black kettle's
Whine and so into the cold
Dark to smother in the thick tide
Of night that drifted about the walls
Of his stark farm on the hill ridge.

It was not the dark filling my eyes
And mouth appalled me; not even the drip
Of rain like blood from the one tree
Weather-tortured. It was the dark
Silting the veins of that sick man
I left stranded upon the vast
And lonely shore of his bleak bed.

Poetry for Supper

'Listen, now, verse should be as natural
As the small tuber that feeds on muck
And grows slowly from obtuse soil
To the white flower of immortal beauty.'

'Natural, hell! What was it Chaucer
Said once about the long toil
That goes like blood to the poem's making?
Leave it to nature and the verse sprawls,
Limp as bindweed, if it break at all
Life's iron crust. Man, you must sweat
And rhyme your guts taut, if you'd build
Your verse a ladder.'

                              'You speak as though
No sunlight ever surprised the mind
Groping on its cloudy path.'

'Sunlight's a thing that needs a window
Before it enters a dark room.
Windows don't happen.'
                              So two old poets,
Hunched at their beer in the low haze
Of an inn parlour, while the talk ran
Noisily by them, glib with prose.

Iago Prytherch

Iago Prytherch, forgive my naming you.
You are so far in your small fields
From the world's eye, sharpening your blade
On a cloud's edge, no one will tell you
How I made fun of you, or pitied either
Your long soliloquies, crouched at your slow
And patient surgery under the faint
November rays of the sun's lamp.

Made fun of you? That was their graceless
Accusation, because I took
Your rags for theme, because I showed them
Your thought's bareness; science and art,
The mind's furniture, having no chance
To install themselves, because of the great
Draught of nature sweeping the skull.

Fun? Pity? No word can describe
My true feelings. I passed and saw you
Labouring there, your dark figure

Marring the simple geometry
Of the square fields with its gaunt question.
My poems were made in its long shadow
Falling coldly across the page.

Ninetieth Birthday

You go up the long track
That will take a car, but is best walked
On slow foot, noting the lichen
That writes history on the page
Of the grey rock. Trees are about you
At first, but yield to the green bracken,
The nightjar's house: you can hear it spin
On warm evenings; it is still now
In the noonday heat, only the lesser
Voices sound, blue-fly and gnat
And the stream's whisper. As the road climbs,
You will pause for breath and the far sea's
Signal will flash, till you turn again
To the steep track, buttressed with cloud.

And there at the top that old woman,
Born almost a century back
In that stone farm, awaits your coming;
Waits for the news of the lost village
She thinks she knows, a place that exists
In her memory only.
                              You bring her greeting
And praise for having lasted so long
With time's knife shaving the bone.
Yet no bridge joins her own
World with yours, all you can do
Is lean kindly across the abyss
To hear words that were once wise.

Those Others

*A gofid gwerin gyfan
Yn fy nghri fel taerni tân.*

Dewi Emrys

I have looked long at this land,
Trying to understand
My place in it – why,
With each fertile country
So free of its room,
This was the cramped womb
At last took me in
From the void of unbeing.

Hate takes a long time
To grow in, and mine
Has increased from birth;
Not for the brute earth
That is strong here and clean
And plain in its meaning
As one of the books are
That tell but of the war

Of heart with head, leaving
The wild birds to sing
The best songs; I find
This hate's for my own kind,
For men of the Welsh race
Who brood with dark face
Over their thin navel
To learn what to sell;

Yet not for them all either,
There are still those other
Castaways on a sea
Of grass, who call to me,

228

Clinging to their doomed farms;
Their hearts though rough are warm
And firm, and their slow wake
Through time bleeds for our sake.

To a Young Poet

For the first twenty years you are still growing,
Bodily that is; as a poet, of course,
You are not born yet. It's the next ten
You cut your teeth on to emerge smirking
For your brash courtship of the muse.
You will take seriously those first affairs
With young poems, but no attachments
Formed then but come to shame you,
When love has changed to a grave service
Of a cold queen.
                              From forty on
You learn from the sharp cuts and jags
Of poems that have come to pieces
In your crude hands how to assemble
With more skill the arbitrary parts
Of ode or sonnet, while time fosters
A new impulse to conceal your wounds
From her and from a bold public,
Given to pry.
                              You are old now
As years reckon, but in that slower
World of the poet you are just coming
To sad manhood, knowing the smile
On her proud face is not for you.

Tramp

A knock at the door
And he stands there,
A tramp with his can
Asking for tea,
Strong for a poor man
On his way – where?

He looks at his feet,
I look at the sky;
Over us the planes build
The shifting rafters
Of that new world
We have sworn by.

I sleep in my bed,
He sleeps in the old,
Dead leaves of a ditch.
My dreams are haunted;
Are his dreams rich?
If I wake early,
He wakes cold.

On the Farm

There was Dai Puw. He was no good.
They put him in the fields to dock swedes,
And took the knife from him, when he came home
At late evening with a grin
Like the slash of a knife on his face.

There was Llew Puw, and he was no good.
Every evening after the ploughing
With the big tractor he would sit in his chair,
And stare into the tangled fire garden,
Opening his slow lips like a snail.

There was Huw Puw, too. What shall I say?
I have heard him whistling in the hedges
On and on, as though winter
Would never again leave those fields,
And all the trees were deformed.

And lastly there was the girl:
Beauty under some spell of the beast.
Her pale face was the lantern
By which they read in life's dark book
The shrill sentence: God is love.

Notes

EVANS. Deathbeds are a favourite subject in the poetry of Thomas and this is one of his best exercises in harsh compassion. The poem gives us a moving insight into the terrible burden of a priest who has to leave a man who is mortally ill, knowing that he is soon to die and that nothing more can be done to help him. The end of the poem is ambiguous; it may be that 'the dark' is simply a metaphor for death, but it may be that it is also a metaphor for disbelief, in which case the real tragedy of Evans would be that he is going to die without the light of God. The poem is a good example of Thomas's favourite rhythm, a heavy four-stressed line which owes something to the beat of traditional Welsh poetry. The other, more recent, ancestor for this kind of rhythm is Gerard Manley Hopkins and his theory of sprung rhythm. Hopkins argued that in any foot there could be a maximum of four syllables as opposed to the three which the Greeks normally allowed, one of which took a heavy stress and the remaining three no stress. Application of this rule led to the gradual break up of traditional iambic poetry throughout the 1930s in the work of poets like Louis MacNeice who wanted something tighter than free verse which would still allow them a certain amount of elbow room. The stress accent writing of R. S. Thomas, however, gives a much more perceptible 'beat' than the work of any of his contemporaries or immediate predecessors.

POETRY FOR SUPPER. This is the nearest Thomas comes to a comic poem. He has an ear for Welsh dialogue, which he seems to use relatively rarely. Despite the imagery one gets a real sense of the two old poets' voices in the poem as they talk over the nature of their art in a country pub. Thomas, one may suppose, is ultimately on the side of the second poet who believes that inspiration needs the vehicle of craftsmanship before it can fully come through.

IAGO PRYTHERCH. The character of Iago Prytherch is a recurring one in Thomas's poems. He seems to be a composite figure (though he may have had a particular real life original) who stands for the endurance and simplicity of the ordinary farm labourer in a hard land. Thomas seems to be fighting a running battle with a number of feelings about this man. These include irritation, compassion, admiration and, as here, feelings too complex to be resolved into any one emotion. The idea of the labourer as a surgeon in the first stanza is a complimentary one, but the description of him 'marring the simple geometry of the square fields' in the last stanza seems to hint at a less flattering interpretation of his role in the landscape. This is a grim, but obscurely moving and deep poem.

NINETIETH BIRTHDAY. This poem describes what must be a routine incident in the life of a country priest – visiting an old woman who is senile now but whom the priest remembers as once wise. The device of writing the whole poem in the second person, as if the poet is addressing someone else, gives it the force of a set of instructions. He is, of course, really addressing himself and the poem is written perhaps to convince himself that what he has been doing is the right thing.

THOSE OTHERS. A poem of mixed bitterness and love for Thomas's own country and countrymen. In simple terms it seems to be in favour of the men of the farms rather than the towns, but I think the distinction should really be treated as a symbolic rather than a literal one. The poem is remarkable in that it is based, unusually for Thomas, on a heavy three-stress rather than a four-stress line, which manages very effectively to avoid any echoes of Yeats in this form. The farms are doomed, presumably, because of increasing industrialisation in Wales.

TO A YOUNG POET. A moving poem of bitterness and despair, tempered by an acceptance of life as it really is in a hard and cruel world. Once again, although written in the second person, the poem is really addressed to the poet himself. This view of the craft of poetry as a kind of hopeless labour is worth comparing with Dylan Thomas's view in his poem 'In My Craft or Solemn Art'. For Dylan Thomas, too, hard work is necessary but there is nothing of R. S. Thomas's sense of inevitable failure.

TRAMP. One of Thomas's relatively rare poems in a two stressed line. The poem's rhythm has a curious sense of jerking rapidly forward and then halting. This seems to mime effectively the abortive attempts of the priest to cross the enormous distance which separates himself from the tramp. The poem ends by summing up their different problems with justice and compassion.

ON THE FARM. A dour vision of a young good-looking girl living with three men, perhaps her father and two brothers, on an outlying farm. The first three stanzas have the power of a painting by Brueghel in his grimmest mood. The last stanza lifts the poem into a different plane. It indicates how the girl is what these brutish men live for, and that she is their means of understanding the ways of God.

Dylan Thomas

Dylan Thomas was born in Wales in 1914 and died while on a
reading tour of America in 1953. The approach to his poetry
is particularly difficult because of the enormous amount of
legend which has gathered round his name and private life.
Whether or not he 'died of drink', whether or not he was unusually debauched, whether he was a great saint or a great
sinner, are not questions of much importance for an assess-
ment of his verse. With the exception of the radio play *Under
Milk Wood* almost all of Dylan Thomas's creative energy went
into his poetry. He wrote very slowly, often at the rate of only
one line a day after hours of hard sober work, and he describes
his poems in the introduction to his *Collected Poems* published
in 1952, as written 'for the love of man and in praise of God'.
Apart from his painstaking craftsmanship, so strangely at odds
with the popular legend of his life, Dylan Thomas's poetry is
perhaps specially interesting for its optimism. No other poet
writing in English since Yeats has responded to life with such
a consistently affirmative and positive note. This may in part
account for Thomas's continuing appeal to readers who don't
normally pay much attention to poetry. Thomas is, with
Wilfred Owen, the greatest Welsh poet of the century and the
Welsh quality of *hwyl* – a sort of high-flown rhetoric – is
perhaps behind what one admires in his poems. Thomas was a
magnificent reader of his own poems and for those who have
heard recordings of his voice it is almost impossible to imagine
other readers for some of his major poems.

The Force that through the Green Fuse Drives the Flower

The force that through the green fuse drives the flower
Drives my green age; that blasts the roots of trees
Is my destroyer.
And I am dumb to tell the crooked rose
My youth is bent by the same wintry fever.

The force that drives the water through the rocks
Drives my red blood; that dries the mouthing streams
Turns mine to wax.
And I am dumb to mouth unto my veins
How at the mountain spring the same mouth sucks.

The hand that whirls the water in the pool
Stirs the quicksand; that ropes the blowing wind
Hauls my shroud sail.
And I am dumb to tell the hanging man
How of my clay is made the hangman's lime.

The lips of time leech to the fountain head;
Love drips and gathers, but the fallen blood
Shall calm her sores.
And I am dumb to tell a weather's wind
How time has ticked a heaven round the stars.

And I am dumb to tell the lover's tomb
How at my sheet goes the same crooked worm.

Especially when the October Wind

Especially when the October wind
With frosty fingers punishes my hair,
Caught by the crabbing sun I walk on fire
And cast a shadow crab upon the land,
By the sea's side, hearing the noise of birds,
Hearing the raven cough in winter sticks,
My busy heart who shudders as she talks
Sheds the syllabic blood and drains her words.

Shut, too, in a tower of words, I mark
On the horizon walking like the trees
The wordy shapes of women, and the rows
Of the star-gestured children in the park.
Some let me make you of the vowelled beeches,
Some of the oaken voices, from the roots
Of many a thorny shire tell you notes,
Some let me make you of the water's speeches.

Behind a pot of ferns the wagging clock
Tells me the hour's word, the neural meaning
Flies on the shafted disk, declaims the morning
And tells the windy weather in the cock.
Some let me make you of the meadow's signs;
The signal grass that tells me all I know
Breaks with the wormy winter through the eye.
Some let me tell you of the raven's sins.

Especially when the October wind
(Some let me make you of autumnal spells,
The spider-tongued, and the loud hill of Wales)
With fists of turnips punishes the land,
Some let me make you of the heartless words.
The heart is drained that, spelling in the scurry
Of chemic blood, warned of the coming fury.
By the sea's side hear the dark-vowelled birds.

Light Breaks where No Sun Shines

Light breaks where no sun shines;
Where no sea runs, the waters of the heart
Push in their tides;
And, broken ghosts with glow-worms in their heads,
The things of light
File through the flesh where no flesh decks the bones.

A candle in the thighs
Warms youth and seed and burns the seeds of age;
Where no seed stirs,
The fruit of man unwrinkles in the stars,
Bright as a fig;
Where no wax is, the candle shows its hairs.

Dawn breaks behind the eyes;
From poles of skull and toe the windy blood
Slides like a sea;
Nor fenced, nor staked, the gushers of the sky
Spout to the rod
Divining in a smile the oil of tears.

Night in the sockets rounds,
Like some pitch moon, the limit of the globes;
Day lights the bone;
Where no cold is, the skinning gales unpin
The winter's robes;
The film of spring is hanging from the lids.

Light breaks on secret lots,
On tips of thought where thoughts smell in the rain;
When logics die,
The secret of the soil grows through the eye,
And blood jumps in the sun;
Above the waste allotments the dawn halts.

This Bread I Break

This bread I break was once the oat,
This wine upon a foreign tree
Plunged in its fruit;
Man in the day or wind at night
Laid the crops low, broke the grape's joy.

Once in this wind the summer blood
Knocked in the flesh that decked the vine,
Once in this bread
The oat was merry in the wind;
Man broke the sun, pulled the wind down.

This flesh you break, this blood you let
Make desolation in the vein,
Were oat and grape
Born of the sensual root and sap;
My wine you drink, my bread you snap.

And Death Shall have no Dominion

And death shall have no dominion.
Dead men naked they shall be one
With the man in the wind and the west moon;
When their bones are picked clean and the clean bones gone,
They shall have stars at elbow and foot;
Though they go mad they shall be sane,
Though they sink through the sea they shall rise again;
Though lovers be lost love shall not;
And death shall have no dominion.

And death shall have no dominion.
Under the windings of the sea
They lying long shall not die windily;

Twisting on racks when sinews give way,
Strapped to a wheel, yet they shall not break;
Faith in their hands shall snap in two,
And the unicorn evils run them through;
Split all ends up they shan't crack;
And death shall have no dominion.

And death shall have no dominion.
No more may gulls cry at their ears
Or waves break loud on the seashores;
Where blew a flower may a flower no more
Lift its head to the blows of the rain;
Though they be mad and dead as nails,
Heads of the characters hammer through daisies;
Break in the sun till the sun breaks down,
And death shall have no dominion.

After the Funeral

(In memory of Ann Jones)

After the funeral, mule praises, brays,
Windshake of sailshaped ears, muffle-toed tap
Tap happily of one peg in the thick
Grave's foot, blinds down the lids, the teeth in black,
The spittled eyes, the salt ponds in the sleeves,
Morning smack of the spade that wakes up sleep,
Shakes a desolate boy who slits his throat
In the dark of the coffin and sheds dry leaves,
That breaks one bone to light with a judgement clout,
After the feast of tear-stuffed time and thistles
In a room with a stuffed fox and a stale fern,
I stand, for this memorial's sake, alone
In the snivelling hours with dead, humped Ann
Whose hooded, fountain heart once fell in puddles
Round the parched worlds of Wales and drowned each sun

(Though this for her is a monstrous image blindly
Magnified out of praise; her death was a still drop;
She would not have me sinking in the holy
Flood of her heart's fame; she would lie dumb and deep
And need no druid of her broken body).
But I, Ann's bard on a raised hearth, call all
The seas to service that her wood-tongued virtue
Babble like a bellbuoy over the hymning heads,
Bow down the walls of the ferned and foxy woods
That her love sing and swing through a brown chapel,
Bless her bent spirit with four, crossing birds.
Her flesh was meek as milk, but this skyward statue
With the wild breast and blessed and giant skull
Is carved from her in a room with a wet window
In a fiercely mourning house in a crooked year.
I know her scrubbed and sour humble hands
Lie with religion in their cramp, her threadbare
Whisper in a damp word, her wits drilled hollow,
Her fist of a face died clenched on a round pain;
And sculptured Ann is seventy years of stone.
These cloud-sopped, marble hands, this monumental
Argument of the hewn voice, gesture and psalm,
Storm me forever over her grave until
The stuffed lung of the fox twitch and cry Love
And the strutting fern lay seeds on the black sill.

A Refusal to Mourn the Death, by Fire, of a Child in London

Never until the mankind making
Bird beast and flower
Fathering and all humbling darkness
Tells with silence the last light breaking
And the still hour
Is coming of the sea tumbling in harness

And I must enter again the round
Zion of the water bead
And the synagogue of the ear of corn
Shall I let pray the shadow of a sound
Or sow my salt seed
In the least valley of sackcloth to mourn

The majesty and burning of the child's death.
I shall not murder
The mankind of her going with a grave truth
Nor blaspheme down the stations of the breath
With any further
Elegy of innocence and youth.

Deep with the first dead lies London's daughter,
Robed in the long friends,
The grains beyond age, the dark veins of her mother,
Secret by the unmourning water
Of the riding Thames.
After the first death, there is no other.

Poem in October

It was my thirtieth year to heaven
Woke to my hearing from harbour and neighbour wood
    And the mussel pooled and the heron
            Priested shore
        The morning beckon
With water praying and call of seagull and rook
And the knock of sailing boats on the net webbed wall
        Myself to set foot
            That second
    In the still sleeping town and set forth.

My birthday began with the water-
Birds and the birds of the winged trees flying my name
   Above the farms and the white horses
       And I rose
     In rainy autumn
And walked abroad in a shower of all my days.
High tide and the heron dived when I took the road
     Over the border
       And the gates
Of the town closed as the town awoke.

   A springful of larks in a rolling
Cloud and the roadside bushes brimming with whistling
   Blackbirds and the sun of October
       Summery
     On the hill's shoulder,
Here were fond climates and sweet singers suddenly
Come in the morning where I wandered and listened
     To the rain wringing
       Wind blow cold
    In the wood faraway under me.

   Pale rain over the dwindling harbour
And over the sea wet church the size of a snail
   With its horns through mist and the castle
       Brown as owls
     But all the gardens
Of spring and summer were blooming in the tall tales
Beyond the border and under the lark full cloud.
     There could I marvel
       My birthday
Away but the weather turned around.

   It turned away from the blithe country
And down the other air and the blue altered sky
   Streamed again a wonder of summer
       With apples
     Pears and red currants

And I saw in the turning so clearly a child's
Forgotten mornings when he walked with his mother
    Through the parables
      Of sun light
  And the legends of the green chapels

  And the twice told fields of infancy
That his tears burned my cheeks and his heart moved in
    mine.
  These were the woods the river and sea
    Where a boy
    In the listening
Summertime of the dead whispered the truth of his joy
To the trees and the stones and the fish in the tide.
    And the mystery
      Sang alive
  Still in the water and singingbirds.

  And there could I marvel my birthday
Away but the weather turned around. And the true
    Joy of the long dead child sang burning
      In the sun.
    It was my thirtieth
Year to heaven stood there then in the summer noon
Though the town below lay leaved with October blood.
    O may my heart's truth
      Still be sung
  On this high hill in a year's turning.

Do not go Gentle into that Good Night

    Do not go gentle into that good night,
    Old age should burn and rave at close of day;
    Rage, rage against the dying of the light.

Though wise men at their end know dark is right,
Because their words have forked no lightning they
Do not go gentle into that good night.

Good men, the last wave by, crying how bright
Their frail deeds might have danced in a green bay,
Rage, rage against the dying of the light.

Wild men who caught and sang the sun in flight,
And learn, too late, they grieved it on its way,
Do not go gentle into that good night.

Grave men, near death, who see with blinding sight
Blind eyes could blaze like meteors and be gay,
Rage, rage against the dying of the light.

And you, my father, there on the sad height,
Curse, bless, me now with your fierce tears, I pray.
Do not go gentle into that good night.
Rage, rage against the dying of the light.

In my Craft or Sullen Art

In my craft or sullen art
Exercised in the still night
When only the moon rages
And the lovers lie abed
With all their griefs in their arms,
I labour by singing light
Not for ambition or bread
Or the strut and trade of charms
On the ivory stages
But for the common wages
Of their most secret heart.

Not for the proud man apart
From the raging moon I write
On these spindrift pages
Nor for the towering dead
With their nightingales and psalms
But for the lovers, their arms
Round the griefs of the ages,
Who pay no praise or wages
Nor heed my craft or art.

Fern Hill

Now as I was young and easy under the apple boughs
About the lilting house and happy as the grass was green,
   The night above the dingle starry,
    Time let me hail and climb
   Golden in the heydays of his eyes,
And honoured among wagons I was prince of the apple towns
And once below a time I lordly had the trees and leaves
    Trail with daisies and barley
  Down the rivers of the windfall light.

And as I was green and carefree, famous among the barns
About the happy yard and singing as the farm was home,
   `In the sun that is young once only,
    Time let me play and be
   Golden in the mercy of his means,
And green and golden I was huntsman and herdsman, the
    calves
Sang to my horn, the foxes on the hills barked clear and cold,
    And the sabbath rang slowly
  In the pebbles of the holy streams.

All the sun long it was running, it was lovely, the hay
Fields high as the house, the tunes from the chimneys, it was
    air
   And playing, lovely and watery

And fire green as grass.
And nightly under the simple stars
As I rode to sleep the owls were bearing the farm away,
All the moon long I heard, blessed among stables, the night-
        jars
    Flying with the ricks, and the horses
        Flashing into the dark.

And then to awake, and the farm, like a wanderer white
With the dew, come back, the cock on his shoulder: it was all
    Shining, it was Adam and maiden,
        The sky gathered again
    And the sun grew round that very day
So it must have been after the birth of the simple light
In the first, spinning place, the spellbound horses walking
        warm
    Out of the whinnying green stable
        On to the fields of praise.

And honoured among foxes and pheasants by the gay house
Under the new made clouds and happy as the heart was long,
    In the sun born over and over,
        I ran my heedless ways,
    My wishes raced through the house high hay
And nothing I cared, at my sky blue trades, that time allows
In all his tuneful turning so few and such morning songs
    Before the children green and golden
        Follow him out of grace,

Nothing I cared, in the lamb white days, that time would take
        me
Up to the swallow thronged loft by the shadow of my hand,
    In the moon that is always rising.
        Nor that riding to sleep
    I should hear him fly with the high fields
And wake to the farm forever fled from the childless land.
Oh as I was young and easy in the mercy of his means,
    Time held me green and dying
        Though I sang in my chains like the sea.

Over Sir John's Hill

Over Sir John's hill,
The hawk on fire hangs still;
In a hoisted cloud, at drop of dusk, he pulls to his claws
And gallows, up the rays of his eyes the small birds of the bay
And the shrill child's play
Wars
Of the sparrows and such who swansing, dusk, in wrangling
 hedges.
And blithely they squawk
To fiery tyburn over the wrestle of elms until
The flash the noosed hawk
Crashes, and slowly the fishing holy stalking heron
In the river Towy below bows his tilted headstone.

Flash, and the plumes crack,
And a black cap of jack-
Daws Sir John's just hill dons, and again the gulled birds hare
To the hawk on fire, the halter height, over Towy's fins,
In a whack of wind.
There
Where the elegiac fisherbird stabs and paddles
In the pebbly dab-filled
Shallow and sedge, and 'dilly dilly,' calls the loft hawk,
'Come and be killed,'
I open the leaves of the water at a passage
Of psalms and shadows among the pincered sandcrabs pranc-
 ing

And read, in a shell,
Death clear as buoy's bell:
All praise of the hawk on fire in hawk-eyed dusk be sung,
When his viperish fuse hangs looped with flames under the
 brand
Wing, and blest shall
Young
Green chickens of the bay and bushes cluck, 'dilly dilly,

Come let us die.'
We grieve as the blithe birds, never again, leave shingle and
    elm,
The heron and I,
I young Aesop fabling to the near night by the dingle
Of eels, saint heron hymning in the shell-hung distant

Crystal harbour vale
Where the sea cobbles sail,
And wharves of water where the walls dance and the white
    cranes silt.
It is the heron and I, under judging Sir John's elmed
Hill, tell-tale the knelled
Guilt
Of the led-astray birds whom God, for their breast of whistles,
Have mercy on,
God in his whirlwind silence save, who marks the sparrows
    hail,
For their souls' song.
Now the heron grieves in the weeded verge. Through win-
    dows
Of dusk and water I see the tilting whispering

Heron, mirrored, go,
As the snapt feathers snow,
Fishing in the tear of the Towy. Only a hoot owl
Hollows, a grassblade blown in cupped hands, in the looted
    elms
And no green cocks or hens
Shout
Now on Sir John's hill. The heron, ankling the scaly
Lowlands of the waves,
Makes all the music; and I who hear the tune of the slow,
Wear-willow river, grave,
Before the lunge of the night, the notes on this time-shaken
Stone for the sake of the souls of the slain birds sailing.

Notes

THE FORCE THAT THROUGH THE GREEN FUSE DRIVES THE FLOWER. All Dylan Thomas's earlier poems are dense with imagery and obscure in structure but this is simpler than most. The point of the poem is to suggest that all life, animal and vegetable, is subject to the same laws of nature, and that all things grow old, decay and die. This idea is far from original. but the severe, slow rhetoric of the poem gives this message an air of great weight and authority. Structurally, the poem consists of four stanzas off rhyming *ababa* followed by a concluding couplet rhyming *aa*. The metre is an even iambic one with four ten-syllable lines in each stanza and a short four and a half or four syllable line. The even stresses and the heavy accents in the poem give it a characteristic heaviness and solemnity.

ESPECIALLY WHEN THE OCTOBER WIND. This poem shows the writer going for a walk in autumn and offering to make some friend, to whom the poem is addressed, a poem about the things he hears and sees in the country as he goes. This slight element of plot, however, is less important to the poem than its incantatory quality – beautifully expressed through the repeated phrase 'some let me make you'. Thomas is constantly suggesting throughout the poem, a connection between landscape and language. Everything he sees and hears on his walk turns into words – the wordy shapes of women and so on.

LIGHT BREAKS WHERE NO SUN SHINES (see Introduction, page xxii). The point of this poem is to suggest that life is like sunshine. The poem is an affirmation of belief in the unending renewal of energy within the body each new day. There is a suggested link between the moods of a human being and the climate of a landscape. Once again, however, the main force of the poem is generated by its rhythm and music.

THIS BREAD I BREAK. This poem links the making of food-stuffs from the vegetable world with a religious ritual involving eating. The poem seems deliberately to aim at maximising rather than minimising the range of application of the terms it contains. Unfortunately, by trying to connect everything Thomas almost ends by connecting nothing. The poem has an air of mystery and significance but ultimately fails to resolve itself into a clear meaning. My own suspicion is that it hints at a kind of pantheism which Thomas would have begun to make clearer and clearer in his poems if he had lived longer. In other words, he seems to want to see divinity in everything, and everything in divinity. In the last stanza Christianity is perhaps being contrasted with the 'sensual root and sap'. The word 'sap' could refer to the brittle wafer of the Host.

AND DEATH SHALL HAVE NO DOMINION. This is Dylan Thomas in more strident mood. One can almost imagine the poem being spoken at a Revivalist meeting with a huge congregation coming in on the refrain 'And death shall have no dominion'. The poem is an obvious, and in some ways a public one: notice how most of the lines are end-stopped, so that there is a unification of sense units and rhythmical ones. This helps to give the feeling its directness and insistence.

AFTER THE FUNERAL. One of the few poems by Dylan Thomas which is securely anchored to a concrete situation. We very quickly know when the poem is being written, where the poet is speaking from and about whom he is talking. The poem has some excellent description of what it is like to be in an old-fashioned room with a corpse. Lines like 'In a room with a stuffed fox and a stale fern' are realistically vivid in a way not common in Thomas's work. At the same time he manages to retain the energy and force of feeling which elsewhere leads him into vagueness and abstraction. The poem is a moving example of how grief can begin to turn into praise.

A REFUSAL TO MOURN THE DEATH, BY FIRE, OF A CHILD IN LONDON. This splendidly original poem maintains the high style more successfully than anyone has done since Yeats. It provides the kind of experience which most ordinary people expect poetry to give: strong feeling, richness of phrasing and an exciting sound. The last line of the poem has been taken to suggest a belief in eternal life, perhaps in the Christian sense, but it need not necessarily do so. I think myself that it refers to the inevitable return in time of all living things to the natural world from which they came. Thomas obviously regards this, of course, as a desirable and acceptable thing. Understanding the syntax of the first stanza depends on reading the whole phrase from 'the mankind making . . .' down to '. . . all humbling darkness' as connected by a series of hyphens.

POEM IN OCTOBER. This has great interest as one of the earliest important poems written in England in syllabics, a metre later to be exploited by Thom Gunn and other poets. The mathematical principle underlying the syllabic form was not always appreciated by early critics of Thomas to whom the rhythms of this poem seemed flaccid and its metrical pattern purely visual and arbitrary. A syllabic metre depends on the presence of a given number of syllables in each line but no given number of feet or stresses as in iambic or accentual verse. In this case the number of syllables per line in each stanza is as follows: 9, 12, 9, 3, 5, 12, 12, 5, 3, 9. This number is repeated in each stanza throughout the poem. The effect is great ease and rapidity of movement combined with a delicate precision of form. Thomas contrives to retain the forcefulness of his earlier poetry by ending each line with a strong word, often a noun. This keeps the metre from becoming too loose. The poem is an exquisitely gay and cheerful one. It describes how a man gets up early in the morning on his birthday and goes out for a walk through the country to a place where he can look down on the town where he lives. The man is almost certainly Thomas himself and the town Swansea, where he was born. The rhyme scheme of the poem is highly original. It seems to depend on normally using the same vowel sound but different consonants, so that the word 'water' can rhyme with the word 'horses'. Thomas is not completely consistent about this but he is consistent enough for the principle to be observable.

DO NOT GO GENTLE INTO THAT GOOD NIGHT. A villanelle, a verse form consisting of nineteen or sometimes twenty-one lines with the first and third lines of the first stanza of three lines repeated throughout the poem as a kind of refrain. The poem is normally based on only two rhymes all the way through as here. The other modern English writer who has produced an important villanelle is William Empson (p. 154). Interestingly enough, Empson's poetry sometimes appears at first sight to be the opposite of Thomas's in its concern for intellectual structure and feeling held in check by wit and irony. Empson greatly admired Thomas's poetry, however, and indeed carried it with him for many years while in the Far East just before the Second World War. The passage of time has made clear the extent to which they come together in their concern for density of phrasing and ambivalence of tone and meaning. Each has been a disastrous influence – Thomas on the poetry of the 1940s, Empson on the poetry of the 1950s. It often seems to be the most obscure poetry which is the easiest to imitate. This poem is about the death of Thomas's own father and is an outburst of protest against the inevitability of death. Its main strength lies in the first three and the last four lines. One has a slight sense that the villanelle form has compelled Thomas to elaborate unnecessarily in the central four stanzas. Nevertheless, the poem is an example of his power to combine what V. Sackville-West called 'vigour and virtuosity' in a remarkable synthesis. The grammar of the word 'do' changes interestingly from a comment to a direct statement in the poem. This helps to keep the tight metre flexible in movement.

IN MY CRAFT OR SULLEN ART. A poem very much in the high style of Yeats, and in the metre which Yeats made his own. Thomas has been more successful than other followers of Yeats, however, in retaining his own individuality in this form. The epithet 'singing' applied to 'light' in the sixth line may seem at first sight to be simply a rhetorical or romantic flourish. If we imagine the words as hyphenated, however, the light becomes the one that Thomas uses for singing or composing poetry by, as one might imagine someone else at a 'reading' light. A surprisingly large number of Thomas's eccentric epithets can be redeemed by this kind of analysis.

FERN HILL. Another poem celebrating the glory and joy of life despite the inevitability of eventual death. Like 'Poem in October' it is in an intricate syllabic form.

OVER SIR JOHN'S HILL. This again is in a complex syllabic stanza. The poem is a prayer on behalf of all the birds whom Thomas hears and sees one evening while walking beside the river Towy and watching a heron fishing.

Keith Douglas

Keith Douglas was born in 1920 and killed in action in Normandy in 1944. Douglas fought through the North Africa campaign as a tank commander and his experiences are vividly recorded in his book *Alamein to Zem-Zem*. In the introduction to this book Douglas says that he went through the battles in the desert like a child at a show. His characteristic note is one of a detached, sophisticated interest in the violence and horror of the war. This contrasts his poetry sharply with Wilfred Owen's. Douglas is greatly admired by Ted Hughes who edited a selection of his work for Faber and Faber in 1964. What Hughes admires seems to be Douglas's general purpose style which does indeed in some ways seem to foreshadow his own. Douglas is a much cooler and drier writer than Hughes, however, and his real affinities are with some of the other Mediterranean poets of the war years like Lawrence Durrell and Terence Tiller.

How to Kill

Under the parabola of a ball,
a child turning into a man,
I looked into the air too long.
The ball fell in my hand, it sang
in the closed fist: *Open Open
Behold a gift designed to kill.*

Now in my dial of glass appears
the soldier who is going to die.
He smiles, and moves about in ways
his mother knows, habits of his.
The wires touch his face: I cry
NOW. Death, like a familiar, hears

and look, has made a man of dust
of a man of flesh. This sorcery
I do. Being damned, I am amused
to see the centre of love diffused
and the waves of love travel into vacancy.
How easy it is to make a ghost.

The weightless mosquito touches
her tiny shadow on the stone,
and with how like, how infinite
a lightness, man and shadow meet.
They fuse. A shadow is a man
when the mosquito death approaches.

Tunisia–Cairo, 1943

Landscape with Figures

I

Perched on a great fall of air
a pilot or angel looking down
on some eccentric chart, a plain
dotted with useless furniture,
discerns dying on the sand vehicles
squashed dead or still entire, stunned
like beetles: scattered wingcases and
legs, heads, appear when the dust settles.

But you who like Thomas come
to poke fingers in the wounds
find monuments and metal posies.
On each disordered tomb
the steel is torn into fronds
by the lunatic explosive.

II

On sand and scrub the dead men wriggle
in their dowdy clothes. They are mimes
who express silence and futile aims
enacting this prone and motionless struggle
at a queer angle to the scenery,
crawling on the boards of the stage like walls,
deaf to the one who opens his mouth and calls
silently. The décor is a horrible tracery
of iron. The eye and mouth of each figure
bear the cosmetic blood and the hectic
colours death has the only list of.
A yard more and my little finger
could trace the maquillage of these stony actors:
I am the figure writhing on the backcloth

Wadi Zem Zem, January, 1943

Aristocrats

('*I think I am becoming a God*')

The noble horse with courage in his eye
clean in the bone, looks up at a shellburst:
away fly the images of the shires
but he puts the pipe back in his mouth.

Peter was unfortunately killed by an 88:
it took his leg away, he died in the ambulance.
I saw him crawling on the sand; he said
It's most unfair, they've shot my foot off.

How can I live among this gentle
obsolescent breed of heroes, and not weep?
Unicorns, almost,
for they are falling into two legends
in which their stupidity and chivalry
are celebrated. Each, fool and hero, will be an immortal.

The plains were their cricket pitch
and in the mountains the tremendous drop fences
brought down some of the runners. Here then
under the stones and earth they dispose themselves,
I think with their famous unconcern.
It is not gunfire I hear but a hunting horn.

Enfidaville, Tunisia, 1943

Vergissmeinicht

Three weeks gone and the combatants gone,
returning over the nightmare ground
we found the place again, and found
the soldier sprawling in the sun.

257

The frowning barrel of his gun
overshadowing. As we came on
that day, he hit my tank with one
like the entry of a demon.

Look. Here in the gunpit spoil
the dishonoured picture of his girl
who has put: *Steffi. Vergissmeinicht*
in a copybook gothic script.

We see him almost with content
abased, and seeming to have paid
and mocked at by his own equipment
that's hard and good when he's decayed.

But she would weep to see to-day
how on his skin the swart flies move;
the dust upon the paper eye
and the burst stomach like a cave.

For here the lover and killer are mingled
who had one body and one heart.
And death who had the soldier singled
has done the lover mortal hurt.

Homs, Tripolitania, 1943

Notes

HOW TO KILL. The title of this poem gives it the air of being a brief infantry manual. In fact the poem beautifully contrasts a highly romantic opening with a cold-blooded down-to-earth second stanza and later goes on to blend the two elements delicately together. It might well be said that Douglas tends to see life through the sights of a rifle. Everything, even death, happens at a great distance. Death is as tiny and remote, but as dangerous, as a mosquito.

LANDSCAPE WITH FIGURES. Here Douglas uses his free style within the framework of the traditional sonnet form. In each sonnet the rhyme scheme is *abba*, *cddc*, *efgefg*. The metre is a loose blend of four- and three-syllable lines. The poems recall certain passages in *Alamein to Zem-Zem* and beautifully express Douglas's feeling of his own irrelevance to the essentially theatrical business of war. This is a highly unusual but not ignoble attitude. Douglas is refusing to fake emotions he does not really feel, and his descriptions are accurate and clear-eyed. The first of the two sonnets makes an interesting comparison with Owen's poem 'The Show' (p. 112).

ARISTOCRATS. The epigraph is an English version of Nero's dying words 'Vae! deus fio'. The point is that the dead English heroes in the poem are god-like in their blend of 'stupidity and chivalry'. The poem makes an interesting modern gloss on the famous remark about the battle of Waterloo being won on the playing fields of Eton. It cleverly identifies the young upper-middle-class officers with the horses they would once have ridden when hunting.

VERGISSMEINICHT. This is Douglas's best poem. It has more energy and compassion than Douglas usually allows himself, but the same detached elegance in its descriptions. 'Vergissmeinicht' is the German for 'forget-me-not'. The poem has a Homeric simplicity.

Philip Larkin

Philip Larkin was born in 1922 at Coventry and educated
at local grammar schools and St John's College, Oxford. He
now works as librarian at Hull University. Larkin is by general
consent one of the two most important poets – with Ted
Hughes – to appear since the war. He is generally considered
as the central figure of the group known as The Movement,
who began publishing widely in the mid-1950s and were first
noticed and named by an anonymous writer in *The Spectator*
in the spring of 1954. The poets with whom Larkin was first
most closely associated are Kingsley Amis and John Wain.
Both of these writers were also educated at St John's College,
Oxford, and John Wain in his autobiography *Sprightly Running*
makes a vivid if slightly over-enthusiastic reference to the circle
in which they were leading figures. 'Kingsley Amis, appearing
on leave from active service, was one of this nebulous group,

and my first casual meetings with him came about because we were both, so to speak, swimming in the thin fluid that solidified only when Philip Larkin arrived.' Adverse critics might regard that last phrase as a fair comment on Movement poetry as a whole. Its virtues – a return to a cool tone, tight form and intellectual backbone after some of the romantic excesses of the 1940s – are all exemplified at their most striking in Larkin's work. The American poet, Robert Lowell, has said that he finds Larkin the most formally satisfying English poet now writing. At the same time, what gives Larkin's poetry its originality and special quality is perhaps a piercing resonance of feeling which reveals a melancholy sensibility as keen as Tennyson's and as tough as Hardy's.

Reasons for Attendance

The trumpet's voice, loud and authoritative,
Draws me a moment to the lighted glass
To watch the dancers – all under twenty-five –
Shifting intently, face to flushed face,
Solemnly on the beat of happiness.

– Or so I fancy, sensing the smoke and sweat,
The wonderful feel of girls. Why be out here?
But then, why be in there? Sex, yes, but what
Is sex? Surely, to think the lion's share
Of happiness is found by couples – sheer

Inaccuracy, as far as I'm concerned.
What calls me is that lifted, rough-tongued bell
(Art, if you like) whose individual sound
Insists I too am individual
It speaks; I hear; others may hear as well,

But not for me, nor I for them; and so
With happiness. Therefore I stay outside,
Believing this; and they maul to and fro,
Believing that; and both are satisfied,
If no one has misjudged himself. Or lied.

Church Going

Once I am sure there's nothing going on
I step inside, letting the door thud shut.
Another church: matting, seats, and stone,
And little books; sprawlings of flowers, cut
For Sunday, brownish now; some brass and stuff
Up at the holy end; the small neat organ;
And a tense, musty, unignorable silence,
Brewed God knows how long. Hatless, I take off
My cycle-clips in awkward reverence,

262

Move forward, run my hand around the font.
From where I stand, the roof looks almost new –
Cleaned, or restored? Someone would know: I don't.
Mounting the lectern, I peruse a few
Hectoring large scale verses, and pronounce
'Here endeth' much more loudly than I'd meant.
The echoes snigger briefly. Back at the door
I sign the book, donate an Irish sixpence,
Reflect the place was not worth stopping for.

Yet stop I did: in fact I often do,
And always end much at a loss like this,
Wondering what to look for; wondering, too,
When churches fall completely out of use
What we shall turn them into, if we shall keep
A few cathedrals chronically on show,
Their parchment, plate and pyx in locked cases,
And let the rest rent-free to rain and sheep.
Shall we avoid them as unlucky places?

Or, after dark, will dubious women come
To make their children touch a particular stone;
Pick simples for a cancer; or on some
Advised night see walking a dead one?
Power of some sort or other will go on
In games, in riddles, seemingly at random;
But superstition, like belief, must die,
And what remains when disbelief has gone?
Grass, weedy pavement, brambles, buttress, sky,

A shape less recognisable each week,
A purpose more obscure. I wonder who
Will be the last, the very last, to seek
This place for what it was; one of the crew
That tap and jot and know what rood-lofts were?
Some ruin-bibber, randy for antique,
Or Christmas-addict, counting on a whiff
Of gown-and-bands and organ-pipes and myrrh?
Or will he be my representative,

Bored, uninformed, knowing the ghostly silt
Dispersed, yet tending to this cross of ground
Through suburb scrub because it held unspilt
So long and equably what since is found
Only in separation – marriage, and birth,
And death, and thoughts of these – for whom was built
This special shell? For, though I've no idea
What this accoutred frowsty barn is worth,
It pleases me to stand in silence here;

A serious house on serious earth it is,
In whose blent air all our compulsions meet,
Are recognised, and robed as destinies.
And that much never can be obsolete,
Since someone will forever be surprising
A hunger in himself to be more serious,
And gravitating with it to this ground,
Which, he once heard, was proper to grow wise in,
If only that so many dead lie round.

Poetry of Departures

Sometimes you hear, fifth-hand,
As epitaph:
He chucked up everything
And just cleared off,
And always the voice will sound
Certain you approve
This audacious, purifying,
Elemental move.

And they are right, I think.
We all hate home
And having to be there:
I detest my room,

Its specially-chosen junk,
The good books, the good bed,
And my life, in perfect order:
So to hear it said

He walked out on the whole crowd
Leaves me flushed and stirred,
Like *Then she undid her dress*
Or *Take that you bastard*;
Surely I can, if he did?
And that helps me stay
Sober and industrious.
But I'd go today.

Yes, swagger the nut-strewn roads,
Crouch in the fo'c'sle
Stubbly with goodness, if
It weren't so artificial,
Such a deliberate step backwards
To create an object:
Books; china; a life
Reprehensibly perfect.

Broadcast

Giant whispering and coughing from
Vast Sunday-full and organ-frowned-on spaces
Precede a sudden scuttle on the drum,
'The Queen', and huge resettling. Then begins
A snivel on the violins:
I think of your face among all those faces,

Beautiful and devout before
Cascades of monumental slithering,
One of your gloves unnoticed on the floor

Beside those new, slightly-outmoded shoes.
Here it goes quickly dark. I lose
All but the outline of the still and withering

Leaves on half-emptied trees, Behind
The glowing wavebands, rabid storms of chording
By being distant overpower my mind
All the more shamelessly, their cut-off shout
Leaving me desperate to pick out
Your hands, tiny in all that air, applauding.

Faith Healing

Slowly the women file to where he stands
Upright in rimless glasses, silver hair,
Dark suit, white collar. Stewards tirelessly
Persuade them onwards to his voice and hands,
Within whose warm spring rain of loving care
Each dwells some twenty seconds. *Now, dear child,
What's wrong*, the deep American voice demands,
And, scarcely pausing, goes into a prayer
Directing God about this eye, that knee.
Their heads are clasped abruptly; then, exiled

Like losing thoughts, they go in silence; some
Sheepishly stray, not back into their lives
Just yet; but some stay stiff, twitching and loud
With deep hoarse tears, as if a kind of dumb
And idiot child within them still survives
To re-awake at kindness, thinking a voice
At last calls them alone, that hands have come
To lift and lighten; and such joy arrives
Their thick tongues blort, their eyes squeeze grief, a crowd
Of huge unheard answers jam and rejoice –

What's wrong! Moustached in flowered frocks they shake:
By now, all's wrong. In everyone there sleeps
A sense of life lived according to love.
To some it means the difference they could make
By loving others, but across most it sweeps
As all they might have done had they been loved.
That nothing cures. An immense slackening ache,
As when, thawing, the rigid landscape weeps,
Spreads slowly through them – that, and the voice above
Saying *Dear child*, and all time has disproved.

Home

Home is so sad. It stays as it was left,
Shaped to the comfort of the last to go
As if to win them back. Instead, bereft
Of anyone to please, it withers so,
Having no heart to put aside the theft

And turn again to what it started as,
A joyous shot at how things ought to be,
Long fallen wide. You can see how it was:
Look at the pictures and the cutlery.
The music in the piano stool. That vase.

Toads Revisited

Walking around in the park
Should feel better than work:
The lake, the sunshine,
The grass to lie on,

Blurred playground noises
Beyond black-stockinged nurses –
Not a bad place to be.
Yet it doesn't suit me,

Being one of the men
You meet of an afternoon:
Palsied old step-takers,
Hare-eyed clerks with the jitters,

Waxed-fleshed out-patients
Still vague from accidents,
And characters in long coats
Deep in the litter-baskets –

All dodging the toad work
By being stupid or weak.
Think of being them!
Hearing the hours chime,

Watching the bread delivered,
The sun by clouds covered,
The children going home;
Think of being them,

Turning over their failures
By some bed of lobelias,
Nowhere to go but indoors,
No friends but empty chairs –

No, give me my in-tray,
My loaf-haired secretary,
My shall-I-keep-the-call-in-Sir:
What else can I answer.

When the lights come on at four
At the end of another year?
Give me your arm, old toad;
Help me down Cemetery Road.

Water

If I were called in
To construct a religion
I should make use of water.

Going to church
Would entail a fording
To dry, different clothes;

My litany would employ
Images of sousing,
A furious devout drench,

And I should raise in the east
A glass of water
Where any-angled light
Would congregate endlessly.

The Whitsun Weddings

That Whitsun, I was late getting away:
   Not till about
One-twenty on the sunlit Saturday
Did my three-quarters-empty train pull out,
All windows down, all cushions hot, all sense
Of being in a hurry gone. We ran
Behind the backs of houses, crossed a street
Of blinding windscreens, smelt the fish-dock; thence
The river's level drifting breadth began,
Where sky and Lincolnshire and water meet.

All afternoon, through the tall heat that slept
   For miles inland,
A slow and stopping curve southwards we kept.

Wide farms went by, short-shadowed cattle, and
Canals with floatings of industrial froth;
A hothouse flashed uniquely: hedges dipped
And rose: and now and then a smell of grass
Displaced the reek of buttoned carriage-cloth
Until the next town, new and nondescript,
Approached with acres of dismantled cars.

At first, I didn't notice what a noise
   The weddings made
Each station that we stopped at: sun destroys
The interest of what's happening in the shade,
And down the long cool platforms whoops and skirls
I took for porters larking with the mails,
And went on reading. Once we started, though,
We passed them, grinning and pomaded, girls
In parodies of fashion, heels and veils,
All posed irresolutely, watching us go,

As if out on the end of an event
   Waving goodbye
To something that survived it. Struck, I leant
More promptly out next time, more curiously,
And saw it all again in different terms:
The fathers with broad belts under their suits
And seamy foreheads; mothers loud and fat;
An uncle shouting smut; and then the perms,
The nylon gloves and jewellery-substitutes,
The lemons, mauves, and olive-ochres that

Marked off the girls unreally from the rest.
   Yes, from cafés
And banquet-halls up yards, and bunting-dressed
Coach-party annexes, the wedding-days
Were coming to an end. All down the line
Fresh couples climbed aboard: the rest stood round;
The last confetti and advice were thrown,

And, as we moved, each face seemed to define
Just what it saw departing: children frowned
At something dull; fathers had never known

Success so huge and wholly farcical;
  The women shared
The secret like a happy funeral;
While girls, gripping their handbags tighter, stared
At a religious wounding. Free at last,
And loaded with the sum of all they saw,
We hurried towards London, shuffling gouts of steam.
Now fields were building-plots, and poplars cast
Long shadows over major roads, and for
Some fifty minutes, that in time would seem

Just long enough to settle hats and say
  I nearly died,
A dozen marriages got under way.
They watched the landscape, sitting side by side
– An Odeon went past, a cooling tower,
And someone running up to bowl – and none
Thought of the others they would never meet
Or how their lives would all contain this hour.
I thought of London spread out in the sun,
Its postal districts packed like squares of wheat:

There we were aimed. And as we raced across
  Bright knots of rail
Past standing Pullmans, walls of blackened moss
Came close, and it was nearly done, this frail
Travelling coincidence; and what it held
Stood ready to be loosed with all the power
That being changed can give. We slowed again,
And as the tightened brakes took hold, there swelled
A sense of falling, like an arrow-shower
Sent out of sight, somewhere becoming rain.

Days

What are days for?
Days are where we live.
They come, they wake us
Time and time over.
They are to be happy in:
Where can we live but days?

Ah, solving that question
Brings the priest and the doctor
In their long coats
Running over the fields.

A Study of Reading Habits

When getting my nose in a book
Cured most things short of school,
It was worth ruining my eyes
To know I could still keep cool,
And deal out the old right hook
To dirty dogs twice my size.

Later, with inch-thick specs,
Evil was just my lark:
Me and my cloak and fangs
Had ripping times in the dark.
The women I clubbed with sex!
I broke them up like meringues.

Don't read much now: the dude
Who lets the girl down before
The hero arrives, the chap
Who's yellow and keeps the store,
Seems far too familiar. Get stewed:
Books are a load of crap.

Ambulances

Closed like confessionals, they thread
Loud noons of cities, giving back
None of the glances they absorb.
Light glossy grey, arms on a plaque,
They come to rest at any kerb:
All streets in time are visited.

Then children strewn on steps or road,
Or women coming from the shops
Past smells of different dinners, see
A wild white face that overtops
Red stretcher-blankets momently
As it is carried in and stowed,

And sense the solving emptiness
That lies just under all we do,
And for a second get it whole,
So permanent and blank and true.
The fastened doors recede. *Poor soul*,
They whisper at their own distress;

For borne away in deadened air
May go the sudden shut of loss
Round something nearly at an end,
And what cohered in it across
The years, the unique random blend
Of families and fashions, there

At last begin to loosen. Far
From the exchange of love to lie
Unreachable inside a room
The traffic parts to let go by
Brings closer what is left to come,
And dulls to distance all we are.

An Arundel Tomb

Side by side, their faces blurred,
The earl and countess lie in stone,
Their proper habits vaguely shown
As jointed armour, stiffened pleat,
And that faint hint of the absurd –
The little dogs under their feet.

Such plainness of the pre-baroque
Hardly involves the eye, until
It meets his left-hand gauntlet, still
Clasped empty in the other; and
One sees, with a sharp tender shock,
His hand withdrawn, holding her hand.

They would not think to lie so long.
Such faithfulness in effigy
Was just a detail friends would see:
A sculptor's sweet commissioned grace
Thrown off in helping to prolong
The Latin names around the base.

They would not guess how early in
Their supine stationary voyage
The air would change to soundless damage,
Turn the old tenantry away;
How soon succeeding eyes begin
To look, not read. Rigidly they

Persisted, linked, through lengths and breadths
Of time. Snow fell, undated. Light
Each summer thronged the glass. A bright
Litter of birdcalls strewed the same
Bone-riddled ground. And up the paths
The endless altered people came,

Washing at their identity.
Now, helpless in the hollow of
An unarmorial age, a trough
Of smoke in slow suspended skeins
Above their scrap of history,
Only an attitude remains:

Time has transfigured them into
Untruth. The stone fidelity
They hardly meant has come to be
Their final blazon, and to prove
Our almost-instinct almost true:
What will survive of us is love.

Notes

REASONS FOR ATTENDANCE. A good example of Larkin's power to convey a speaking voice through the rhythms of the ten-syllable iambic line. The poem is about being middle-aged and unmarried and feeling out of touch with the younger generation. Its immense technical control can be indicated by the placing of the last two words 'or lied'. By themselves these do not, of course, make a grammatical sentence, but a special rhythmical stress is placed on them by the full stop after the preceding word 'himself'. The effect is to sum up the whole poem and at the same time comment on it. Larkin gives us a tragic and yet bracing sense that everybody needs both experience of life and experience of art if they are to be complete people.

CHURCH GOING. One of Larkin's most famous poems. It represents a highly serious attempt by a reverent agnostic to express and come to terms with his feelings about religion, particularly about Christianity. The poem moves from the light-hearted, chatty tone of the first two stanzas through the literary and rather intellectual mood of the middle three stanzas to an elevated and moving conclusion in the last two. The diction is flexible enough to include conversational phrases like 'God knows how long' (although in its context this has a double meaning) and romantic and obsolete words like 'blent'. The brilliant accuracy of Larkin's poetry is apparent in a phrase like 'tense, musty, unignorable silence'. The word 'un-ignorable' is a good example of what Yeats once called the surprising word that seems inevitable.

POETRY OF DEPARTURES. A beautiful defence of conventional morality and ordinary routine living against the glamorised romanticising to which all of us, and perhaps particularly artists, are sometimes prone. The poem manages to defend the humdrum without sounding pompous. It does this by its natural, throwaway language, humour and willingness to see the other man's point of view. To maintain these prose virtues in a carefully written piece of verse is an amazing achievement. The poem is written in a stress accent form with three stresses in one line and two in the next line all the way through, and with the second and fourth, sixth and eighth, first and fifth and third and seventh lines rhyming. The argument at the end of the poem is unusual and interesting: it seems to be that thinking conformity is more desirable than arbitrary and un-thought-out originality. It may be that Larkin is thinking of the kind of minor and bad romantic poet who believes that scanda-lous living is a substitute for good writing.

BROADCAST. One of Larkin's rare love poems. It describes a man listening to a concert broadcast from a large auditorium. The man pictures the girl he is thinking about in the audience as he listens to the music and the applause at the end of the concert. I say 'a man' because one can never assume that a poem in the first person is necessarily autobiographical. Larkin's poems often seem to have the vividness and authenti-city of real life, but it would be wrong to suppose the poet has entirely renounced his right to elements of invention or imagi-nation.

FAITH HEALING. A clear, straightforward poem about an American evangelist, described with a mixture of accuracy and pathos. The image of the frozen landscape thawing at the end of the poem has the same power to lift the tone on to a more emotional plane as the image of the arrow shower at the end of 'The Whitsun Weddings'. The words 'all time has disproved' which end the poem can be taken in one of two senses: they may mean either 'everything that time has disproved' or 'the voice which the whole of time has disproved'. William Empson's book *Seven Types of Ambiguity* had a powerful influence on the poetry of the 1950s and double meaning was highly prized in the verse of the period. Sometimes it led to pointless trickery but, when handled by a craftsman as skilful as Larkin, as here, it has the effect of enriching and deepening a poem's meaning.

HOME. This short poem is about the idea of home conceived as one's childhood home and not the place one now lives in.

The décor in the last line suggests a particularly old-fashioned home, perhaps Edwardian or late Victorian. The word 'bereft' in the third line of the first stanza is a piece of archaic diction. Does it help the 'old-fashioned' flavour of the poem, or is it simply a convenient rhyme word for 'left' and 'theft'?

TOADS REVISITED. The point of the title is that Larkin had already written a poem called 'Toads' and this is a sequel. Both are light-hearted, half serious poems about the oppressive, tedious nature of work. The idea of a toad squatting on one is a forceful and at the same time funny image for this. There really is a road called Cemetery Road not far from where Larkin works in Hull.

WATER. This unrhymed poem is written in a stress accent rhythm which goes like this: 2 2 3, 2 2 3, 2 2 3, 3 2 3 2. The poem is an unusually bare and direct one for Larkin. There is a hint of the influence of Robert Graves in the phrase 'a furious devout drench'.

THE WHITSUN WEDDINGS. This is Philip Larkin's most famous poem and one of the major poems written since 1945. It has the same blend of restrained feeling and spectacular technical control as Gray's 'Elegy in a Country Churchyard' and its place in English literature already seems as secure. Philip Hobsbaum has said that a new landscape gets into English poetry in the lines:

> An Odeon went past, a cooling tower,
> And someone running up to bowl.

John Betjeman, the living English poet whom Larkin most admires, had already done the same sort of thing and his influence is apparent elsewhere in 'The Whitsun Weddings', notably in the description of the relatives in the fourth stanza, which some readers have found slightly patronising. In fact, like 'Reasons for Attendance' this poem is about not belonging, about watching other people's attempts to obtain enduring love without being directly involved oneself. The people getting married seem slightly ridiculous in Larkin's description, but this is a deliberate device to suggest his distance from them and inability to enter fully into their happiness. The magnificent image of the arrow shower at the end of the poem has been taken by a perceptive critic of Larkin, Anthony Thwaite, to be a sad one since rain is usually an image for tragedy and failure in Larkin, but it could alternatively be regarded as a happy one since falling rain makes crops grow, just as the marriages now being celebrated will one day lead to the bearing of children.

DAYS. This is a direct simple-looking poem about time and death. The one concrete detail, the 'long coats' of the priest and the doctor, brings the poem to life with a sinister vividness. It also suggests the timeless rituals we associate with the poetry of R. S. Thomas. Like 'Water' this poem seems to be aiming at a plain, timeless quality quite different from the practical everyday flavour of most of Larkin's poetry.

A STUDY OF READING HABITS. At first reading, this may seem just a very good funny poem. Even at the technical level, however, the rhyming (e.g. 'fangs' and 'meringues') is superb. On closer reading the point the poem is making appears as a subtle and serious one. The speaker in the poem is represented as someone who began by reading for escapism and ended up abandoning reading because the villains in the fantasies he used to enjoy turned out to be too true to life, and so failed to give him the kick he was looking for. This *persona* is closely related to the *persona* in many of Larkin's more obviously serious poems. He even wears very thick spectacles, as Larkin does himself. The last line 'Books are a load of crap' is an ironic attack on, and at the same time defence of, serious literature. Coming from a writer who is a librarian, of course, it also greatly adds to the fun of the poem.

AMBULANCES. A good example of Larkin's characteristic power to treat abstract description with a peculiar sense of concreteness. The phrase 'something nearly at an end', for example, as a sort of euphemism for a dying man, is frightening, original and moving all at once. The syntax towards the end of the poem, notably in the last sentence, has the intricacy which Larkin sometimes aims at when trying to be particularly formal. A paraphrase of the last sentence might go something like this: 'When you're being taken away from your friends to hospital in an ambulance, ordinary life seems very far away and death rather close.' The way Larkin puts it it is no longer banal but resonant and touching. It gives dignity to the experience in a way the language of an eighteenth-century poet could sometimes do by the use of words deriving from Latin or Greek. Larkin's originality lies in his ability to get this kind of dignity without resorting to any but simple Anglo-Saxon words.

AN ARUNDEL TOMB. The tomb referred to in the poem is in Chichester Cathedral. The detail of the linked hands which the poet admires is thought to be a nineteenth-century addition, but this in no way weakens the delicacy and tenderness of the poem. The simply worded but clearly profoundly felt maxim in the last line 'what will survive of us is love' is built up to and in a way earned by the down-to-earth exactness of the rest of the poem.

Donald Davie

Donald Davie was born in 1922. He is now a Professor of Literature at the University of Essex in Colchester. Like Eliot and Empson before him, Davie has written criticism which illuminates and prepares the way for his own poetry. His two critical books, *Purity of Diction in English Verse* and *Articulate Energy*, seem to me the best criticism published in book form since the war. Davie has half-ironically described himself in one poem as 'a pasticheur of late Augustan styles', but this description is only applicable to his earlier work. His work as a translator from Polish and as a student of contemporary American literature, has led him towards a new and looser style whose full resources he has perhaps still to exploit. In some ways Davie stands to Larkin as MacNeice stands to Auden – he is widely regarded as the second most important member of the group to which he was first considered as belonging. In fact, however, Davie is increasingly seeming to have more affinities with poets whose interests are in art and in connections between art and ethics, particularly Charles Tomlinson and Edward Lucie-Smith.

Remembering the 'Thirties

I

Hearing one saga, we enact the next.
We please our elders when we sit enthralled;
But then they're puzzled; and at last they're vexed
To have their youth so avidly recalled.

It dawns upon the veterans after all
That what for them were agonies, for us
Are high-brow thrillers, though historical;
And all their feats quite strictly fabulous.

This novel written fifteen years ago,
Set in my boyhood and my boyhood home,
These poems about 'abandoned workings', show
Worlds more remote than Ithaca or Rome.

The Anschluss, Guernica – all the names
At which those poets thrilled or were afraid
For me mean schools and schoolmasters and games;
And in the process some-one is betrayed.

Ourselves perhaps. The Devil for a joke
Might carve his own initials on our desk,
And yet we'd miss the point because he spoke
An idiom too dated, Audenesque.

Ralegh's Guiana also killed his son.
A pretty pickle if we came to see
The tallest story really packed a gun,
The Telemachiad an Odyssey.

II

Even to them the tales were not so true
As not to be ridiculous as well:
The ironmaster met his Waterloo,
But Rider Haggard rode along the fell.

'Leave for Cape Wrath tonight!' They lounged away
On Fleming's trek or Isherwood's ascent.
England expected every man that day
To show his motives were ambivalent.

They played the fool, not to appear as fools
In time's long glass. A deprecating air
Disarmed, they thought, the jeers of later schools;
Yet irony itself is doctrinaire,

And, curiously, nothing now betrays
Their type to time's derision like this coy
Insistence on the quizzical, their craze
For showing Hector was a mother's boy.

A neutral tone is nowadays preferred.
And yet it may be better, if we must,
To find the stance impressive and absurd
Than not to see the hero for the dust.

For courage is the vegetable king,
The sprig of all ontologies, the weed
That beards the slag-heap with his hectoring,
Whose green adventure is to run to seed.

To a Brother in the Mystery

Circa 1290

The world of God has turned its two stone faces
One my way, one yours. Yet we change places
A little, slowly. After we had halved
The work between us, those grotesques I carved
There in the first bays clockwise from the door.
That was such work as I got credit for
At York and Beverley: thorn-leaves twined and bent
To frame some small and human incident

Domestic or of venery. Each time I crossed
Since then, however, underneath the vast
Span of our Mansfield limestone, to appraise
How you cut stone, my emulous hard gaze
Has got to know you as I know the stone
Where none but chisels talk for us. I have grown
Of my own way of thinking yet of yours,
Seeing your leafage burgeon thère by the doors
With a light that, flickering, trenches the voussoir's line;
Learning your pre-harmonies, design
Nourished by exuberance, and fine-drawn
Severity that is tenderness, I have thought,
Looking at these last stalls that I have wrought
This side of the chapter's octagon, I find
No hand but mine at work, yet mine refined
By yours, and all the difference: my motif
Of foliate form, your godliness in leaf.

   And your last spandrel proves the debt incurred
Not all on the one side. There I see a bird
Pecks at your grapes, and after him a fowler,
A boy with a bow. Elsewhere, your leaves discovered
Of late blank mask-like faces. We infect
Each other then, doubtless to good effect . . .
And yet, take care: this cordial knack bereaves
The mind of all its sympathy with leaves,
Even with stone. I would not take away
From your peculiar mastery, if I say
A sort of coldness is the core of it,
A sort of cruelty; that prerequisite
Perhaps I rob you of, and in exchange give
What? Vulgarity's prerogative,
Indulgence towards the frailties it indulges,
Humour called 'wryness' that acknowledges
Its own complicity. I can keep in mind
So much at all events, can always find
Fallen humanity enough, in stone,
Yes, in the medium; where we cannot own
Crispness, compactness, elegance, but the feature

Seals it and signs it work of human nature
And fallen though redeemable. You, I fear,
Will find you bought humanity too dear
At the price of some light leaves, if you begin
To find your handling of them getting thin,
Insensitive, brittle. For the common touch
Though it warms, coarsens. Never care so much
For leaves or people, but you care for stone
A little more. The medium is its own
Thing, and not all a medium, but the stuff
Of mountains: cruel, obdurate, and rough.

A Meeting of Cultures

Iced with a vanilla
Of dead white stone, the Palace
Of Culture is a joke

Or better, a vast villa
In some unimaginable suburb
Of Perm or Minsk.

Ears wave and waggle
Over the poignant Vistula
Horns of a papery stone,

Not a wedding cake but its doily!
The Palace of Culture sacks
The centre, the dead centre

Of Europe's centre, Warsaw.
The old town
Rebuilt is a clockwork toy.

I walked abroad in it
Charmed and waylaid
By a nursery joy:

Hansel's and Gretel's city!
Their house of gingerbread
That lately in

Horrific forest glooms
Of Germany
Bared its ferocity

Anew, resumes its gilt
For rocking-horse rooms
In Polish rococo.

Diseased imaginations
Extant in Warsaw's stone
Her air makes sanative.

How could a D.S.O.
Of the desert battles live,
If it were otherwise,

In his wooden cabin
In a country wood
In the heart of Warsaw,

As the colonel did, who for
The sake of England took
Pains to be welcoming?

More jokes then. And the wasps humming
Into his lady's jam
That we ate with a spoon

Out in the long grass. Shades,
Russian shades out of old slow novels,
Lengthened the afternoon.

Notes

REMEMBERING THE 'THIRTIES. An excellent example of Davie's favourite form in his early work, the four-line stanza rhyming *abab* with a very even, smooth iambic beat and carefully observed regular, natural syntax. Some people have thought this style a kind of straitjacket, but it has, when one acquires a taste for it, the satisfying quality of a good piece of craftsmanship. The poem is a good example of the contrasting attitudes of two generations – the 'thirties and the 'fifties. The mingled criticism and admiration of Auden, particularly in the second section of the poem, is subtle and honest. The phrase 'a neutral tone is nowadays preferred' could be taken as the leading article in the charter of The Movement.

TO A BROTHER IN THE MYSTERY. A dramatic monologue in the manner of some of Browning's. The speaker is a stone carver in a great cathedral in the thirteenth century. The interest of the poem, however, does not lie in the revelation of character, as it would in a Browning poem, but in the laying bare of two contrasting attitudes to artistic creation. The carver about whom the speaker is talking is prone to a certain coldness and classicism, whereas he himself is liable to the romantic excesses of crudity and vagueness. The end of the poem is a moving plea for ultimate obedience to the material of art for one's subject or meaning. In literary terms, this would amount to saying that the first essential is to be able to write. As always with Davie, the interlacing of the vowel and consonant sounds is extremely musical. His poems all need to be read aloud with the consonants heavily stressed to bring out their full verbal richness. Like all good poetry, they work as a taste in the mouth. Davie's own voice has a trace of Yorkshire accent, as Ted Hughes's does, and this fact is important to remember in reading poems by them.

A MEETING OF CULTURES. An example of Davie's later style in which he attempts to draw on the free-flowing rhythm of some of the American poet Robert Lowell's later work. At the same time one can hear remotely the three heavy stresses of the familiar Yeats line which he used in 'Easter, 1916'. The poem is set in Warsaw and records some of Davie's interest in the culture of modern Eastern Europe. The Hansel and Gretel reference is to Humperdinck's opera in the second act of which the two children encounter a witch who turns children into ginger bread in an oven: Davie is linking this with the incinerators at Auschwitz. The poem is interesting for its ability to yoke together a wide range of scenes and subjects.

Christopher Middleton

Christopher Middleton was born in 1926. He teaches German at King's College in London and is the author of many translations from modern German poets. Of all the younger English poets now writing his work seems most closely in tune with the tradition of the modern movement as initiated by Eliot and Pound. Indeed, if Eliot has written the best French poetry in the English language, it could be said that Middleton has written the best German. At a time when most younger poets have believed that poetry can and should be capable of paraphrase, Middleton has resolutely refused to be bound by the restrictions of prose sense. Some of his best poems defy analysis and maintain the deliberate irrationality of Surrealist and Expressionist poetry. Middleton's work has also drawn to some extent on the explorations of the Black Mountain school of poets in America led by Charles Olson and Robert Creeley. These poets believe that verse structure should have a physiological basis related to a man's breathing, and even his heart beat. In practice this leads them towards a sort of mimetic free verse, following out a rapid, rhetorical sequence of ideas in long lines (as in Ginsberg's poem 'Howl)' and a hesitant sequence of ideas in short lines (as in parts of Creeley's 'For Love').

Seven Hunters

I

On skins we scaled the snow wall,
seven hunters; roped, leaning
into claws of wind; we climbed,
wisely, for no fixed point.
There was no point we knew.

Staggered upon it at noon.
Drifts half buried it. The coils
horns eyes had to be hacked free.
We lashed, as the moon rose,
its black flesh to sledges.

It was dead as a doornail,
thank God. Labouring
the way down, by luck
we found a hut, beer and bread.

II

Some came in cars, some barefoot,
some by air, some sprang from ships,
some tore in by local train,
some capered out of bed
and biked there with babies.

Like flies they filled the hot square.
The cordon, flung round that heap
of black tubes, when the eye blazed,
could not see. The crowd did.
Then we heard the first shout.

Now in our town the streets
and houses have gone.
Here, underground, we
who were seven are one.

At Porthcothan

A speck of dark at low tide on the tideline,
It could not be identified as any known thing,
Until, as one approached, a neck was clear
(It is agreed that logs, or cans, are neckless),
And then a body, over which the neck stood
Curved like a questionmark, emerged
As oval, and the whole shape was crouching
Helpless in a small pool the sea had left.

The oval body, with green sheen as of pollen
Shading off into the black plumage, and the neck
Surmounted by the tiny wide-eyed head,
Were not without beauty. The head was moving,
So like a cobra it seemed rash to offer
An introductory finger to the long hooked bill
Stabbing the air. Danger had so
Sharpened what intelligence the bird possessed,
It seemed to pierce the mind of the observer.
In fact we were afraid, yes afraid of each other.

Finally though I picked it up and took it
To a quiet side-bay where dogs were rarer.
Here the shag sat, happy in the sun,
Perched on a slab of rock where a pool was,
In which I caught five fish for it
With a pocketknife, a handkerchief
And a plunging forefinger. But at six o'clock
It left the rock and waddled off seaward.

Though breakers came in high and curling
It straddled them, bouncing, buoyant,
Borne along the sealine sideways, with head up,
Slithering across the bay's whole width, and then
Drifted ashore again, to scuttle flapping
With webbed feet flat like a Saturday banker's
To shelter on a level rock. Here it studied,

With the air of one of whom something is expected,
The turbulent Atlantic slowly rising.
What could I do but leave it meditating?

Early next morning, on the bay's north side,
I found it cuddled under the cliff. The tide
Was low again. What hungry darkness
Had driven so the dark young shag to shelter?
It did not resist when I picked it up.
Something had squeezed the cobra out of it.

I took it to a cave where the sun shone in,
Then caught two fish. It opened one green eye,
And then another. But though I cut
The fish into portions, presenting these
To the bill's hooked tip, it only shook its head.
Noon came. The shag slept in the cave. At two
I hurried back. The shag was stone dead,
With its fine glossy head laid back a little
Over the left shoulder, and a few flies
Were pestering its throat and the fish scraps
Now unlikely to get eaten.
                                        Ten minutes perhaps
I sat there, then carried it up the cliff path
And across the headland to a neighbouring cove
Where oystercatchers and hawks flew and far
Far below in loose heaps small timber lay, tickled
By a thin finger of sea. There I flung the shag,
For in some such place, I thought,
Such bodies best belong, far from bathers, among
The elements that compose and decompose them,
Unconscious, strange to freedom, but perceptible
Through narrow slits that score the skin of things.

Or perhaps (for I could not see the body falling)
A hand rose out of air and plucked the corpse
From its arc and took it, warm still,
To some safer place and concealed it there,
Quite unobtrusively, but sure, but sure.

The Forenoon

All the long forenoon, the loitering of insects;
Their invisible wings, whirring in choir and alley,
By lemon pyramids, in domes of organpounded air,
Over golden loaves that cool on glass in Greek Street.

One has flown to the vine slopes of a gated city,
One is crushed in a tube; one is a foreign king,
Stern in his carriage, popular, waving;
One with a whip stumbled after office girls,
And woke smiling. In iron shade
To one on a bench his nostril's curlew pipings bring
Concomitant visions of vacant moors.
One has dwelled among the springs and heard
A throbbing in the ark above their mountain.
One sidesteps a banker with a beak
And a dead baby dangling on a string from it.
One wisecracks. One darts giggling under a hat,
To munch a matchstick. One reads words
ARBOGAST FACTION PACT BUT HEAT RISES

One: severed from the great root the strong shrivel
One: the voluminous black fire answers their cry of terror
One: the plumed waves have burst long enough on this
    shore
One: scattering the blind swarms that drink at the carcass.

Navajo Children
Canyon de Chelly, Arizona

You sprouted from sand,
running, stopping, running;
beyond you tall red
tons of rock rested
on the feathery tamarisk.

Torn jeans, T-shirts
lope and skip, toes drum
and you're coming
full tilt
for the lollipops,

hopefully
arrive, daren't
look, for our stares
(your noses dribble)
prove too rude

in your silence,
can't break, either,
your upturned
monkey faces into smiles.
It's no joke,

as you grope
up, up
to the driver's door, take
them reverently, the
lollipops –

your smallest, too small,
waited three
paces back, shuffling,
then provided,
evidently

by a sister on tiptoe who
takes his hand, helps
unwrap the sugar totem.
And we are swept
on, bouncing,

look back,
seeing walls
dwarf you. But how
could you get any
more thin, small, far.

Lenau's Dream

Scares me mad, that dream;
wish I could tell my-
self I slept without

a dream! But what of
these tears pouring down
still, loud throb of heart?

Waking, I was done up.
My handkerchief wet
(had I just buried

someone?). Don't know how
I got hold of it,
and me fast asleep –

but they were there, the
visitors, evil,
I gave them my house

for their feast, then got
off to bed, while they
tore the place to bits,

the wild fool ele-
mentals! Gone out now,
leaving their trail, these

tears and from tables
great wine pools dripping
slowly to the floor.

Notes

SEVEN HUNTERS. This poem is written as two syllabic sonnets. The number of syllables in the lines are: 7 7 7 6 6, 7 7 7 6 6, 7 5 5 7. The poem seems to be about a group of primitive hunters who discover the corpse of some enormous beast, perhaps a kind of mammoth, which they believe to be dead but which later comes to life. At the end of the poem the monster has killed all the people who had come to see it and seems also to have eaten the hunters. The poem really depends, however, not on understanding this plot but on responding to the associations which elements in it conjure up. The poem has some of the evocative power of a Surrealist painting by Salvador Dali or Max Ernst.

AT PORTHCOTHAN. This long, slow moving, meditative poem is unique in Middleton's published work for its clarity of structure and unambiguous expression of feeling. To be able to convey this kind of sentiment about the death of a young bird without lapsing into sentimentality is an amazing achievement in the mid-twentieth century. Even the optimistic gesture of the conclusion seems to come off. When people speak of the kind of Georgian poem which Eliot's revolution made impossible, this is the sort of thing they mean. Of all the poems in this book it has most in common with Lawrence's 'Snake' (p. 39) which was in fact published in one of Edward Marsh's anthologies of Georgian poetry. The success of the poem seems to depend largely on the skill with which the rhythm departs relatively slightly from the iambic norm with which it begins and then does so only to follow out the natural movement of the poet's thought. In fact the poem oscillates between a basic five-syllable and a basic four-syllable stress pattern, but one is not aware of this as in any way obtrusive or odd.

THE FORENOON. This forms the third section of the poem-sequence 'Herman Moon's Hourbook', and is one of Middleton's most important and ambitious poems so far. Many elements in it seem to stand in a direct line from *The Waste Land*. Although each poem in the sequence is independent, all are connected by the consciousness of Herman Moon, a sort of mid-century Everyman living in London. This section can be interestingly compared with 'The Fire Sermon' (p. 87). The sensuous vividness of the description anchors and gives added weight to the horrifying and irrational images which proliferate as the poem develops. The sinister quality of the poem depends on the connection, implied but never stated, between insects and people. Whenever the word 'one' occurs it seems to refer to the same species of creature, which is never clearly defined. This catalogue effect is in some ways reminiscent of Auden.

NAVAJO CHILDREN CANYON DE CHELLY, ARIZONA. A beautifully mimetic poem recalling an incident during a drive in the Arizona desert. The short free verse lines are skilfully dovetailed together and sometimes abruptly halted to reproduce the movement of the vehicle and the children. The poem perhaps owes a little to the style of a Black Mountain poet like Robert Creeley.

LENAU'S DREAM. This is a sort of modern Grimm's fairy tale. The attractiveness of the poem comes from the contrast between the unconcern, even jauntiness, of the narrator, and our own sense that what he is talking about is particularly ominous and terrifying. Who were the visitors in the night? Who, for that matter, is Lenau? We never know, and not knowing gives the poem its peculiar quality. The poem is all written in lines of five syllables.

Thom Gunn

Thom Gunn was born in 1929. He was educated at Cambridge, and now lives in America, where he teaches at the University of California at Berkeley. Gunn's first book, *Fighting Terms*, was published by the Fantasy Press in Oxford when he was only twenty-five and immediately established him as one of the most interesting poets of his generation. The passage of time has made it clearer that Gunn is not a Movement poet in the way that Philip Larkin or Kingsley Amis is. His work forms an important bridge between the poetry of Larkin and the poetry of Hughes: he writes with the formal precision and elegance of a 1950s poet but with the interest in energy and violence of a 1960s one. The tension between the grace of his style and the bite of his subject matter gives Gunn's poetry its peculiar quality. Like Auden, his future career is perhaps likely to form a closer part of the American than the English poetic tradition. Already his later poems have something in common with the syllabic work of academic poets such as Donald Hall and, from an older generation, Marianne Moore.

The Wound

The huge wound in my head began to heal
About the beginning of the seventh week.
Its valleys darkened, its villages became still:
For joy I did not move and dared not speak,
Not doctors would cure it, but time, its patient skill.

And constantly my mind returned to Troy.
After I sailed the seas I fought in turn
On both sides, sharing even Helen's joy
Of place, and growing up – to see Troy burn –
As Neoptolemus, that stubborn boy.

I lay and rested as prescription said.
Manoeuvred with the Greeks, or sallied out
Each day with Hector. Finally my bed
Became Achilles' tent, to which the lout
Thersites came reporting numbers dead.

I was myself: subject to no man's breath:
My own commander was my enemy.
And while my belt hung up, sword in the sheath,
Thersites shambled in and breathlessly
Cackled about my friend Patroclus' death.

I called for armour, rose, and did not reel.
But, when I thought, rage at his noble pain
Flew to my head, and turning I could feel
My wound break open wide. Over again
I had to let those storm-lit valleys heal.

Incident on a Journey

One night I reached a cave: I slept, my head
Full of the air. There came about daybreak
A red-coat soldier to the mouth, who said
'I am not living, in hell's pains I ache,
    But I regret nothing'.

His forehead had a bloody wound whose streaming
The pallid staring face illuminated.
Whether his words were mine or his, in dreaming
I found they were my deepest thoughts translated.
    '*I regret nothing:*

'Turn your closed eyes to see upon these walls
A mural scratched there by an earlier man,
And coloured with the blood of animals:
Showing humanity beyond its span,
    Regretting nothing.

'No plausible nostalgia, no brown shame
I had when treating with my enemies.
And always when a living impulse came
I acted, and my action made me wise.
    And I regretted nothing.

'I as possessor of unnatural strength
Was hunted, one day netted in a brawl;
A minute far beyond a minute's length
Took from me passion, strength, and life, and all.
    But I regretted nothing.

'Their triumph left my body in the dust;
The dust and beer still clotting in my hair
When I rise lonely, will-less. Where I must
I go, and what I must I bear.
    And I regret nothing.

'My lust runs yet and is unsatisfied,
My hate throbs yet but I am feeble-limbed;
If as an animal I could have died
My death had scattered instinct to the wind,
    Regrets as nothing.'

Later I woke. I started to my feet.
The valley light, the mist already going.
I was alive and felt my body sweet,
Uncaked blood in all its channels flowing.
    I would regret nothing.

On the Move
'Man, you gotta Go'

The blue jay scuffling in the bushes follows
Some hidden purpose, and the gust of birds
That spurts across the field, the wheeling swallows,
Have nested in the trees and undergrowth.
Seeking their instinct, or their poise, or both,
One moves with an uncertain violence
Under the dust thrown by a baffled sense
Or the dull thunder of approximate words.

On motorcycles, up the road, they come:
Small, black, as flies hanging in heat, the Boys,
Until the distance throws them forth, their hum
Bulges to thunder held by calf and thigh.
In goggles, donned impersonality,
In gleaming jackets trophied with the dust,
They strap in doubt – by hiding it, robust –
And almost hear a meaning in their noise.

Exact conclusion of their hardiness
Has no shape yet, but from known whereabouts
They ride, direction where the tires press.

They scare a flight of birds across the field:
Much that is natural, to the will must yield.
Men manufacture both machine and soul,
And use what they imperfectly control
To dare a future from the taken routes.

It is a part solution, after all.
One is not necessarily discord
On earth; or damned because, half animal,
One lacks direct instinct, because one wakes
Afloat on movement that divides and breaks.
One joins the movement in a valueless world,
Choosing it, till, both hurler and the hurled,
One moves as well, always toward, toward.

A minute holds them, who have come to go:
The self-defined, astride the created will
They burst away; the towns they travel through
Are home for neither bird nor holiness,
For birds and saints complete their purposes.
At worst, one is in motion; and at best,
Reaching no absolute, in which to rest,
One is always nearer by not keeping still.

California

Black Jackets

In the silence that prolongs the span
Rawly of music when the record ends,
   The red-haired boy who drove a van
In weekday overalls but, like his friends,

   Wore cycle boots and jacket here
To suit the Sunday hangout he was in,
   Heard, as he stretched back from his beer,
Leather creak softly round his neck and chin.

Before him, on a coal-black sleeve
Remote exertion had lined, scratched, and burned
   Insignia that could not revive
The heroic fall or climb where they were earned.

   On the other drinkers bent together,
Concocting selves for their impervious kit,
   He saw it as no more than leather
Which, taut across the shoulders grown to it,

   Sent through the dimness of a bar
As sudden and anonymous hints of light
   As those that shipping give, that are
Now flickers in the Bay, now lost in night.

   He stretched out like a cat, and rolled
The bitterish taste of beer upon his tongue,
   And listened to a joke being told:
The present was the things he stayed among.

   If it was only loss he wore,
He wore it to assert, with fierce devotion,
   Complicity and nothing more.
He recollected his initiation,

   And one especially of the rites.
For on his shoulders they had put tattoos:
   The group's name on the left, The Knights,
And on the right the slogan Born To Lose.

Considering the Snail

The snail pushes through a green
night, for the grass is heavy
with water and meets over
the bright path he makes, where rain
has darkened the earth's dark. He
moves in a wood of desire,

303

pale antlers barely stirring
as he hunts. I cannot tell
what power is at work, drenched there
with purpose, knowing nothing.
What is a snail's fury? All
I think is that if later

I parted the blades above
the tunnel and saw the thin
trail of broken white across
litter, I would never have
imagined the slow passion
to that deliberate progress.

My Sad Captains

One by one they appear in
the darkness: a few friends, and
a few with historical
names. How late they start to shine!
but before they fade they stand
perfectly embodied, all

the past lapping them like a
cloak of chaos. They were men
who, I thought, lived only to
renew the wasteful force they
spent with each hot convulsion.
They remind me, distant now.

True, they are not at rest yet,
but now that they are indeed
apart, winnowed from failures,
they withdraw to an orbit
and turn with disinterested
hard energy, like the stars.

Notes

THE WOUND. This is Gunn writing in the vein of Hemingway in *A Farewell to Arms*. The speaker in the poem, which is a monologue of the Trojan War, is one of Gunn's characteristic *personae* – the mercenary who fights for himself and his friends and is subject to no country or cause. The 'wound' seems to be a symbol either for sensitivity or for some specific psychological trauma in the past which interferes with the speaker's freedom to act.

INCIDENT ON A JOURNEY. An 'encounter' poem which has something in common with Wilfred Owen's 'Strange Meeting'. The journey referred to in the title of the poem is the journey through life. The attitudes expressed by the dead soldier who comes to the narrator of the poem in his dream are the typically tough-minded ones of Gunn's early poems. Of all the younger poets in England, Gunn is perhaps the one with the most clearly articulated group of basic attitudes. These seem to be that man is a creature possessing free will whose destiny lies in his power to choose and pick his future by his own actions. This philosophy derives from the existentialism of Jean-Paul Sartre and Albert Camus. The refrain echoes a French song made famous by Edith Piaf.

ON THE MOVE. The central image of the roving motorcyclist in this poem derives from the film 'The Wild Ones', starring Marlon Brando, which enjoyed a widespread secret vogue in the early 1950s after it had been banned in England for general release. The Motorcyclist emerges in Gunn's second book as one of his representative modern heroes. His independence and urge for exciting action stamp him as the moral examplar of a whole generation of 'rebels without a cause', from James Dean to the Rolling Stones. Gunn has succeeded in voicing the attitudes of this generation as few other poets have. The last three lines of the poem have immense authority and might stand for Gunn's central philosophy of life.

BLACK JACKETS. This poem expresses the fetishistic interest in uniforms and insignia which tends to appear in some of Gunn's later poems. A line like 'Concocting selves for their impervious kit' brings a new and vivid life to the cliché 'clothes make the man'. The poem shows considerable sociological insight, and reminds us of how much Hitler's success depended upon the jackboot. It has a certain danger as a poem that seems to advocate the comradeship and aristocracy of a doomed élite.

CONSIDERING THE SNAIL. Gunn was one of the key figures in the syllabics revival in English poetry in the early 1960s and this poem is an excellent example of his skill in the manipulation of this metre. There are seven syllables to each line and the rhyme scheme in each stanza is *abcabc*. Gunn manages to retain his own note, though drawing on a subject we would normally have expected to come across in the poems of Ted Hughes. Gunn is interested in the 'power' which seems to stand to the snail as 'will' stands to human beings.

MY SAD CAPTAINS. A moving poem about freeing oneself from the dross of human passions and becoming wholly subject to one's own independence of mind and will, as the stars are in their courses. It has a rather cold, haughty quality but seems to be deeply felt. Once again the poem is written in lines of seven syllables, rhyming *abcabc* in each stanza. As with other poets. Gunn sometimes tends to repeat himself in a successful form,

Peter Porter

Peter Porter was born in Australia in 1929 and now lives in London, where he works in an advertising agency. Porter's main subject is the decadence of western commercial society, to the analysis of which he brings a jaundiced and witty eye. His interest in history gives his explorations of contemporary violence a depth and solidity which the work of some of his contemporaries lacks. Porter sometimes seems to conceive London as the capital city of a latter-day Roman empire, and hence he feels no sense of exile as an Australian living abroad. All his best poems have been written in England and his work forms part of the central English poetic tradition in the 1960s.

Annotations of Auschwitz

I

When the burnt flesh is finally at rest,
The fires in the asylum grates will come up
And wicks turn down to darkness in the madman's eyes.

II

My suit is hairy, my carpet smells of death,
My toothbrush handle grows a cuticle.
I have six million foulnesses of breath.
Am I mad? The doctor holds my testicles
While the room fills with the zyklon B I cough.

III

On Piccadilly underground I fall asleep –
I shuffle with the naked to the steel door,
Now I am only ten from the front – I wake up –
We are past Gloucester Rd, I am not a Jew,
But scratches web the ceiling of the train.

IV

Around staring buildings the pale flowers grow;
The frenetic butterfly, the bee made free by work,
Rouse and rape the pollen pads, the nectar stoops.
The rustling railway ends here. The blind end in Europe's gut.
Touch one piece of unstrung barbed wire –
Let it taste blood: let one man scream in pain,
Death's Botanical Gardens can flower again.

V

A man eating his dressing in the hospital
Is lied to by his stomach. It's a final feast to him
Of beef, blood pudding and black bread.
The orderly can't bear to see this mimic face
With its prim accusing picture after death.
On the stiff square a thousand bodies
Dig up useless ground – he hates them all,

These lives ignoble as ungoverned glands.
They fatten in statistics everywhere
And with their sick, unkillable fear of death
They crowd out peace from executioners' sleep.

VI

Forty thousand bald men drowning in a stream –
The like of light on all those bobbing skulls
Has never been seen before. Such death, says the painter,
Is worthwhile – it makes a colour never known.
It makes a sight that's unimagined, says the poet.
It's nothing to do with me, says the man who hates
The poet and the painter. Six million deaths can hardly
Occur at once. What do they make? Perhaps
An idiot's normalcy. I need never feel afraid
When I salt the puny snail – cruelty's grown up
And waits for time and men to bring into its hands
The snail's adagio and all the taunting life
Which has not cared about or guessed its tortured scope.

VII

London is full of chickens on electric spits,
    Cooking in windows where the public pass.
This, say the chickens, is their Auschwitz,
    And all poultry eaters are psychopaths.

Your Attention Please

The Polar DEW has just warned that
A nuclear rocket strike of
At least one thousand megatons
Has been launched by the enemy
Directly at our major cities.
This announcement will take
Two and a quarter minutes to make,

You therefore have a further
Eight and a quarter minutes
To comply with the shelter
Requirements published in the Civil
Defence Code – section Atomic Attack.
A specially shortened Mass
Will be broadcast at the end
Of this announcement –
Protestant and Jewish services
Will begin simultaneously –
Select your wavelength immediately
According to instructions
In the Defence Code. Do not
Take well-loved pets (including birds)
Into your shelter – they will consume
Fresh air. Leave the old and bed-
ridden, you can do nothing for them.
Remember to press the sealing
Switch when everyone is in
The shelter. Set the radiation
Aerial, turn on the geiger barometer.
Turn off your Television now.
Turn off your radio immediately
The Services end. At the same time
Secure explosion plugs in the ears
Of each member of your family. Take
Down your plasma flasks. Give your children
The pills marked one and two
In the C.D. green container, then put
Them to bed. Do not break
The inside airlock seals until
The radiation All Clear shows
(Watch for the cuckoo in your
perspex panel), or your District
Touring Doctor rings your bell.
If before this, your air becomes
Exhausted or if any of your family
Is critically injured, administer

The capsules marked 'Valley Forge'
(Red pocket in No. 1 Survival Kit)
For painless death. (Catholics
Will have been instructed by their priests
What to do in this eventuality.)
This announcement is ending. Our President
Has already given orders for
Massive retaliation – it will be
Decisive. Some of us may die.
Remember, statistically
It is not likely to be you.
All flags are flying fully dressed
On Government buildings – the sun is shining.
Death is the least we have to fear.
We are all in the hands of God,
Whatever happens happens by His Will.
Now go quickly to your shelters.

Soliloquy at Potsdam

There are always the poor –
Getting themselves born in crowded houses,
Feeding on the parish, losing their teeth early
And learning to dodge blows, getting
Strong bodies – cases for the warped nut of the mind.
The masterful cat o'nine tails, the merciful
Discipline of the hours of drill – better
Than being poor in crowded Europe, the swan-swept
Waters where the faces dredge for bread
And the soggy dead are robbed on their way to the grave.
I can hear it from this window, the musket-drill
On the barrack square. Later today I'll visit
The punishment block. Who else in Europe
Could take these verminous, clutching creatures
And break them into men? What of the shredded back

And the broken pelvis, when the side-drum sounds,
When the uniformed wave tilts and overwhelms
The cheese-trading burghers' world, the aldermanic
Principalities. The reformers sit at my table,
They talk well but they've never seen a battle
Or watched the formed brain in the flogged body
Marching to death on a bellyful of soup and orders.
There has to be misery so there can be discipline.
People will have to die because I cannot bear
Their clinging to life. Why are the best trumpeters
Always French? Watch the west, the watershed
Of revolution. Now back to Quantz. I like to think
That in an afternoon of three sonatas
A hundred regiments have marched more miles
Than lie between here and Vienna and not once
Has a man broken step. Who would be loved
If he could be feared and hated, yet still
Enjoy his lust, eat well and play the flute?

The World of Simon Raven

Rooks are raging where great elms were felled,
Family silver's been lent for the Fête,
Nanny's facing Nigel with stained sheets,
Telegrams announce James is expelled,
Mrs Diamond from Sea View Estate
Tempts a team in training with boiled sweets.

Meanwhile sturgeon from Odessa packed
For Black's and Tan's, renowned St James's Clubs,
Laced with spanish fly, cause randy scenes
At Ascot, a Bishop's face is smacked;
Debs and guardsmen break up Chelsea pubs,
Blackmailers send snaps to dons at Queen's.

Unpaid Mess Bills get a Blue cashiered,
Boys from Balham pelt a First in Greats
With Latin Grammars, Israeli agents
Put public lice in Prince Muhammad's beard,
Doctor Boyce cuts off his cousin Kate's
Clitoris – the favourite fails the fence,

Bookies' reminders frighten Adjutants,
Crockford's man is found with a marked deck.
Somewhere beyond Maidenhead an old
Lady rings her bank for an advance
On her pension, sends her son a cheque,
Watches with the cat as it gets cold.

Homage to Gaetano Donizetti

There was a sugar farmer's son (hyperthyroid)
I knew who was just like Nemorino,
And a girl in the Everest Milk Bar
Whose tits rubbed the cold of the ice cream churn
As she reached down with her cheating scoop –
You saw more if you asked for strawberry –
She had a cold Christ hung over that defile
Crucified in silver, his apotheosis
In dry ice fumes. She was just like bel'Adina,
All the magic in the world wouldn't get
Your hand down her front unless she'd heard
Your rich uncle had just died.
Transistors behind her played Pat Boone,
But only to make a money music
In the till. Dear Master, what they say
About your big guitar is academic prejudice.
The truth is Dr Dulcamara's got
The Times Music Critic's job; the rustici
Are cooking on Sicilian gas, Venetian composers

Are setting Goethe to gongs and spiels and phones,
Teutons still come south to add a little
Cantilena to their klangschönheit
(Not to mention the boys of Naples), and those apostles,
The Twelve Notes, are at work on their Acts
To beautify our arrogance. Why should you care
That your audience are stuffed shirts if you know
That half at least have paid up for their seats.

Notes

ANNOTATIONS OF AUSCHWITZ. This is a good example of Porter's technique of using a number of short, independent sections to cast light from several angles on a central theme, in this case the Nazi concentration camps. The total effect manages to be fragmentary and cumulative at the same time. Section VII, for example, could be detached and printed separately as a neat, rather sick epigram. On the other hand it fulfils a useful role in the overall structure of the poem as a wry, deflating comment on the pure horror of some of the earlier descriptions. The poem has the quality of first class journalism which Porter admires in the work of Auden, who is his main influence. The rhythm is more rugged, however, than Auden's and the tone more bracing.

YOUR ATTENTION PLEASE. The monologue of a radio announcer giving warning of an imminent nuclear attack. The flat, calm tone of a news broadcast is well maintained, but at the same time injected with strong elements of black comedy. The poem is both frightening and funny at the same time in the way a film like *Dr Strangelove: or How I learned to Stop Worrying and Love the Bomb* was. It is loosely (and therefore, strictly speaking, badly) written in a syllabic form. Porter frequently uses difficult traditional or modern metres but tends to treat them with a cavalier unconcern for precision. The originality of his work depends on this curious mixture of energy and straitlacing.

SOLILOQUY AT POTSDAM. The speaker in this dramatic monologue is Frederick the Great, King of Prussia in the late eighteenth century. Quantz was his court composer. The last two and a half lines of the poem are an excellent example of Porter's power to create pithy and quotable maxims. Porter, it should be said, has described himself as 'an unhelpful supporter of the Labour Party'. The attitudes of Frederick the Great are being presented here for understanding and moral judgement, not for approval.

THE WORLD OF SIMON RAVEN. Simon Raven is a novelist whose subject matter tends to be the predicaments of upper-middle-class young men involved in various kinds of scandals. Porter's poem forms a kind of fantastic, imaginary synopsis for an unwritten Raven novel. The poem is written with considerable technical tightness and accuracy of invention, and Cyril Connolly has called it one of the funniest poems he knows. Its excellence as a piece of humour lies, I think, in its power to amuse even if one has read none of Raven's novels. The point is that his books are a good example of one kind of class attitude which Porter wants to poke fun at, though with general insight and, underneath the poem's surface, a considerable degree of sympathy. One might, in fact, describe Porter as the Betjeman of the Left.

HOMAGE TO GAETANO DONIZETTI. Donizetti was a prolific Italian composer of operas at the beginning of the nineteenth century. The poem successfully blends the grace and poise of late Auden with a strong dose of randiness and satire. Porter has said that he would like to blend his career as a poet with one as a musical hack and he clearly admires Donizetti, as he admires Auden, for his professionalism. Nemorino, bel'Adina and Dr Dulcamara and the rustics are characters in Donizetti's opera *L'Elisir d'Amore*. The poem is also to some extent an attack on fashionable modernism in musical technique, as in twelve-note composition.

Ted Hughes

Ted Hughes was born in 1930 in Yorkshire. He is generally regarded, with Philip Larkin, as one of the two most important English poets to appear since the war. Already his energy and rough-hewn style have fathered a host of imitators. If Larkin is the voice of the 1950s, then Hughes is just as surely the voice of the 1960s. Until her death in 1963 Hughes was married to Sylvia Plath and there is much evidence of mutual influence in their work. Indeed, her last poems seem to push to the limit the latent violence of his earlier work. The great American poet Robert Lowell has said that Ted Hughes's animal poems are 'like a thunderbolt' and indeed many of them seem to spring from the page with the energy of a force of nature. The future development of Hughes's poetry is hard to predict. He has (in my view without success) tried his hand at children's verse, and at radio plays, and it seems clear that some form of poetic drama is likely to be his next step forward. Nobody now writing poetry in English seems to me to have more latent power or be more likely to improve his existing reputation. Hughes is already a major poet and his career is rich in promise.

The Thought-Fox

I imagine this midnight moment's forest:
Something else is alive
Beside the clock's loneliness
And this blank page where my fingers move.

Through the window I see no star:
Something more near
Though deeper within darkness
Is entering the loneliness:

Cold, delicately as the dark snow,
A fox's nose touches twig, leaf;
Two eyes serve a movement, that now
And again now, and now, and now

Sets near prints into the snow
Between trees, and warily a lame
Shadow lags by stump and in hollow
Of a body that is bold to come

Across clearings, an eye,
A widening deepening greenness,
Brilliantly, concentratedly,
Coming about its own business

Till, with a sudden sharp hot stink of fox
It enters the dark hole of the head.
The window is starless still; the clock ticks,
The page is printed.

Esther's Tomcat

Daylong this tomcat lies stretched flat
As an old rough mat, no mouth and no eyes.
Continual wars and wives are what
Have tattered his ears and battered his head.

Like a bundle of old rope and iron
Sleeps till blue dusk. Then reappear
His eyes, green as ringstones: he yawns wide red,
Fangs fine as a lady's needle and bright.

A tomcat sprang at a mounted knight,
Locked round his neck like a trap of hooks
While the knight rode fighting its clawing and bite.
After hundreds of years the stain's there

On the stone where he fell, dead of the tom:
That was at Barnborough. The tomcat still
Grallochs odd dogs on the quiet,
Will take the head clean off your simple pullet,

Is unkillable. From the dog's fury,
From gunshot fired point-blank he brings
His skin whole, and whole
From owlish moons of bekittenings

Among ashcans. He leaps and lightly
Walks upon sleep, his mind on the moon.
Nightly over the round world of men,
Over the roofs go his eyes and outcry.

Hawk Roosting

I sit in the top of the wood, my eyes closed.
Inaction, no falsifying dream
Between my hooked head and hooked feet:
Or in sleep rehearse perfect kills and eat.

The convenience of the high trees!
The air's buoyancy and the sun's ray
Are of advantage to me;
And the earth's face upward for my inspection.

My feet are locked upon the rough bark.
It took the whole of Creation
To produce my foot, my each feather:
Now I hold Creation in my foot

Or fly up, and revolve it all slowly –
I kill where I please because it is all mine.
There is no sophistry in my body:
My manners are tearing off heads –

The allotment of death.
For the one path of my flight is direct
Through the bones of the living.
No arguments assert my right:

The sun is behind me.
Nothing has changed since I began.
My eye has permitted no change.
I am going to keep things like this.

View of a Pig

The pig lay on a barrow dead.
It weighed, they said, as much as three men.
Its eyes closed, pink white eyelashes.
Its trotters stuck straight out.

Such weight and thick pink bulk
Set in death seemed not just dead.
It was less than lifeless, further off.
It was like a sack of wheat.

I thumped it without feeling remorse.
One feels guilty insulting the dead,
Walking on graves. But this pig
Did not seem able to accuse.

It was too dead. Just so much
A poundage of lard and pork.
Its last dignity had entirely gone.
It was not a figure of fun.

Too dead now to pity.
To remember its life, din, stronghold
Of earthly pleasure as it had been,
Seemed a false effort, and off the point.

Too deadly factual. Its weight
Oppressed me – how could it be moved?
And the trouble of cutting it up!
The gash in its throat was shocking, but not pathetic.

Once I ran at a fair in the noise
To catch a greased piglet
That was faster and nimbler than a cat,
Its squeal was the rending of metal.

Pigs must have hot blood, they feel like ovens.
Their bite is worse than a horse's –
They chop a half-moon clean out.
They eat cinders, dead cats.

Distinctions and admirations such
As this one was long finished with.
I stared at it a long time. They were going to scald it,
Scald it and scour it like a doorstep.

Relic

I found this jawbone at the sea's edge:
There, crabs, dogfish, broken by the breakers or tossed
To flap for half an hour and turn to a crust
Continue the beginning. The deeps are cold:
In that darkness camaraderie does not hold:
Nothing touches but, clutching, devours. And the jaws,
Before they are satisfied or their stretched purpose
Slacken, go down jaws; go gnawn bare. Jaws
Eat and are finished and the jawbone comes to the beach:
This is the sea's achievement; with shells,
Vertebrae, claws, carapaces, skulls.

Time in the sea eats its tail, thrives, casts these
Indigestibles, the spars of purposes
That failed far from the surface. None grow rich
In the sea. This curved jawbone did not laugh
But gripped, gripped and is now a cenotaph.

An Otter

I

Underwater eyes, an eel's
Oil of water body, neither fish nor beast is the otter:
Four-legged yet water-gifted, to outfish fish;
With webbed feet and long ruddering tail
And a round head like an old tomcat.

Brings the legend of himself
From before wars or burials, in spite of hounds and vermin-
poles;
Does not take root like the badger. Wanders, cries;
Gallops along land he no longer belongs to;
Re-enters the water by melting.

Of neither water nor land. Seeking
Some world lost when first he dived, that he cannot come at
      since,
  Takes his changed body into the holes of lakes;
    As if blind, cleaves the stream's push till he licks
    The pebbles of the source; from sea

    To sea crosses in three nights
Like a king in hiding. Crying to the old shape of the starlit
      land,
  Over sunken farms where the bats go round,
    Without answer. Till light and birdsong come
    Walloping up roads with the milk wagon.

II

The hunt's lost him. Pads on mud,
Among sedges, nostrils a surface bead,
The otter remains, hours. The air,
Circling the globe, tainted and necessary,

Mingling tobacco-smoke, hounds and parsley,
Comes carefully to the sunk lungs.
So the self under the eye lies,
Attendant and withdrawn. The otter belongs

In double robbery and concealment –
From water that nourishes and drowns, and from land
That gave him his length and the mouth of the hound.
He keeps fat in the limpid integument

Reflections live on. The heart beats thick,
Big trout muscle out of the dead cold;
Blood is the belly of logic; he will lick
The fishbone bare. And can take stolen hold

On a bitch otter in a field full
Of nervous horses, but linger nowhere.
Yanked above hounds, reverts to nothing at all,
To this long pelt over the back of a chair.

Pike

Pike, three inches long, perfect
Pike in all parts, green tigering the gold.
Killers from the egg: the malevolent aged grin.
They dance on the surface among the flies.

Or move, stunned by their own grandeur,
Over a bed of emerald, silhouette
Of submarine delicacy and horror.
A hundred feet long in their world.

In ponds, under the heat-struck lily pads –
Gloom of their stillness:
Logged on last year's black leaves, watching upwards.
Or hung in an amber cavern of weeds

The jaws' hooked clamp and fangs
Not to be changed at this date;
A life subdued to its instrument;
The gills kneading quietly, and the pectorals.

Three we kept behind glass,
Jungled in weed: three inches, four,
And four and a half: fed fry to them –
Suddenly there were two. Finally one

With a sag belly and the grin it was born with.
And indeed they spare nobody.
Two, six pounds each, over two feet long,
High and dry and dead in the willow-herb –

One jammed past its gills down the other's gullet:
The outside eye stared: as a vice locks –
The same iron in this eye
Though its film shrank in death.

324

A pond I fished, fifty yards across,
Whose lilies and muscular tench
Had outlasted every visible stone
Of the monastery that planted them –

Stilled legendary depth:
It was as deep as England. It held
Pike too immense to stir, so immense and old
That past nightfall I dared not cast

But silently cast and fished
With the hair frozen on my head
For what might move, for what eye might move.
The still splashes on the dark pond,

Owls hushing the floating woods
Frail on my ear against the dream
Darkness beneath night's darkness had freed,
That rose slowly towards me, watching.

Snowdrop

Now is the globe shrunk tight
Round the mouse's dulled wintering heart.
Weasel and crow, as if moulded in brass,
Move through an outer darkness
Not in their right minds,
With the other deaths. She, too, pursues her ends,
Brutal as the stars of this month,
Her pale head heavy as metal.

Thistles

Against the rubber tongues of cows and the hoeing hands of
   men
Thistles spike the summer air
And crackle open under a blue-black pressure.

Every one a revengeful burst
Of resurrection, a grasped fistful
Of splintered weapons and Icelandic frost thrust up

From the underground stain of a decayed Viking.
They are like pale hair and the gutturals of dialects.
Every one manages a plume of blood.

Then they grow grey like men.
Mown down, it is a feud. Their sons appear
Stiff with weapons, fighting back over the same ground.

The Brother's Dream

In a blue, deadly brilliance, a parched madness of rock, of dust
And a pounding ache of blood
I go upward
                  In a mountain world of fear
And leathery grass.
Of pine-trees, blasted like gibbets,
Holding out fistfuls of needles, bunched at the branch-end,
Bristling, still as coral.
A mountain is lifting me into terror.
With a clatter of little stones
I climb out onto eternity.
My shadow trails with me.
I have come here of my own will.
My voice is ready for any cries needed.

Like a grave, the cave-hole is watching,
In appalling quiet.
                    I stand, part of the stillness –
Not the alert lizard's trigger stillness.
Stillness of some skulls, lying in the open.
And a lilac scent of rottenness
Hanging, like a veil, over the retina.
And a scream going on and on, too fierce for the ear-nerve,
Too deep in the air's stillness.
The masked hills trying to tell me, straining their stillness.
Flies meander in and out of the cave.
They settle on the sunny rocks to clean their wrists and behind
    their heads.
They settle on my shirt.
The rocks, that stare through the end,
Stare deep into me
With their final faces.
I am very frail, almost nothing.
Not here, yet here. A moment ago, not here.
Suddenly shouting into the cave: 'Come out!'
And 'Come out! Come out!' the echo
Brightens the hills like a bombflash.
Somewhere under the ground, the bear is at home.
The brain, flickering, quicker than any of these flies;
The bunched talons, contented;
The fangs, in their own kingdom,
And the happy blood –
The black well
Too deep to glitter
Where my shout, that clangs among open mountains,
Is already being digested.

For the pine-trees,
And for the sprawled hills, pasturing their shadows,
It is ordinary morning.

But the bear is filling the cave-mouth.
Its aimed gullet, point-blank, blasting

Into my face, the risen bear
Walks to embrace me,
With a scream like a weapon
Twisting into my midriff,
The rib-roofed gape measuring at my head,
And I see black lips, the widening curtains of saliva,
The small eyes brown and wet and full of evil
Locked in a fever of annihilation,
Lifted talons spread out like dungforks
Reaching to drag the sky down
Over my eyes, the bear crashes its mass
Onto me like a conifer

And at that moment I grip it.
I push away those eyes, the maniacs,
And the ripsaw scream,
The hatred like agony,
The jaws like a ghastly injury, widening, widening –

I grip it with my left hand by the shag
And cordage of its gullet and I hold it
At my locked arms length and with my dagger
In this other hand I rip it up
From the belly – up, up, up
I rip it. I am a steel madman.
The bear's scream is sawing at my brains
But I rip upward till the heart-muscle
Kicks at the dagger haft.
And I have opened a river.
And the bear slides from me like a robe
I have cut the cords of. I wade
Out of the daze.
    A long while I stand
Like a man awakening.
      The rocks
Wait for me, landmarks
Back to enormous mountain silence.
Time tries to move.

I watch blood
Crawling to touch my boot, slowly, blindly
Tasting the dust.

And the treetops stir.
The bluetits are busy and inquisitive.

But the rocks, and the engraved hills, are altered.
Their incomprehensible faces stare at me
With a new fear.

I come back down through the fir-trees
To my companions and the eyes of the dogs
That were afraid to come with me.
I'm bloody as a Caesarian babe – not my blood.
I send them up to strip the carcass.
I sleep, exhausted.

Notes

THE THOUGHT-FOX. This is a poem about composing poetry, or rather about being visited by the muse. Appropriately enough, in Hughes's case, this muse is an animal, a fox. Hughes has said it was the first animal poem he wrote.

ESTHER'S TOMCAT. An energetic hymn of praise to the elegance, bravery, toughness and gaiety of an old cat. It successfully avoids the fatal 'twee' charm which often affects writers about cats, but at the same time it is wholly free from anthropomorphism or moralising. The poem is written in one of Hughes's favourite loose forms – four-line stanzas, off rhyming in an initially regular and later irregular way. Like Peter Porter, Hughes has a careless disregard for symmetry which at his worst, though not here, leads him into vagueness and crudity.

HAWK ROOSTING. This is perhaps Hughes's greatest poem. It is the monologue of a hawk sitting in the top of a wood. Hughes has said, however, that he had in mind the personality of someone like Hitler and the poem is best interpreted as a remarkable insight into the nature of Fascist psychology. At the same time it never gets away from the essential nature of the bird which is the outward subject of the poem. The headlong violence and the tensed arrogance of the poem is enormously exciting and something quite new in English poetry. One has to turn back towards Jacobean drama for this kind of uninhibited expression of villainy. The poem's influence on the revival of the dramatic monologue form in the early 1960s was crucial.

VIEW OF A PIG. A sort of funeral speech over the body of a dead pig. Hughes is trying to be extremely accurate about his feelings as he sees the pig's body. The object of the poem is to drain death of all its nobility and false trappings. Even the brief spurt of praise for the pig's energy in its lifetime in the second last stanza is abruptly stamped out at the end of the poem. The pig has become just a stone, to be treated like an inanimate object. Ultimately what comes through, I think is a muted unglamourised pathos.

RELIC. Another celebration of natural energy and violence. No political parallels are to be inferred between life in the depths of the sea and life in contemporary society. On the other hand, Hughes does seem to be approving of resolution and integrity. The English conception of themselves as 'the bulldog breed' takes on a new form in this poem. If anything, the tone suggests that energetic activity is doomed but praiseworthy as long as it lasts.

AN OTTER. This is not simply an excellent poem about an otter. The key to its deeper meaning seems to lie in the phrase 'so the self under the eye lies' in the second stanza of the second section. I think that Hughes is using the amphibian otter as a metaphor for the double nature of man, which he sees as partly passive and receptive (living in water) and partly aggressive and active (able to impress its shape and nature on land). The tension between these two elements, as Hughes conceives it, is mimed by the life of the otter which can 'linger nowhere' and is seeking 'some world lost when first he dived.'

PIKE. The last four stanzas of this poem serve as a reminder that Hughes's world in these animal poems is the world of his own childhood in south Yorkshire. Unlike Lawrence, whose animals are almost all exotic and foreign ones which he studied abroad, Hughes's beasts are the native fauna of England seen as part of the unchanging landscape.

SNOWDROP. What might in the hands of another poet have been a delicate and romantic lyric about this flower in the hands of Hughes becomes a transformation of the flower into a thing of armour and hard purpose. It is a tribute to Hughes's skill that this in no way seems arbitrary. He succeeds in persuading us that the snowdrop really is a thing of ice and iron.

THISTLES. This magnificent poem is a short paean of praise to the unkillable virtue of heroism. By presenting this quality through the nature of part of the vegetable, rather than the

animal, kingdom, Hughes contrives to give it an air of naturalness and inevitability, as if heroism like the flowers in spring
is something which must go on for ever.

THE BROTHER'S DREAM. A long narrative poem based on a
dream. Its description of a man's fight with a bear is beautifully
worked out, but the underlying force of this episode is symbolic. In a sense it seems to be a reworking of the legend of St
George and the Dragon in modern psychological terms. The
bear is perhaps an image for our animal nature, or more
precisely the emotion of fear, which can only be controlled by
the ruthless cruelty of the will. The poem's great strength,
however, lies in its surface vividness and narrative power.
The freedom of the rhythm suggests that Hughes is beginning
to forge a new style very close to the boundaries of prose.

Sylvia Plath

Sylvia Plath was born in America in 1932 and died in London in 1963. She was married to Ted Hughes and they had two children, a girl and a boy. At the time of her death Sylvia Plath was writing in a state of extreme nervous and creative tension, sometimes producing as many as three or four poems a day. She once described these last poems as 'long and thin, like myself'. They seem to be like herself in far more than shape. As the record of an attempt to grapple with a number of over-riding obsessions in a state of extreme neurotic excitement, these poems are almost without parallel in the English language. As A. Alvarez has grimly said, 'Poetry of this order is a murderous art'. Whether Sylvia Plath could have taken this kind of poetry further if she had lived longer, no one can say. Her death and the quality of the last poems seem inextricably connected. Her name and work are already beginning to take on something of the quality of a legend, and she has become one of the heroes of her time in the way that Rupert Brooke did at the beginning of the First World War. We are too close to her work at the moment to assess clearly its final place in English literature, but there is some danger that it may eventually seem too hectic and too native of the mood of the early 1960s to retain its full intensity of impact for other generations.

Lady Lazarus

I have done it again.
One year in every ten
I manage it —

A sort of walking miracle, my skin
Bright as a Nazi lampshade,
My right foot

A paperweight,
My face a featureless, fine
Jew linen.

Peel off the napkin
O my enemy.
Do I terrify? —

The nose, the eye pits, the full set of teeth?
The sour breath
Will vanish in a day.

Soon, soon the flesh
The grave cave ate will be
At home on me

And I a smiling woman.
I am only thirty.
And like the cat I have nine times to die.

This is Number Three.
What a trash
To annihilate each decade.

What a million filaments.
The peanut-crunching crowd
Shoves in to see

Them unwrap me hand and foot —
The big strip tease.
Gentlemen, ladies

These are my hands
My knees.
I may be skin and bone,

Nevertheless, I am the same, identical woman.
The first time it happened I was ten.
It was an accident.

The second time I meant
To last it out and not come back at all.
I rocked shut

As a seashell.
They had to call and call
And pick the worms off me like sticky pearls.

Dying
Is an art, like everything else.
I do it exceptionally well.

I do it so it feels like hell.
I do it so it feels real.
I guess you could say I've a call.

It's easy enough to do it in a cell.
It's easy enough to do it and stay put.
It's the theatrical

Comeback in broad day
To the same place, the same face, the same brute
Amused shout:

'A miracle!'
That knocks me out.
There is a charge

For the eyeing of my scars, there is a charge
For the hearing of my heart —
It really goes.

And there is a charge, a very large charge
For a word or a touch
Or a bit of blood

Or a piece of my hair or my clothes.
So, so, Herr Doktor.
So, Herr Enemy.

I am your opus,
I am your valuable,
The pure gold baby

That melts to a shriek.
I turn and burn.
Do not think I underestimate your great concern.

Ash, ash –
You poke and stir.
Flesh, bone, there is nothing there —

A cake of soap,
A wedding ring,
A gold filling.

Herr God, Herr Lucifer
Beware
Beware.

Out of the ash
I rise with my red hair
And I eat men like air.

Daddy

You do not do, you do not do
Any more, black shoe
In which I have lived like a foot
For thirty years, poor and white,
Barely daring to breathe or Achoo.

Daddy, I have had to kill you.
You died before I had time —
Marble-heavy, a bag full of God,
Ghastly statue with one grey toe
Big as a Frisco seal

And a head in the freakish Atlantic
Where it pours bean green over blue
In the waters off beautiful Nauset.
I used to pray to recover you.
Ach, du.

In the German tongue, in the Polish town
Scraped flat by the roller
Of wars, wars, wars.
But the name of the town is common.
My Polack friend

Says there are a dozen or two.
So I never could tell where you
Put your foot, your root,
I never could talk to you.
The tongue stuck in my jaw.

It stuck in a barb wire snare.
Ich, ich, ich, ich,
I could hardly speak.
I thought every German was you.
And the language obscene

An engine, an engine
Chuffing me off like a Jew.
A Jew to Dachau, Auschwitz, Belsen.
I began to talk like a Jew.
I think I may well be a Jew.

The snows of the Tyrol, the clear beer of Vienna
Are not very pure or true.
With my gypsy ancestress and my weird luck
And my Taroc pack and my Taroc pack
I may be a bit of a Jew.

I have always been scared of *you*,
With your Luftwaffe, your gobbledygoo.
And your neat moustache
And your Aryan eye, bright blue.
Panzer-man, panzer-man, O You —

Not God but a swastika
So black no sky could squeak through.
Every woman adores a Fascist,
The boot in the face, the brute
Brute heart of a brute like you.

You stand at the blackboard, daddy,
In the picture I have of you,
A cleft in your chin instead of your foot
But no less a devil for that, no not
Any less the black man who

Bit my pretty red heart in two.
I was ten when they buried you.
At twenty I tried to die
And get back, back, back to you.
I thought even the bones would do.

But they pulled me out of the sack,
And they stuck me together with glue.

And then I knew what to do.
I made a model of you,
A man in black with a Meinkampf look

And a love of the rack and the screw.
And I said I do, I do.
So daddy, I'm finally through.
The black telephone's off at the root,
The voices just can't worm through.

If I've killed one man, I've killed two —
The vampire who said he was you
And drank my blood for a year,
Seven years, if you want to know.
Daddy, you can lie back now.

There's a stake in your fat black heart
And the villagers never liked you.
They are dancing and stamping on you.
They always *knew* it was you.
Daddy, daddy, you bastard, I'm through.

The Arrival of the Bee Box

I ordered this, this clean wood box
Square as a chair and almost too heavy to lift.
I would say it was the coffin of a midget
Or a square baby
Were there not such a din in it.

The box is locked, it is dangerous.
I have to live with it overnight
And I can't keep away from it.
There are no windows, so I can't see what is in there.
There is only a little grid, no exit.

I put my eye to the grid.
It is dark, dark,
With the swarmy feeling of African hands
Minute and shrunk for export,
Black on black, angrily clambering.

How can I let them out?
It is the noise that appals me most of all,
The unintelligible syllables.
It is like a Roman mob,
Small, taken one by one, but my god, together!

I lay my ear to furious Latin.
I am not a Caesar.
I have simply ordered a box of maniacs.
They can be sent back.
They can die, I need feed them nothing, I am the owner.

I wonder how hungry they are.
I wonder if they would forget me
If I just undid the locks and stood back and turned into a tree.
There is the laburnum, its blond colonnades,
And the petticoats of the cherry.

They might ignore me immediately
In my moon suit and funeral veil.
I am no source of honey
So why should they turn on me?
Tomorrow I will be sweet God, I will set them free.

The box is only temporary.

Edge

The woman is perfected.
Her dead

Body wears the smile of accomplishment,
The illusion of a Greek necessity

Flows in the scrolls of her toga,
Her bare

Feet seem to be saying:
We have come so far, it is over.

Each dead child coiled, a white serpent,
One at each little

Pitcher of milk, now empty.
She has folded

Them back into her body as petals
Of a rose close when the garden

Stiffens and odours bleed
From the sweet, deep throats of the night flower.

The moon has nothing to be sad about,
Staring from her hood of bone.

She is used to this sort of thing.
Her blacks crackle and drag.

Notes

LADY LAZARUS. This poem uses the *persona* of an imaginary woman who, like Lazarus in the Bible, rises from the dead to say a number of things about the impulse to suicide. The poem has a sinister, witch-like and magical quality. It conveys both the horror and fascination of death, and at the same time the theatricality of attempted suicide as a means of drawing attention to oneself. The poem's impact is enriched and deepened by the conception of death as a doctor in a Nazi concentration camp. The reference to 'a cake of soap, a wedding ring, a gold filling' towards the end of the poem, brings to mind the products and the relics of the incinerators at Auschwitz. The point about the lampshade reference at the beginning of the poem is that one prominent Nazi commandant of a concentration camp had a lampshade made out of human skin.

DADDY. This is perhaps Sylvia Plath's most famous poem. It records an obsession with her father which she had already begun to explore in her earlier work. She once spoke in a broadcast of an Electra complex – a fascination with one's father, like Electra's for her father Agamemnon in the myth – and this poem could be symptomatic of it. The concept of the father as a Fascist is an imaginary but vividly apt one to express the love–hate relationship which is under presentation. At the same time the concept of herself as possibly being a Jew, enables Sylvia Plath in the poem to draw – as in 'Lady Lazarus', and this time even more appropriately – on the history of Nazi oppression. The poem's use of a nursery rhyme rhythm with an insistent rhyme on one word all the way through, helps to emphasise the psychologically immature and subordinate position in which the girl speaking feels in relation to her dead father. The paradox and the tragedy of the poem is that despite what is explicitly said the tone suggests that the obsession has not in fact fully been sloughed off or lived through.

THE ARRIVAL OF THE BEE BOX. There is a poem in Sylvia Plath's first book, *The Colossus* (1960), called 'The Beekeeper's Daughter', and she returned several times to the theme of bees in her last poems. This poem is an excellent example of her power to generate one image from another in a sequence governed only by the logic of feeling, but at the same time powerfully convincing in context. For example, the initial idea of the bees as a Roman mob suggests that their unintelligible noise is the language of Latin, and this in its turn suggests to the poet that she in relation to the bees is a dictator or a general like Caesar. The poem skilfully mixes fear, pity, irritation and tenderness. It would be easy to read in some symbolism to the pent up, frustrated bees in the box, but I am sure none is explicitly intended. Nevertheless, their nature and their plight, as presented in the poem, clearly corresponds to the state of mind of the poet.

EDGE. The edge referred to in the title is perhaps the brink of nervous breakdown or suicide. Under the pseudonym of Virginia Lucas, Sylvia Plath published a novel called *The Bell Jar* about a girl's experiences in a mental hospital, and the material of this book is (though in a much more intense form) redeployed in some of her last poems. This poem manages to be both morbid and serene at the same time. It gives a new energy to the familiar nineteenth-century cliché of the beauty of a dead woman's body. The last image in the poem seems to be presenting the moon as an old woman with a rustling skirt of darkness.